Baedeker

Hawaii

Contents

The Principal Places of Tourist Interest at a Glance

Preface

This book is one of the new generation of Baedeker guides.

These guides, illustrated throughout in colour, are designed to meet the needs of the modern traveller. They are quick and easy to consult, with the principal places of interest described in alphabetical order, and the information is presented in a format that is both attractive and easy to follow.

This guide is concerned with the eight principal islands of the Hawaiian archipelago in the Pacific Ocean – Hawaii, Kahoolawe, Kauai, Lanai, Maui, Molokai, Niihau and Oahu.

The guide is in three parts. The first part gives a general account of the islands, their climate, flora and fauna, population, religions, economy, history, famous people, art and culture. A selection of quotations and a number of suggested itineraries provide a transition to the second part, in which the places and features of tourist interest in the individual islands – their towns and villages, national parks and scenery – are described. The third part contains a variety of practical information. Both the sights and the practical information are listed in alphabetical order.

The new Baedeker guides are noted for their concentration on essentials and their convenience of use. They contain numerous specially drawn plans and colour illustrations; and at the end of the book is a large map making it easy to locate the various places described in the "A to Z" section of the guide with the help of the co-ordinates given at the head of each entry.

How to use this book

Following the tradition established by Karl Baedeker in 1844, sights of particular interest are distinguished by either one ★ or two ★★ stars.

To make it easier to locate the various sights listed in the "A to Z" section of the Guide, their co-ordinates on the large map of Hawaii are shown in red at the head of each entry.

Only a selection of hotels, restaurants and shops can be given: no reflection is implied, therefore, on establishments not included.

The symbol ⓘ on a town plan indicates the local tourist office from which further information can be obtained. The post-horn symbol indicates a post office.

In a time of rapid change it is difficult to ensure that all the information given is entirely accurate and up to date, and the possibility of error can never be completely eliminated. Although the publishers can accept no responsibility for inaccuracies and omissions, they are always grateful for corrections and suggestions for improvement.

Facts and Figures

Note

The term "Hawaii" can refer to both the island of Hawaii and the state of Hawaii, i.e. all of the Hawaiian islands. In order to avoid confusion the term "Hawaii" is used in this guide to refer to the state. When the island of Hawaii is intended it is called either the Island of Hawaii or "Big Island".

It should also be pointed out that the phrase "in Hawaii" means in the state of Hawaii whereas "on Hawaii" means on the Island of Hawaii.

General

Lying in the north Pacific the chain of Hawaiian Islands stretches over 1518 miles/2436km from the south-east to the north-west crossing the Tropic of Cancer. Its geographical location is between longitude 154° 40' and 178° 75' west and latitude 18° 54' and 28° 15' north. The eight main islands lie within the tropical zone with the Northwestern Hawaiian Islands situated chiefly to the north of the Tropic of Cancer. Their remote location in the middle of the Pacific Ocean makes them the most isolated group of islands in the world.

Location

The Hawaiian archipelago stretches from the Kure Atoll in the north-west to the Island of Hawaii in the south-east and encompasses 132 islands, coral reefs and sandbanks. The Northwestern Hawaiian or Leeward Islands, with a total surface area of only 2.7sq.miles/7sq.km are regarded as separate from the eight main islands in the south-east which cover an area of 10,277sq.miles/16,540sq.km. These main islands consist of the inhabited islands of Hawaii, Maui, Oahu, Kauai, Molokai, Lanai and Nihau along with the uninhabited island of Kahoo-lawe. The results of excavations on the Northwestern Hawaiian Islands suggest that some of these islands were also inhabited earlier.

The five Midway Islands in the extreme north-west do not belong to the US state of Hawaii but are under the jurisdiction of the US navy,

Groups of islands

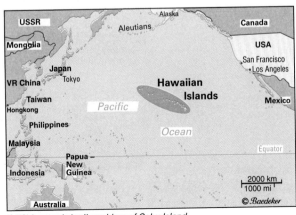

◀ "Chinaman's hat"; emblem of Oahu Island

which maintains a naval and air support base there with 500 personnel. The Kure Atoll is the site of a US coastguard navigation station with about 20 staff, the only inhabitants of these islands.

Northwestern
Hawaiian Islands

The Northwestern Hawaiian Islands were for the most part not discovered until the last century. They are the oldest islands in the entire archipelago; being estimated at 6–25 million years old. At the beginning of the 20th century all the islands, with the exception of the Midways, were placed under protection by the then President of the United States Theodore Roosevelt and the entire area was declared the "Hawaiian Islands National Park Refuge".

Origins of the Hawaiian Islands

Volcanic activity

The Hawaiian archipelago consists of the peaks of cooled down volcanoes with the mass of the lava being under water. The mountains of the Hawaiian Islands are therefore without exception formed from cooled down volcanoes; only two volcanoes are still active on the island of Hawaii: the Mauna Loa and the Kilauea.

Hawaii's volcanic origins date from the Middle Tertiary period, geologically a relatively young development. The formation of the chain of Hawaiian Islands covered a period of approximately 70 million years.

Hawaii belongs to a seismographically unstable zone of the Pacific which has the highest incidence of land volcanoes and earthquakes.

Over millions of years magma builds up in certain "hot spots" below the earth's crust erupting through cracks and fissures in the form of volcanic explosions. As Hawaii lies on part of the earth's crust, the Pacific basin, which is in turn subject to the movement of the giant plates of the earth's surface, in this case the "Pacific Plate", which is moving south-east to north-west, Hawaii is shifting about 3–4in./8–10cm annually in a northwesterly direction. Instead of just a single volcano this plate movement has led to the formation of a chain of volcanoes from north-west to south-east above the "hot spot" below Hawaii. The oldest volcanoes are in the north-west (Kure Atoll), the youngest are found on the southeasterly island of Hawaii.

The differing ages of the volcanoes is reflected in the various stages of erosion. Whereas the island of Hawaii is growing through volcanic activity the neighbouring northwesterly islands are being worn down by weathering and erosion by the sea. On the Kure Atoll and the

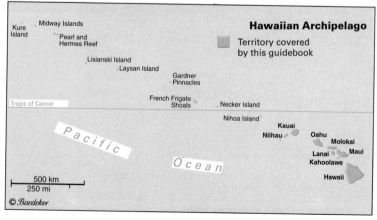

Kure Island — Midway Islands

Pearl and Hermes Reef

Lisianski Island

Laysan Island

Gardner Pinnacles

French Frigate Shoals — Necker Island

Nihoa Island

Kauai
Niihau
Oahu
Molokai
Lanai — Maui
Kahoolawe
Hawaii

Tropic of Cancer

Hawaiian Archipelago

Territory covered by this guidebook

Pacific Ocean

500 km
250 mi

© Baedeker

Formation of the Hawaiian Archipelago

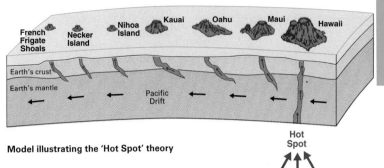

Model illustrating the 'Hot Spot' theory

© *Baedeker*

Midway Islands, 1553 miles/2,500km north-west only limestone reefs project from the sea.

The lava streams on Hawaii fall into two distinct types. Their Polynesian names have become adopted into the terminology of volcanic research. The "aa" lava has a rough, angular structure whereas the flowing "pahoehoe" lava is smooth and rounded. It is this hot, gaseous lava which on cooling and degassing can turn into "aa" lava. The chemical composition of both types of lava is identical.
    The black sandy beaches consist of lava which has been eroded and worn down by sea water.

Lava formations

As well as volcanic eruptions on the Hawaiian Islands earthquakes are another result of this unstable area within the earth's core. Often they are so weak that they pass unnoticed. The earthquakes either accompany volcanic errUption or are the result of faults, cracks in the rock stratum, which can be caused by the movement of the Pacific Plate on the floor of the Pacific Ocean.

Earthquakes and tsunamis

Submarine earthquakes give rise to the tsunami, a giant tidal wave, that is capable of causing considerable damage. The tsunami are caused by earthquakes on the sea bed which produce exceptionally long wave formations. On meeting the coastal waters the tsunami, which can reach speeds of up to 62mph/100kph slows down but increases in height. Tidal waves of 115ft/35m have been observed. The centres of these submarine earthquakes can be seen far away from the Hawaiian Islands so that most tsunamis that reach Hawaii start from the edge of the Pacific Ocean.
    The island of Hawaii has been particularly badly hit by tsunamis and the other islands have also been affected.
    The Tsunami Information Center in Honolulu collates and evaluates seismographical data and information about the tidal patterns and issues early warnings of tsunamis.

Administration

In March 1959 Hawaii was proclaimed the 50th member of the United States of America. Its capital is Honolulu on the island of Oahu.
    The state of Hawaii, named after the island of the same name, is the only island state of the USA. It covers a small surface area and is the

50th US state

9

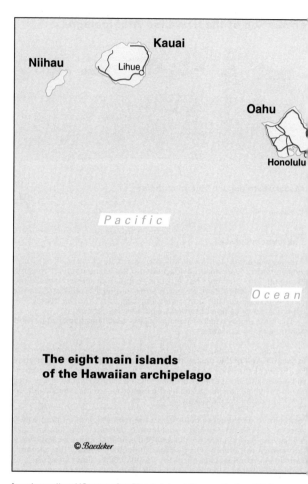

**The eight main islands
of the Hawaiian archipelago**

© *Baedeker*

fourth smallest US state after Rhode Island, Connecticut and Delaware. It is the only state which does not share a common border with any other state and it does not belong to the North American landmass.

Government

The state is headed by a governor who is elected every four years. Parliament consists of two chambers, the House of Representatives with 51 delegates and the Senate with 25 members. The House of Representatives is re-elected every two years, the Senate every four years. A delegate is sent to the US House of Representatives.

Counties

The state of Hawaii is divided into four counties which, apart from Hawaii County, each includes several islands. Municipal administration also comes under the auspices of the counties as there is no independent local system of administration. At the head of the county is the mayor, who has the right to appoint all officials within the county.

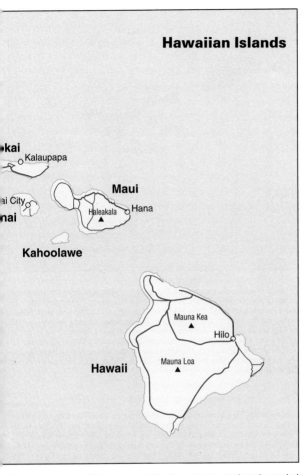

Hawaiian Islands

kai
Kalaupapa

Maui

ai City

nai

Haleakala ▲ Hana

Kahoolawe

Mauna Kea ▲
Hilo

Hawaii

Mauna Loa ▲

The disadvantage of this system is that large towns, such as the capital Honolulu and larger places on the islands, do not have their own local administration to deal more effectively with their specific problems.

There are two main political parties in Hawaii: the "Democrats" and the "Republicans". Since the recognition of Hawaii as a member of the United States in 1959 the island's politics have been firmly under Democratic control. An unusual feature is that the ethnic variety of the population is reflected in the make up of its political representatives. George Ariyoshi, Governor of Hawaii from 1974 to 1986, was of Japanese descent. The first governor of Hawaiian descent was John Waihee, who held office from 1986 to 1994. The present governor is Ben Cayetano.

Politics

The Hawaiian politicians have the reputation of being reserved and media-shy, unlike the usual American media spectacle.

11

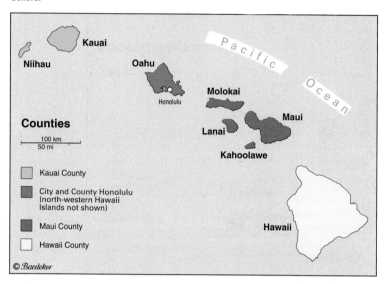

Political influence is exerted particularly by representatives of the most important economic branches of Hawaii (tourism, sugar and banana production, building). The trade union organisations are also politically powerful. With the increase in the number of jobs in the service industries the public service union was able to expand its area of influence. The International Longshoremen and Warehousemen's Union, which represents the interests of the sugar and banana workers, has become less influential through the gradual restructuring of the economy.

National symbols

Flag

The national flag was originaly designed in 1816 for King Kamehameha I and is a combination of the British Union Jack and the American "Stars and Stripes" flag. It is made up of eight alternating white, red and blue stripes (representing the eight main islands including Kahoolawe) and the British Union Jack in the top left corner. The origin of the Hawaiian flag is not absolutely clear but it is suspected that the English seafarer George Vancouver Kamehameha brought the British flag as a present. During the 1812 war, in which British and American war ships fought each other in Hawaiian waters, Kamehameha is said to have created the new flag as a diplomatic solution thereby avoiding conflicts with both sides.

Seal

The great state seal bears the inscription "State of Hawaii", the national motto and the date 1959, the year in which Hawaii became the 50th state of the USA. In the centre is the coat of arms which has the figure of King Kamehameha I on the left and the goddess of liberty holding the Hawaiian flag on the right with the wings of a phoenix outstretched below. The figures are entwined with taro, banana leaves and ferns.

Coat of arms

The coat of arms of the monarchy, which originated in 1845, is very ornate and can be seen, for example, on the gates of the Iolani Palace.

Coat of Arms of the State on the gate of Iolani Palace

In the centre of the quartered shield is the ancient triangular flag of the Hawaiian chiefs with two crossed spears. Above it is a crown and it is flanked by representations of Chief Kamanawa holding a spear on the left and Chief Kameeiamoku hoding a "kahli" (feather bush) on the right.

Both chiefs are said to have supported the late King Kamehameha I in his efforts to unite the land. The national motto appears below. The coins minted by the monarchy also bear the coat of arms.

The state anthem also has royal origins and was adopted by parliamentary decree in 1967. The text of the anthem "Hawai'i pono" (see Quotations) was written in 1874 by King David Kalakaua in honour of Kamehameha I and was to have been sung to the tune of the British state anthem "God Save the King". But two years later Heinrich Berger from Potsdam, leader of the Royal Hawaiian Band, composed a melody which appealed to the Hawaiians.

Anthem

In 1923 the hibiscus, a type of mallow, was chosen as the state flower. Owing to its short flowering period it is also known as the hour flower. Although it is usually the red hibiscus which features as the state flower it must be pointed out that the colour was not prescribed in the almost 70 year old decree.

State flower

Hawaii also has a state tree, the "kukui" or candlenut tree, a nut tree, which is very important to the Hawaiians because of the many applications of the nut oil it produces. Until 1959 the coconut palm was the offical tree.

State tree "kukui"

The state animal is the humpback whale, a species of whale threatened with extinction. Of about 1000 of these animals in the North Pacific between 250 and 600 swim into the waters of the Hawaiian Islands to give birth.

State animal Humpback whale

13

Climate

State bird "nene"	The state bird is also threatened with extinction. The "nene" or Hawaiian goose, which is only found on Hawaii and Maui islands, choose to live on the lava-covered ground between 3937 and 7874ft/1200 and 2400m. Attempts to return birds bred in captivity back to the wild have so far been unsuccesful.
State fish "humuhumunuku-nukuapua'a"	Even the Hawaiians have difficulty in pronouncing correctly the name of the state fish. It is the "humuhumunukunukuapua'a", a small fish which belongs to the "humuhumu" family. It has been immortalised in a song:

"I want to go back
to my little grass shack
in Ke-ala-ke-kua, Hawaii
where the humuhumunukunukukuapuaa goes swimming by".

Aloha State	The official name of Hawaii is Aloha State (aloha=welcome), which means that the "Aloha spirit", the feeling of joy at being alive and friendship, should be deeply rooted in both political and daily life.

Climate

General	The climate in the region of the Hawaiian archipelago is constant throughout the year with mild temperatures and sunny weather which is frequently interrupted by heavy rainfall, especially on the east side of the islands. The main influence is the trade winds which blow continually from the north-west and, cooled by the Pacific Ocean, make the tropical climate pleasant and bearable.

There are only two seasons on Hawaii; summer from May to October and winter from October to April. In winter the temperatures are somewhat lower and it is often overcast with showers. This is caused by the cool, damp winds which temporarily interrupt the trade winds.

Influential factors	The climate of Hawaii is determined by a combination of factors:

Its location within the tropics results in the relatively even climate all year round with little differences in temperature and a constantly high level of annual sunshine. The vast waters of the Pacific Ocean with an almost constant temperature of 24°C/75°F to 27°C/81° all year act as a "thermostat". It cools warm air currents and warms cold air masses.

In winter, when the sun heads south, the Hawaiian Islands may be influenced by the Pacific low pressure areas. They bring cloudy, wet weather which can even become very stormy.

The size of the islands and their topography – especially the high mountains – influence the local climate. They cause the air masses to rise and divide the islands into the wet windward side and the dry leeward side. The different types of upland climate result in the summit of the Mauna Kea on Hawaii island even occasionally being snow-capped.

Temperatures	The distinctive feature of the climate of the Hawaiian Islands is that temperature differences between summer and winter are less than those between day and night. Even though the temperature extremes in Honolulu have been recorded at 33°C/91°F and 15°C/59°F the overall range is narrow.

The average annual temperatures range from 22°C/72°F (January) and 26°C/79°F (August). In the winter months between November and March the temperatures can fall to 18°C/64°F, in the summer months it can reach 30°C/86°F.

The differences between the coast and mountains are more striking. In the mountains the temperature decreases as altitude increases and it can be noticably cooler there. When walking in the mountains warm clothing must be worn.

The amount of rainfall and its distribution is dependent on the island's relief and the direction of the trade winds. The leesides of the mountains have lower levels of precipitation than the exposed windward sides.

The frequent rainfall on the slopes causes the highest levels of precipitation to fall in the middle altitudes on the windward sides. As a result of this the 5167ft/1575m high Waialeale on Kauai is the rainiest place in the world with an average total of 12,000mm. On the other hand Puako on Hawaii island is one of the driest places on the islands with 230mm of rainfall per annum. The average annual rainfall for Honolulu is 600mm. Typical of rainfall on Hawaii are the irregular showers which only affect a restricted area but are very heavy and short.

In winter the amount of rainfall decreases but there is no fixed rainy season.

Climatic Chart Months	Temperatures in °C		Hours of sunshine per day	No of days of rainfall	Amount of rainfall in mm
	Average maximum	Average minimum			
January	24.2	20.6	7.3	14	104
February	24.4	19.4	7.7	11	66
March	25.0	19.4	8.3	13	78
April	25.6	20.0	8.6	12	48
May	26.7	21.1	8.8	11	25
June	27.2	22.2	9.4	14	23
July	27.8	22.8	9.4	14	23
August	28.3	23.3	9.3	13	28
September	28.3	23.3	9.2	13	36
October	27.8	22.2	8.3	13	48
November	26.7	21.1	7.5	13	64
December	25.6	20.6	6.2	15	104
Annual	26.7	21.1	8.3	154	643

(Climatic statistics from Honolulu measuring station (Oahu))

Because of the geographical proximity to the equator the sun is high in the sky all year. In total the mean amount of sunshine is higher in summer but it should be mentioned that the sun shines the most in the coastal regions, in contrast to the central upland areas which are often veiled in cloud.

On Oahu the average monthly amounts of sunshine vary from 129 hours in February to 270 hours in June, which constitute 40% and 72% respectively of the possible amount of sunshine. The mean daily amount of sunshine in Honolulu varies from 6 hours in December to 9.4 hours in July.

The difference between the shortest and longest day is only slight. In December it remains light for 11½ hours and in June 13 hours (for comparison: Southern California 10 and 14½ hours, Northeast coast of USA 8½ and 15½ hours).

Flora and Fauna

Flora

The isolation of the Hawaiian Islands (1988 miles/3200km is the shortest distance from the mainland) meant that it took a long period of time for plants to colonise the islands. Most seeds and spores were carried

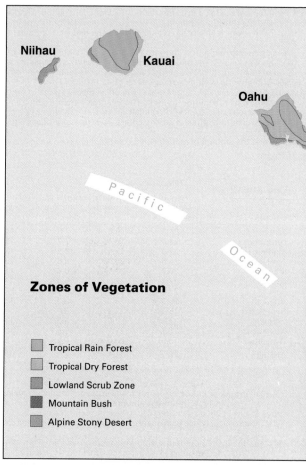

Niihau

Kauai

Oahu

Pacific

Ocean

Zones of Vegetation

Tropical Rain Forest

Tropical Dry Forest

Lowland Scrub Zone

Mountain Bush

Alpine Stony Desert

to the islands by birds. The variety of landscapes – coastline, mountains, valleys and moors – together with the different climatic zones, the wet windward side and the dry leeward side provided ideal conditions for a wide range of vegetation. A large number of endemic plants found only on the Hawaiian Islands evolved. Nowadays only few of the original species can still be found in the remote inaccessible areas. Many plants have died out or are threatened with extinction. Artificially introduced decorative or commercially grown plants predominate in many parts of the islands.

Information about the original variety of plants was brought back by word of mouth and later in the form of sketches by the seafarers James Cook, George Vancouver, Otto von Kotzebue and the first Hawaiian scientists.

Vegetation zones

The distribution of plants on the island is directly related to the climate and topography. The average annual rainfall and temperatures are the

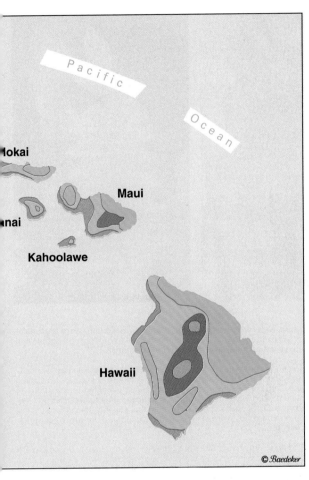

P a c i f i c

O c e a n

lokai

nai

Maui

Kahoolawe

Hawaii

© *Baedeker*

most important climatic factors. The differing altitudes have resulted in the following vegetation zones: shrub vegetation in the coastal areas, rainforest in the wetland areas and in the upland mountain regions forest with almost bare rock on the peaks.

In the lower-lying regions the vegetation has been pushed back by the cultivation of commercial crops. Plants introduced from Asia, Africa, Australia and tropical regions of America have developed well here. In the urban regions many tropical plants have been introduced.

The beauty and richness of the plant world in Hawaii can be appreciated in the numerous public and private parks and botanical gardens.

The first settlers, the Polynesians, who came to Hawaii from Marquesas and Tahiti, brought coconuts, bananas, sugar cane, sweet potatoes, breadfruit, yam roots and taro, a tuber rich in starch,. Fruits,

Introduced plants

17

Torch Ginger

Heliconia

which we today regard as exotic or even Hawaiian, were also introduced by the settlers. These include the papaya, mango, pineapple and guava which mostly come from South America.

The numerous types of flowers which are often described as "typically Hawaiian" are also indigenous to other countries such as Java, India and China. Examples include the hibiscus (elevated to the status of state flower), plumerias, proteas, anthurias, ginger, strelitzias and heliconias. Of the many species of orchid there is only one native species, all other species were originally introduced and are grown commercially today.

Trees

There are only two indigenous types of tree on Hawaii, the koa tree, a type of acacia impressive for its considerable size with a trunk of up to 10ft/3m thick and a height of more than 65ft/20m, and the "ohia" which occurs both in its shorter form as a shrub and as a tree of up to 98ft/30m. The koa tree is recognisable by its crescent-form leaves and yellow flowers. The Polynesians use its wood for canoes, surf boards and calabashes. The "ohia" is the most common tree in Hawaii. Its especially hard wood was used both in the production of basic commodities, furniture and house building. Another widespread tree is the "kukui" or candlenut tree, a nut tree, the oil of which was used as fuel for oil lamps. The nuts are still used as a spice. The paper mulberry tree was important in the production of "kapa". Its bark was used together with the bark of other trees and shrubs to make barkcloth out of the raffia fibres, which was the original clothing of the islanders.

Silver sword plant

The silver sword plant is a botanical rarity. It grows in upland areas over 6561ft/2000m and can only be found on the edge of the Haleakala crater. It is 5–10 years before it produces a huge bloom which can reach a height of 6½ft/2m. After flowering it forms seeds and dies.

Fauna of the Hawaiian Islands

The indigenous animal kingdom of the Hawaiian Islands consists of relatively few species which is accounted for by the isolated location of the islands. There are no amphibians or reptiles and thus the islands are a paradise free from snakes. On the other hand there are many species of insects and snails. Similarly the Hawaiian waters are rich in fish and coral.

General

Many of the species of birds which used to be found on the Hawaiian Islands have become extinct. Only a few species can survive in remote upland areas.

Domestic animals such as deer, horses and sheep, pigs, goats, chickens and dogs were introduced as the islands were settled. Rats and mice were undesirable imports. The grazing animals, in particular, have had a noticeable effect on the local eco-system. The damage caused by their hooves and grazing in the lower lying regions has changed the local vegetation and also the occurence of native plants and animals. The birds have disappeared from these regions; some species became extinct, others withdrew to the higher upland forests.

Mammals

Only two mammals can be considered to be "original inhabitants" of the island: a species of seal, the Hawaiian monk seal and the hair-covered bat. The monk seal is threatened with extinction and only to be found on the Northwestern Hawaiian Islands. The bat is still to be found in the mountain areas between heights of 4276ft/1300m and 6579ft/2000m.

The humpback whale appears in the waters of the Hawaiian Islands, especially off Maui Island, where it brings up its young as well as the sperm whale and the 16–20ft/5–6m long narwhal. Dolphins which belong to the tooth-whaled family are present all year round. The largest colony of extremely rare green turtles lives on French Frigate Shoals, a group of 12 small sandbanks within the Northwestern Hawaiian Islands.

Only a few species of well known Hawaiian birds remain. The clothes bird and the various types of honey eaters, from whose feathers the royal robes were made, have mainly become extinct. Out of around 70 species 23 have already disappeared and a further 31 are endangered. On Oahu there is not one bird from the original species and on the other islands many of the native birds have retreated to mountain regions over 3280ft/1000m. The national bird, the "nene" or Hawaiian goose only numbered 40 during the Forties on the island of Hawaii and on Maui it had completely disappeared. Since it has been protected its numbers have increased on the slopes of the Mauna Loa and Mauna Kea on Hawaii and the Haleakala on Maui to a total of 600.

Birds

There are also a considerable number of migratory birds which break their annual journey on the unpopulated Northwestern Hawaiian Islands. Particularly impressive is the Pacific golden plover which briefly interrupts its flight from Alaska or Siberia to the southern Pacific to land on Hawaii.

Several million sea birds breed on the small northwestern islands and atolls; examples include the Laysan albatross, the largest of Hawaii's sea birds, various species of gannet and terns.

Of the 10,000 species of Hawaiian insects, which according to entomologists have developed from only 150 original species, many are only to be found on one of the islands. Their existence is often dependent on the presence of a single species of plant.

Insects

The first pests – fleas, lice and flies – were brought by the Polynesian settlers. Mosquitos, termites, ants and cockroaches probably came later with the seafarers as did the fruit and vegetable pests.

Flora and Fauna

The ethnic variety . . .

. . . of the Hawaiian people

It is a complete mystery how almost 1000 species of snail could have developed, of which many are endemic, i.e. only found here. There are approx. 100 tree snails which have striking colourful, patterned shells.

The underwater world of the offshore coral reefs and the many caves in the volcanic rock of the coastline are home to 700 species of fish alone. A short selection includes the blue-lipped fish, coral fish, red hine fish, the "kihikihi", butterfly, parrot and goat fish. Most of the varieties of fish are not restricted to Hawaiian waters but are distributed throughout the entire tropical regions of the Indian and Pacific oceans.

Nowadays the coral reefs are threatened by the destruction of the coral for souvenirs and the jewellery trade. Care must be taken to avoid damaging the coral when diving or snorkelling.

Population

According to 1989 estimates the population of the state of Hawaii stands at 1,112,000 inhabitants. The population is distributed unevenly over the individual islands. Four fifths of the population live on the island of Oahu. About half the inhabitants of Oahu are concentrated in the capital Honolulu. The next largest towns are Hilo (Hawaii) with 43,500 inhabitants, Pearl City (Oahu) with 43,000 inhabitants, followed by five other places on Oahu: Kailua (35,000), Kaneohe (29,000), Waipahu (29,000), Mililani (22,000) and Wahiawa (17,000). The remaining towns have populations which are mostly under 15,000. Even though the majority of the towns have relatively low populations the level of urbanisation on the islands is high. Only a fifth of the population lives in the towns. The trend towards moving into urban areas is slowing down. At 63 per sq.km the population density on the Hawaiian Islands is very low. However, it varies from island to island. By far the most densely populated island is Oahu with 546 inhabitants per sq.km.

Ethnic pluralism

The population of Hawaii is made up of 50 different ethnic groups and as such constitutes the most far-reaching mixture of races in such a small area. The ethnic roots of Hawaii's population can be traced to both Asia and Europe. The Hawaiian Islands are not just a geographical link between east and west but socially Hawaii is the only state of the USA made up of ethnic minorities and – despite the current rapid increase in the white population with the arrival of many Californians – does not have a white majority.

About 60% of the inhabitants were born on the islands, 25% come from the American mainland and 15% were born abroad.

According to the 1980 census the population of Hawaii is made up as follows:

Whites	318,770	33.0%
Japanese	239,750	25.0%
Filipinos	113,900	12.0%
Hawaiians	115,000	10.0%
Chinese	56,300	6.0%
Puerto Ricans	19,350	2.0%
Blacks	17,350	2.0%
Koreans	17,950	2.0%
Samoans	14,100	1.5%
Mexicans	8,700	1.0%
Vietnamese	3,500	0.4%
Indians	2,650	0.3%
Guamese	1,700	0.2%
Others	85,000	5.0%

Population

The biggest ethnic groups are the whites and Japanese whose numbers continue to grow. During the last decade the number of Vietnamese increased the most. Not included in these statistics are the military personnel of the US forces and their relatives who are mainly stationed in Pearl Harbor and Schofield Barracks, in total about 100,000 people.

Population development

Hawaiians

The Hawaiians, the first settlers on the islands, are a mixture of different Polynesian races and may have come to Hawaii in the 6th or 7th c. A.D. from the Marquesas Islands, about 994 miles/1600km to the south. In the 12th c. Hawaii was conquered by the inhabitants of Tahiti who brought far-reaching changes to the existing culture and religions. When the British seafarer James Cook discovered Hawaii in 1778 the islands were populated by about 300,000 Hawaiians. They relied mainly on agriculture and were described as tall, strong and peaceful people.

The number of Hawaiians was decimated by the imported diseases against which they had no resistance or immunity.

When the first missionaries arrived in Hawaii 40 years later the Hawaiian population had fallen by more than a half to 140,000. According to one report almost 100,000 Hawaiians died in a typhoid or cholera epidemic (the Hawaiians called it "okuu") in 1804. In the years that followed tuberculosis, leprosy, measles, smallpox and other infectious diseases spread, usually with fatal consequences.

In 1882 the census by King David Kalakaua recorded 48,000 Hawaiians.

These conditions together with a high infant mortality rate and a high proportion of mixed marriages have resulted in there being only 10,000 "real" Hawaiians today. According to the law all inhabitants with a Hawaiian grandparent count as Hawaiian so that officially 10% (115,000) of the island's population are Hawaiian.

Statistical data
(selected)

The fall in population figures owing to the decrease in the Hawaiian population and the renewed increase with the migration of other nationalities are illustrated in the following statistics:

1778	300,000	inhab. (estimated)
1832	130,000	inhab. (estimated)
1882	48,000	inhab.
1900	154,000	inhab.
1950	499,769	inhab.
1980	893,428	inhab.
1989	1,112,000	inhab. (estimated)

Other ethnic
groups

The first major change in the Hawaiian population occured with the immigration of the contract workers for the plantations. The first group consisted of Chinese agricultural workers. In the second half of the 19th c. and beginning of the 20th c. Japanese and Filipinos followed and from 1878 Portuguese, who, as supervisors ("lunas") enjoyed quite high social status from the beginning. Koreans and Puerto Ricans were also originally signed up as plantation workers and contribute to the present day melting pot. This planned pattern of immigration continued until the end of the Second World War.

The most recent group to arrive here are the Samoans who came to Hawaii from American Samoa in order to improve their standard of living. Equally the number of mainland Americans is growing since Hawaii became a US state.

Today the Hawaiians are often regarded as a problem group. The level *Social problems* of unemployment among them is above average as is the incidence of sickness and crime rate. They are at the bottom end of the social hierarchy and feel themselves to be socially marginalised. They have no part in the economic development which was unleashed by the tourist boom and so their incomes are below average. The present day problems of the Hawaiians must be seen in connection with the historical development of the Hawaiian Islands. Until today one of the causes of the social misery of the Hawaiians was seen as the unfair distribution of land. The land claims of the Hawaiians to the so-called Crown Land have not been met fully today. In comparison one third of the privately owned land belongs to only seven landowners.

In contrast to the Hawaiians' situation other members of the population were able to demonstrably improve their social position. An example are the Japanese who have extended their social and economic influence since the Seventies. High Japanese investment in real estate and tourism are causing concern that Hawaii is increasingly coming under Japan's influence.

Similarly the Chinese achieved social elevation from plantation workers to the Hawaiian upper class. Together with the whites these three political groups determine to a large extent the economic and political prosperity of Hawaii.

Religion

The different religions on Hawaii reflect the different social groups. The *Religious diversity* religious freedom laid down in the constitution of 1840 has given rise to an almost infinite variety of religions and sects.

The first wave of Christianity began with the arrival of the first American missionaries in 1820. In the following years almost every Christian faith spread. At the same time the Hawaiian religion declined in importance and almost completely disappeared. The Catholics are numerically the strongest group with 290,000 followers attending 68 churches.

Among the Protestant churches the following creeds are represented: Mormons, Baptists, Unitarians, Adventists, Lutherans, United Church of Christ, Methodists, Assembly of God, Anglican High Church, Jehovah's Witnesses and others. The Jewish community numbers 2000 believers.

Alongside the Christian religious communities large numbers of eastern religions have established themselves. The Japanese and Chinese who came to Hawaii as the first plantation workers brought Buddhism, Shintoism, Taoism and Confucianism.

Today Buddhists with over 65,000 believers and almost 80 temples form the second largest religious community in Hawaii. Since the beginning of this century the increasing influence of Shintoism has been apparent from the growing number of Shinto shrines.

The Asian religious communities number over 100,000 members. Indian temples, pagodas, synagogues and mosques are further evidence of Hawaii's active religions.

More than 300,000 islanders do not belong to any religious community.

Missionaries

On October 23rd 1819 a ship carrying the first missionaries destined for *Protestants* Hawaii set sail. A young Hawaiian theology student, Henry Opukahaia from Napoopoo (Kauai), who had gone to New England arranged for the American Board of Commissioners for Foreign Missions to send

Statue of Buddha . . .

Kauahaao Church

missionaries to Hawaii. He was unable to take part in this journey himself as he died of typhoid shortly before the ship's departure (see Famous People, Henry Oppukahaia). On April 4th 1820 the crew of the two-master "Thaddeus" landed at Kailua-Kona (Hawaii) after a 200 day journey and began the task of converting the Hawaiians to Christianity. By 1863 this mission was completed: Hawaii was a Christian, and from the missionaries point of view, a civilised land.

Catholics

The Catholics did not want to be left behind by the successful Protestant missionaries. In 1827 the first Catholic priests arrived but were turned back by Queen Kaahumanu who had already been converted to Christianity. With the influx of Portuguese and Filipinos, who belonged to the Catholic faith, the Catholic Church was able to gradually strengthen its influence.

Mormons

The Mormons arrived in Hawaii in 1850 with plans to build a community and a town on Lanai Island based on the model of Salt Lake City, Utah, USA. However, they were recalled to Utah in 1858. Following their return to Hawaii in 1864 they settled in Laie (Ohau) and established a sugar cane plantation and a temple. In the Mormon community which still exists today is the Polynesian Cultural Center (see A–Z, Oahu) and the largest Mormon temple, built 1919.

With 32,000 followers the "Church of Jesus Christ of Latterday Saints" – the full description for the Mormons – is the biggest Protestant community in Hawaii.

Hawaiian religion

Religious life

Religion permeated many areas of the everyday life of the Hawaiians with nature playing an important role. Significant patterns and symbols in nature and also certain plants were attributed spiritual power. Hawaiians believe that the spirit of the gods can be embodied in living and dead objects. Natural events such as volcanic eruptions or tsunamis were understood to be the moods of the gods.

The Hawaii social life was controlled by a large number of rules and bans. This code of behaviour, called "kapu", extended into all areas of life. Men and women were not allowed to eat together. Women were forbidden to consume certain foods such as fish and bananas. Transgression of these strict rules was punishable with death. The only escape was to flee to a protective temple.

"kapus"

In total the not insignificant sum of 40,000 gods and demi-gods were worshipped. For every aspect of daily life there was a god, with men and women having different gods. They took the form of idols, normally carved from wood and sometimes reaching the height of humans. Some were also made from feathers, straw or stone with human hair usually covering the heads.

Hawaiian gods

In the Bishop Museum in Honolulu these idols are on display but the tourist is more likely to come across them with wide mouths and huge sparkling teeth as cheap imitations in the numerous souvenir shops.

The main gods in Hawaii were Ku, Hina, Kane, Kanaloa, Lono and Pele. Ku, the protective god of war and man's reproductive power, and Hina, the moon goddess, embody the feminine and masculine side of nature.

Chief gods

Kane, the Hawaiian god for man and husband, was the most popular Hawaiian god. He was the god of life, of sunlight, of fresh water and forest. As Kane is the god of life he renounces sacrifices and generally is not idolised.

Kanaloa, the god of oceans and winds, was also honoured as the protective god of healing. He did battle with Kane thereby becoming the god of death.

Two gods outlasted the overthrow of the gods by King Kamehaha II as well as the missionaries' attempts at conversion to Christianity and have retained their popularity until the present day: Pele, the goddess of fire, whose seat is the Kilauea volcano on Hawaii and the demi-god Maui, after whom the island was named. Many legends surround his heroic deeds; above all, he is said to have held the sun still to create more daylight for the islanders to carry out their work.

Lono was the god of the clouds, the harvest and the rain – in other words a god who brought prosperity. The harvest festival ("makahiki") was held in his honour.

The Hawaiians worshipped their gods in various temples called "heiaus". A "heiau" consisted of a square uncovered stone wall, possibly enclosing an area the size of a football field. In the centre a platform was built as a sacrificial table – often this is all that remains today from that period.

Hawaii temples "heiau"

The protective temples were refuges for people who had broken the Hawaiian code of conduct, the "kapus".

Fish, chicken, dogs and fruit were sacrificed to please the gods. However, from the 12th c., influenced by the Tahitians, humans were sacrificed to certain gods in the "heiaus".

The death of Kamehameha I in 1819, the founder of the Hawaiian kingdom, signalled the end of the old system of religion. His two favourite wives – polygamy was the norm in old Hawaii and Kamahameha made good use of it – Kaahumanu and Keopuolani used the new king Kamahameha II to break the "kapus", the multitude of bans which the old beliefs imposed on the Hawaiians. Two of the most sacred "kapus" fell in November 1819: first of all men and women ate

Breakdown of Hawaiian religion

together and in addition to this women were allowed to eat the forbidden fruit – bananas and certain fish.

Kaahumanu, made "kuhia nui" or regent for the weak and reputedly alcoholic young king, was the real ruler of the country. She sat next to the king at the first "free" meal, the "ai noa", and with the first bite which they took together the fate of the Hawaiian religion was sealed.

On the command of Kamehameha II the "heiaus", which until then had been regarded as holy, were destroyed and the idols burnt so that only scant ruins are left today, some of which have recently been restored.

The collapse of the Hawaiian religion and closely related Hawaiian culture must also be seen alongside contemporary developments on the island. The emergence of the missionaries from New England and the later immigration of plantation workers from China, Japan and the Philippines altered the communal and social life to such a degree that the base for the Hawaiian religion, the intact Hawaiian community, was gradually eroded.

Economy

General situation

The state of the Hawaiian economy is characterised by the consequences of one-sided development. The exclusive concentration on banana and sugar cane production from the middle of the last century combined with increasing competition on the world markets and general overproduction has led to a susceptible and unbalanced agricultural structure.

Since the Sixties the main pillar of the Hawaiian economy has changed from agriculture to tourism.

Sugar cane . . .   *and pineapple growing*

In the industrial sector the construction industry has profited from the effects of population expansion and from the rapid growth of tourist projects and the associated infrastructure. The mainstay of Hawaiian industry is the sugar and pineapple industry. Smaller local firms specialise in textiles and clothes. Industry is centred mainly on Oahu Island.

With the gradual change of Hawaii into a society based on service industries both tourism and providing for the American troops based here are becoming increasingly important.

To alleviate the generally unstable situation of the Hawaiian economy efforts have been made in recent years to attract investment in the areas of modern technology (news technology, production of computer software and electrical goods, biotechnology, oceanic research and astronomy) and regenerative sources of energy (wind and thermal energy) thereby achieving a degree of diversification in the economy.

Agriculture and food processing

Agriculture, formerly the most important factor in the islands' economy, is decreasing in importance. Falling prices for sugar and pineapples – for many years the mainstay of the agricultural economy – have brought about restructuring: the number of plantations and area under cultivation have decreased whereas the production on other areas has increased. Other crops are becoming more important.

Decline

The Polynesians introduced sugar cane when they settled on Hawaii as wind protection and to sweeten foods. The Hawaiians chewed the cane and also extracted the juice which was used as a food and for medicinal purposes. Sugar cane also played a part in religious rites.

Sugar cane

The successful commercial production of sugar cane began in the middle of the 19th c. following the development of equipment for removing the sugar. The molasses could be separated from the sugar syrup by using centrifuges producing white sugar crystals. The large number of producers soon resulted in the "Big Five", five producers who gradually bought up their competitors. The feudal structure of the sugar industry was soon established. One of the "Big Five" was Claus Spreckels, already sugar king of California. He came to Hawaii in 1876, acquired large areas of land on Maui Island and set up Hawaii's first sugar refinery. Sugar cane production requires a lot of water and the irrigation system developed by Spreckels solved one of the main problems of commercial production.

Commercial sugar cane production

Spreckels was the pathfinder for the profitable production of sugar cane resulting in numerous plantations. At this time sugar production faced no economic competition.

Owing to the acute shortage of labour brought about by the continual disappearance of the Hawaiian population and the simultaneous rise in the Hawaiian sugar industry, plantation workers were recruited from Asia in the first instance. The first contract workers came from China, followed by Japanese and later other nationalities which are all to be found in today's mixed population: Filipinos, Mexicans, Samoans, Portuguese and a number of freed slaves from the southern states of America who found conditions here little better.

Work on the sugar plantations was hard and the conditions were appalling. The situation only gradually improved when the workers formed trade unions after the Second World War.

Today there has been a considerable reduction in the number of sugar farms to about 300 plantations. The main areas of cultivation are on the four biggest islands: Hawaii, Maui, Oahu and Kauai.

Economy

Sugar cane production is reduced to 16 companies. The five most influential concerns have branched out into other areas of the economy.

Pineapples

Pineapple fields form part of the familar picture of Hawaii yet economically sugar cane is more important. Pineapples arrived in 1820 from Brazil and at first were only grown in small quantities.

The type which is now grown almost exclusively in Hawaii is the Cayenne fruit, a very sweet and exceptionally large fruit weighing between 2–3kg. This type comes from the Caribbean island of Jamaica and was first introduced into Hawaii in 1886.

Widespread cultivation and industrial processing of pineapple was initiated by James Drummond Dole of Boston. He was the first to recognise the importance of the pineapple and planted an area of 24 hectares in Wahiawa on Oahu Island. Even today there are still large pineapple fields. He built a canning factory for processing the pineapple and tinned pineapple soon conquered the American market and later the world market.

In 1922 Dole bought the whole of Lanai Island where the largest pineapple plantation in the world is to be found. Although as a result of worldwide overproduction the acreage under pineapples is annually decreasing more than 90% of all American pineapples still come from Lanai.

Taro

Taro, a tuber which requires a plentiful supply of water for its growth is only cultivated for home consumption and goes to make "poi" the national dish. The main areas of cultivation are on Kauai.

Cona coffee

Cona coffee plants grow especially well on the often cloud-covered west coast of Hawaii Island.

Cona coffee, a connoisseur blend which has recently become profitable, is produced primarily by small companies which deliver their September harvest to some large roasting houses. The lava earth in the shadow of Mt Mauna Loa combined with a climate of dew at dawn, sunshine in the morning and cumulus clouds providing shade in the afternoon create ideal conditions.

In comparison with other sorts of coffee the expensive cona coffee is a full-bodied aromatic coffee which can be enjoyed in many of the island's restaurants.

Macadamia nuts

The macadamia nut tree, like pineapples and coffee, is not native to Hawaii but comes from Australia.

It is grown on the east coast of Hawaii Island. The nut tree first bears fruit after seven or eight years.

The two largest plantations are situated to the south and north of Hilo; the Mauna Loa Macadamia Nut Corporation, about 5½ miles south of Hilo has more than 800,000 trees and manufactures numerous products from macadamia nuts in its factory. The second large factory is the Hawaiian Holiday Macadamia Nut Factory in Honokaa, north of Hilo on road 18.

Fruits

Papayas, mangoes, coconuts, bananas, guavas, passion fruit, avocados, water melons and oranges are all grown in large quantities in Hawaii. The Kahuku papayas are the best and of these a variety called Kamiya papaya which grows on the north coast of Oahu is the most prized. On Kauai strawberry papayas with red flesh predominate. The best mangoes are said to come from Waianae (Oahu) and from the west coast of Kauai. Papayas, pineapples and bananas ripen throughout the year, mangoes during the summer months. Fruit and vegetable growing has become important in view of attempts to diversify agricultural production.

Orchids

Flower and orchid growing on the island of Hawaii and in the area surrounding Hilo is a lucrative source of income. Orchids are grown for both the home and export market. Flowers

Cattle rearing is of considerable importance for Hawaiian agriculture and takes place on the islands of Hawaii and Molokai. Near the north coast of Hawaii is the biggest private ranch of the US, the Parker ranch with about 50,000 head of cattle and on Molokai the Puu O Hoku ranch which breeds exclusively French Charolais cattle on 5,500 hectares. Hawaii can only provide 40% of its meat requirements. Cattle rearing

The total amount of agricultural production stands at about 500 million US dollars with cattle production netting just under 100 million US dollars, not much more than one tenth of the income from tourism in Hawaii.

Military

Hawaii's geographical location makes it of strategic importance. Numerous military support units of the United States navy, air force and land forces are based on the Hawaiian Islands.

Approximately 60,000 military personnel and their families are stationed in Hawaii. A large number of highly qualified civilians are also employed on the military bases. Catering for this section of the population provides employment for the service industries. The finances which Hawaii receives from the national defence budget represent the second largest source of income of the state of Hawaii.

The area devoted to military installations is enormous. On Oahu Island especially, where 80% of the population live, the military occupies 26% of the area.

Tourism

General

Hawaii is a part of the world which has tremendous tourist potential with its favourable climate, varied scenery and dream beaches. Whereas in 1959, when Hawaii became the 50th US state, only about 250,000 tourists travelled to Hawaii, in 1993 almost 6.2 million visitors made tourism into the most important area of the economy. Owing to this trend the gross national product has increased tenfold over three decades to 20 billion US dollars and the unemployment rate has fallen to 3.5%, the lowest of all US states. Today 40% of all jobs are to be found in the ever-growing tourist sector and related industries.

Capacity

There are 70,500 hotel beds available for tourists, a third under Japanese ownership. In addition, there is a considerable number of condominiums, self-contained bungalows comparable with holiday apartments.

Development plans

The number of hotel rooms has increased by several thousand over the past few years. Several hotel concerns such as the Ritz Carlton, Embassy Suites and Four Seasons have opened their first hotels on Hawaii or have hotels under construction. Following the development of mega-complexes such as Hyatt Regency Waikoloa on Hawaii Island and Westin Kauai there does not seem to have been a moment's pause for thought. Several of the older hotels are being partly or completely renovated in order to maintain high standards of quality. This applies particularly to Waikiki where a new Japanese hotel still under construction, the Prince Hotel, is providing competition. The bigger hotels are trying to attract congresses and meetings to Hawaii in order to increase their potential occupancy. The average occupancy rates at present are between 60 and 65%.

The crowded beach of Waikiki

In 1987 65% of the tourists came from the American mainland, 22% from Japan and 13% from Canada, Europe and the South Pacific, including Australia and New Zealand. It is not surprising that in several large hotels such as the Hilton Hawaiian Village in Waikiki the morning alarm call is in English and Japanese and many restaurants offer Japanese specialities even for breakfast.

Of the relatively small number of European tourists (in 1990 out of a total 6,971,000 only 220,000 came from Europe) the 54,000 Germans make up a large proportion.

Where the tourists come from

Statistical evidence shows that Japanese tourists in Hawaii spend four times as much as Americans. It is a Japanese custom to return home laden with presents. A comprehensive shopping trip is an absolute necessity. It is quite a sight to see long queues of Japanese shoppers forming in front of the smallest shops along Kalakaua Avenue during the Japanese main holiday season, so-called Golden Week, and who are only admitted when others have left the shop.

Tourist expenditure

On average the tourist spends nine days on Hawaii. All travellers arrive by air which results in the length of stay being much shorter than in the past. When travellers came by boat in the Fifties they took the week-long sea voyage into account and stayed longer in the resort, usually a month on average.

Length of stay

The most popular destination is Waikiki on Oahu Island. Approximately 70% of tourists stay on Oahu, 15% on Maui, and 7% on both Kauai and less than 1% on Molokai and Lanai. Waikiki is the tourist stronghold and attracts as many tourists as all other five islands together.

Regional distribution

Effects of tourism

The rapidly increasing number of visitors to the islands and further expansion of tourist development, not only on Oahu Island, but also on the less well known islands, such as Molokai, have brought far-reaching changes.

Further development

Land speculation has driven up land prices and accelerated the sale of the islands. Japanese capital which in recent years has flowed into Hawaii was chiefly invested in tourist projects. Out of 20 luxury hotels on Waikiki beach 18 were in Japanese hands by 1988. The Japanese, who also represent the second strongest tourist group, are gaining more and more influence in economic activities and especially tourism in Hawaii.

The lion's share of tourist investment is in the control of six multi-national concerns. As the returns from sugar cane and pineapple growing are falling the descendants of the former sugar barons are also investing in large-scale tourist projects.

Land speculation and large-scale tourist projects

The new trend towards luxurious developments on islands hardly opened up to tourists increases the social divide between the native population living in the rural areas and the wealthy tourists in their luxury hotels. On the thinly populated islands an imbalance can easily arise between the numbers of the local population and the numerous tourists.

Social effects

A further problem is the quality of jobs which tourism has created. The frequently unqualified jobs in the tourist service sector are often not very attractive and not exactly well paid. The indigenous population

Quality of jobs

Economy

profits only to a limited extent from the tourist development on their islands.

Environmental damage

Environmental damage is growing with the increasing number of visitors especially on the heavily populated island of Oahu. The results are increased traffic, increased consumption of drinking water, growing rubbish dumps and large quantities of sewage.

Dependencies

The most sensitive area of Hawaiian tourism is the dependency on the only means of transport, the aeroplane. The fear of flying at the time of the Gulf War at the beginning of 1991 has led to an extreme drop in bookings with entire American airline companies. Hawaii was especially hard hit as both the Japanese and the Americans stayed away. The extensive dependency on tourism, which in the event of a recession in the USA and Japan, the two most important tourist countries for Hawaii, could have disastrous consequences, caused the government to look for ways and means to strengthen other branches of the economy, but which so far have not been very successful.

South sea myths

Not least it should be mentioned here that most tourists who travel to Hawaii expect to find paradise. Every tourist should be aware that the world of the natives despite their friendliness and Alohan spirit is not as unproblematic and bright as that of the tourists. Every visitor should come with an open mind to the problems of the islanders and an acceptance and appreciation of the Hawaiian way of life and culture.

History

The first settlers on Hawaii arrive from Polynesia presumably via the Marquesas Islands, situated 2600 miles/4160km away. **Around 750**

Over the next two centuries sea-going canoes ply between the island of Tahiti, 2740 miles/4380km away and Hawaii. **1100**

The landing of a Spanish expedition in Hawaii led by Juan Gaetani is a matter of historical dispute. James Cook is therefore acknowledged to have discovered Hawaii. **1535**

The future king Kamehameha I is born in Kohala, in the north of Hawaii Island. **1758**

On January 18th Cook sights the northwestern islands of the Hawaiian archipelago and names them after his employer and commissioner, the Earl of Sandwich, the Sandwich Islands. Three days later he goes ashore with the crews of his ships "Resolution" and "Discovery" in Waimea (Kauai) and is received with great ceremony. Following his return from the Arctic he sights Maui for the first time on November 26th. **1778**

On January 17th the British ships land in Kealakekua Bay on the Kona coast of Hawaii, where 10,000 Hawaiians have turned out to greet them. On February 14th Cook, four sailors and several Hawaiians meet their death during an incident in which Cook allegedly tries to take a chief captive. **1779**

The first trading ship on its return voyage from China anchors in Hawaii. **1785**

In May English and French ships land in Hawaii, soon followed by Russian, Spanish and American vessels. **1786**

Kamehameha seeks to rule the Hawaiian Islands. His troops invade Maui. **1789**

A massive eruption of the volcano Kilauea destroys the forces of Kamehameha's opponent Keoa Kuahuula on Maui. **1790**

The first ships under the command of the British seafarer George Vancouver land at Kealakekua Bay (Hawaii). He introduces the first cattle to Hawaii. **1792**

His victory in the battle of Nuuanu Pali on Oahu allows Kamehameha to unite all the islands, with the exception of Kauai, under his rule. **1795**

Kamehameha's attempts to take Kauai are thwarted by a storm in which his ships are destroyed. **1796**

The first horses are brought to Hawaii on board an American freighter. **1803**

A renewed invasion attempt on Kauai by Kamehameha fails owing to a sudden epidemic. **1804**

Under pressure King Kaumualii agrees to relinquish his island to the Hawaiian Kingdom of Kamehameha I. **1810**

Landing of the "Resolution" and "Discovery" in Waimea (Kauai)

1815   John Palmer Parker settles in Waimea (Hawaii) and is given the right to hunt the wild cattle for the sale of their meat and skins: this is the start of the Parker Ranch.

1816   On May 21st Kaumualii of Kauai signs an agreement with the German doctor Georg Anton Scheffer in which Kauai is placed under the protection of the Russian tsar. Six months later a Russian two-master arrives in Hawaii under the command of Otto von Kotzebues to a splendid welcome by King Kamehameha. One year later Kaumualii revokes his declaration in return.

1819   Kamehameha I dies on May 8th; his son Liholiho is declared the new king, Kamehameha II, on May 20th.
         On September 29th the first whaling ships dock in Kealakekua Bay (Hawaii).
         In November King Kamehameha II abolishes the Hawaiian religion and drops the "kapa" laws.

1820   On March 31st the first ship carrying US missionaries arrives on the Kona coast (Hawaii).

1821   Kumualii is brought to Honolulu as a hostage and pledges loyalty again to the Royal family. He marries Kaahumanu, the regent and favourite wife of Kamehameha I.

1823   On November 27th King Kamehameha II and Queen Kamamalu set out on board a British whaling ship for Great Britain. Both succumb to measles; their mortal remains do not arrive in Honolulu until 3 May 1825 on board a British warship.

1825   On June 6th Prince Kauikeaouli, just 9 years old, is proclaimed the new king (Kamehameha III); his stepmother Kaahumanu remains regent.

1826   The first American warship the two-master "Dolphin" arrives on January 16th.

The first Catholic missionaries arrive from France but are soon expelled by Kaahumanu.   1827

From California, still part of Mexico, the first "paniolos", future cowboys, arrive on the islands to tend the cattle.   1830

In Lahaina (Maui) the Lahainaluna seminary is founded, a Christian educational institute for young Hawaiians.   1831

On June 5th the regent ("kuhina nui") Kaahamanu dies.   1832
    The missionaries carry out the first census; the population is estimated at 130,000.
    The missionaries also define the Hawaiian alphabet as having seven consonants and five vowels; the first translation of the New Testament is published soon afterwards.

The sixth and final group of North American missionaries arrive in Hawaii.   1833

On February 14th the first printed edition of a Hawaiian weekly magazine appears, "Ka Lama Hawaii", consisting of four pages. The first printing press is in the Lahainaluna seminary.   1834

The first Hawaiian-English dictionary containing 5700 words appears.   1836
On July 30th the first English language weekly newspaper "Sandwich Island Gazette" is published in Honolulu by two Americans.

In Wailuku (Maui) a central girls' boarding school is opened to educate suitable women for the Hawaiian graduates of the Lahainaluna seminary.   1837
    Catholic missionaries return to Hawaii for the first time since their expulsion.

The missionaries publish the first literary magazine the "Hawaiian Spectator".   1838

On June 17th Kamehameha III announces the introduction of civil rights for all Hawaiians and simultaneously proclaims an edict of tolerance towards all religions.   1839

The first edition of the newspaper "The Polynesian" appears; its publisher writes the first history of Hawaii three years later: "The History of the Hawaiian or Sandwich Islands".   1840

Admiral Lord Paulet, captain of the British two-master "Carysfort" wants to compel Hawaii to become a British protectorate. For almost six months the "Union Jack" flies over Hawaii until the appearance of Admiral Richard Thomas with another warship to revoke the cession.   1843
    On November 28th a joint Anglo-French declaration is signed in London recognising the independence of the Sandwich Islands; a similar declaration is made by the US government in the summer of 1844.

The first English-Hawaiian dictionary is published by the Lahainaluna Press.   1845
    The first coffee produced in Kailua Kona is exported, 124kg precisely.
    The capital of the Kingdom of Hawaii is transferred from Lahaina to Honolulu.

Increasing numbers of whaling ships land at Lahaina (596) and Honolulu (429).   1846

The first government with six ministers and a Privy Council is formed as the executive body of the kingdom. At the end of April the second part of the constitution on the distribution of land, the "Great Mahele" is announced. It becomes law in 1848.

1847   In Honolulu the first theatre is founded under the name of the Thespian Theatre. It only opens for one season and is followed by the Royal Hawaiian Theatre.

1848   Land distribution takes place with a third being awarded each to the Royal Family, the government and the people. For the first time the Hawaiian population have rights of land ownership.

1850   The first post office is established in Honolulu and the first stamps are issued.
A law allows the engagement of urgently needed foreign contract workers.

1851   Kamehameha III signs a secret agreement which states that in the event of the further spread of French imperialism Hawaii will be protected by the United States.

1852   The old constitution of 1840 is replaced on June 8th by one in which all men are summoned to participate in the government of the country.

1853   The first official census reveals a population of only 73,000; 30% of all inhabitants belong to Christian churches.
Within eight months a smallpox epidemic claimed the lives of almost 2500 Hawaiians.

Rulers of the Kingdom of Hawaii

Kamehameha I (1758?–1819)
Kamehameha the Great, king from 1795 until 1819, married to Kaahumanu

Kamehameha II (1799–1824)
Liholiho, eldest son of Kamehameha I, king from 1819 to 1824, married to Keopuolani, joint regency of Kaahumanu

Kamehameha III (1814–54)
Kauikeaouli, younger brother of Kamehameha II, king from 1825 to 1854, Kaahumanu and later Kihau, eldest half-sister of Kamehameha III, are regents

Kamehameha IV (1834–63)
Alexander Liholiho, son of Kinau and grandson of Kamehameha I, king from 1855 to 1863

Kamehameha V (1830–72)
Lot Kapulaiwa, brother of Kamehameha IV, king from 1863 to 1872

William C. Lunalilo (1835–74)
King from 1873 to 1874, first elected king of Hawaii

David Kalakaua (1836–91)
King from 1874 to 1891, elected

Liliuokalani (1838–1917)
Lydia Kamekaeha Kaolamalii, Queen from 1891 to 1893, elected, last queen of Hawaii

A particularly productive type of sugar cane, "Lahaina", is imported from Tahiti giving the sugar industry an extra boost.
    Ten schools are established which provide English lessons for the Hawaiian youth.
    On December 15th Kamehameha III dies, he is succeeded by Prince Alexander Liholiho as Kamehameha IV. — **1854**

The first regular boat service between Hawaii and the mainland is opened by the "Regular Dispatch" Line. A letter from New York arrives in Honolulu in the record time of 55 days.
    The Mauna Loa volcano erupts threatening the town of Hilo. — **1855**

The newspaper "Pacific Commercial Advertiser" is founded. It is the forerunner of the present day "Honolulu Advertiser", one of Hawaii's chief newspapers. — **1856**

The first Hawaiian bank is opened in Honolulu by Frank Reed Bishop under the name Bank of Bishop & Co, Ltd, the present day First Hawaiian Bank. — **1858**

The population figures continue to fall dramatically. A new census registers just 70,000 inhabitants.
    In Honolulu the foundation stone for the first Hawaiian hospital, the Queen's Hospital, is laid. — **1860**

The outbreak of the American Civil War drives up the price of sugar, causing a boom in the Hawaiian sugar industry. — **1861**

The North American Missionary Society ends its activities in Hawaii and leaves its future work to the Hawaii Evangelical Association. On November 30th Kamehameha IV dies; he is succeeded by his elder brother Lot Kapulaiwa as Kamehameha V. — **1863**

Kamehameha V announces a new constitution which affords him greater powers. He sells Nihau Island to the Sinclair Robinson family for 10,000 dollars. — **1864**

King Kamehameha V ordains the founding of a leper colony in Kalawao (Molokai), where sufferers are isolated, often by force. Within the first seven years the number of patients reaches 800. — **1866**

Hawaii and the USA sign a trade agreement to facilitate the import of sugar to the USA. — **1867**

A new eruption of Mauna Loa along with earthquakes endangers Hawaii Island. — **1868**

Heinrich Berger, German conductor at the court of Kamehameha V, gives his first concert with the Royal Hawaiian Band, which he leads until 1915.
    On December 11th Kamehameha V dies and as he has not appointed a successor, in accordance with the constitution, a new king must be elected by Parliament. — **1872**

On January 8th William Charles Lunalilo is elected king.
    In September he defeats a rebellion by his bodyguards. — **1873**

On February 3rd King Lunalilo dies; Parliament elects David Kalakaua as his successor. On November 17th the new ruler sets off on a visit to the United States and only returns in February 1875. — **1874**

A new trade agreement with the USA comes into force under which sugar exports are considerably increased. By 1890 they will have increased tenfold. — **1876**

The Royal Hawaiian Band

1878	The first party of Portuguese workers arrives from Madeira; by the end of the century their numbers increase to 18,000.
1879	The foundation stone of the Iolani Palace in Honolulu, the future home of the King, is laid.
1881	King Kalakaua goes on a tour round the world.
1882	Parliament assigns a large area of Crown Property to the sugar industrialist Claus Spreckel near Wailuku (Maui).
1883	Kalakaua and Queen Kapiolani are the first Hawaiian monarchs to be crowned in the purpose-built pavilion in the park of Iolani Palace.
1884	For the first time the population of Hawaii has increased; a census records 86,000 people.
1886	Owing to the relaxation of the Japanese emigration laws the number of Japanese contract workers increases rapidly. Within a decade they make up a quarter of the total Hawaiian population.
1887	Kalakaua's extravagant lifestyle increases the national debt considerably. The newly founded "Hawaiian League", set up to combat corruption among other things, introduces a new constitution, which limits the privileges of the monarch and the Hawaiians in favour of foreign economic interests. The Americans sign a treaty ensuring their exclusive use of Pearl Harbor.
1891	On January 20th Kalakaua dies in San Francisco, he is succeeded by his sister Liliuokalani nine days later.

The Bishop Museum founded in 1889 in Honolulu, the centre of South Pacific culture, is opened. — 1892

On January 17th Queen Liliuokalani is overthrown in a bloodless coup. She tried to increase her powers through a new constitution. Her opponents, who urged annexation by the US, put Sandford B. Dole at the head of a provisional government. Dole abolishes the monarchy, but the desired annexation is rejected by the American president Grover Cleveland. — 1893

On July 3rd the constitution of the Republic of Hawaii is accepted and Dole is elected president the following day. — 1894

On January 6th a counter-revolution occurs, which attempts to re-instate Liliuokalani. However, the revolt is defeated and on January 24th the Queen declares her willingness to abdicate and recognise the republic. — 1895

The population rises to 109,000 with the number of those born off the island, half-Hawaiians and foreigners surpassing the Hawaiian population. — 1896

With the outbreak of the Spanish-American war the American forces use Oahu as a military base.
    On July 7th US President William McKinley signs a congress declaration for the annexation of Hawaii. Hawaii's sovereignty is ended on August 12th, but the republican state apparatus remains until 1900. — 1898

On June 14th Hawaii officially becomes the territory of the United States of America with Dole as the first governor.
    A fire supposed to destroy plague-ridden houses gets out of control and an area of 37 acres/15 hectares in Chinatown, Honolulu, is destroyed in the blaze. — 1900

The first meeting of the territorial parliament takes place and fixes the rate of income tax.
    Electric-powered trams replace the horse-drawn carriages in Honolulu. — 1901

The County system of administration is introduced in Hawaii. The parliament petitions Congress for the first time to accept Hawaii as a state of the union. — 1903

The first Philippino workers come to Hawaii. — 1906

With only five students the College of Agriculture and Mechanic Arts is founded and renamed the College of Hawaii in 1911. It becomes the University of Hawaii in 1920 and today has about 50,000 students spread between Honolulu and Hilo as well as seven associated Community Colleges.
    Jack London and his wife travel to Hawaii on their first visit, other visits follow in 1915 and 1916. — 1907

The Hawaiian Pineapple Growers Association is founded.
    Congress decides to establish a naval base at Pearl Harbor. — 1908

Schofield Barracks, which are later extended into the largest permanent military support base of the USA, are built in Wahiawa (Oahu). — 1909

The first public Library of Hawaii is founded. — 1913

The American submarine "Skate" sinks in Honolulu harbour resulting in the loss of all the crew. — 1915

History

1916	The Hawaii National Park is opened on Hawaii and on Maui.
1917	The USA enters the First World War declaring war against Germany. The Hawaiian National Guard is mobilised for active service.
1918	The dry dock at Pearl Harbor is officially opened.
1919	The great Mormon temple in Laie (Oahu) is consecrated.
1920	The population has risen to 256,000; the proportion of Japanese reaches a peak at 42.7%
1922	The Hawaiian Pineapple Co. acquires Lanai Island and ships the pineapples to its canning factory in Honolulu. Two radio stations in Honolulu transmit their first broadcasts.
1924	An eight month strike on a sugar plantation in Hanapepe (Kauai) ends with the death of 17 strikers and four policeman, 101 people are arrested.
1925	On August 31st the first flight is undertaken from San Francisco to Hawaii in a twin-engined sea plane of the American army, but it runs out of fuel 300 miles (500km) from the islands; the five-man crew are not rescued until September 10th by a submarine.
1927	The Honolulu Academy of Arts is opened as the first art museum of Hawaii. Whereas the first flight from the mainland by two lieutenants in a triple-engined Fokker aeroplane succeeds, two weeks later two civilian pilots in a Travelair Discoverer have to make an emergency landing after a 25 hour flight on the coast of Molokai.
1932	The first radio telephone service Honolulu–London is opened and soon after extended to the capital cities of Europe and South America.
1934	Franklin D. Roosevelt is the first American president to visit Hawaii. A regular airmail postal service between the islands begins.
1935	An airmail postal service California–Hawaii is introduced with the four-engined Pan Am plane "China Clipper".
1941	With the Japanese bomb attack on Pearl Harbor which claims almost 2400 lives and sinks several warships the USA enters the Second World War. On December 30th Japanese submarines attack the harbours of Hilo (Hawaii), Nawiliwili (Kauai) and Kahului (Maui).
1942	On January 28th a Japanese submarine sinks a US transport ship in Hawaiian waters. On March 2nd a Japanese plane bombs Honolulu.
1946	The worst tsunami ever to have hit Hawaii causes tremendous damage around Hilo (Hawaii). It results in 150 dead, 160 injured and damage in excess of 25 million US dollars. A committee of the US House of Representatives is in favour of the immediate acceptance of Hawaii into the union, but opposition by the Senate thwarts all attempts over the following ten years.
1949	On May 1st a six-month long strike by the dockworkers' union almost brings the port of Honolulu to a standstill.
1950	The population continues to expand. In comparison with 1900 the population has more than trebled to almost 500,000.

On 1 December the first Hawaiian television station KGMB in Honolulu comes into service. 1952

The alleged Communist infiltration of the Hawaiian trade unions further delays the acceptance of Hawaii as a US state. 1955

On March 11th and 12th the Senate votes 76:15 and the US House of Representatives 323:89 for Hawaii's acceptance as a US state. A referendum in Hawaii produces a majority of 17:1. The inhabitants of Nihau are opposed to this new status. 1959

In a 93% turnout of the electorate the governor, two state senators and a deputy are elected.

On August 21st Hawaii is officially declared the 50th US state.

A jet airliner belonging to the Australian airline Quantas lands for the first time at Honolulu. Regular jet services bring about a new phase in tourism.

Within a decade the population rises by more than 20% to 609,000. 1960

Congress approves the creation of the East-West Center at the University of Hawaii with the purpose of promoting the cultural and technological co-operation between Eastern Asia, the Pacific nations and the United States.

Hawaii Island is hit by another tsunami causing 27 deaths; at the same time there are volcanic eruptions and earthquakes around Puna (Hawaii).

The first underwater cable is laid between Hawaii and Tokyo at a cost of 84 million US dollars. 1964

Seven US airlines are granted landing permission. Hawaii can now be reached from 35 mainland airports. As a result the number of tourists rises to 1 million this year. 1967

The meteoric population increase continues: within a decade the population of Hawaii has increased by a further 25%. 1970

On April 2nd the schoolteachers go on strike for three weeks demanding improved pay and conditions. 1973

Hilo (Hawaii) is badly damaged by an earthquake.

The 40 year old sugar laws expire leading to the sugar price shooting up from 11 to 65%. 1974

The Democrat, George Ariyoshi, is the first American of Japanese descent to be elected Governor of Hawaii.

In a symbolic occupation of the unpopulated island of Kahoolawe, which is used by the army for weapons testing, the first demands are made for its return. 1976

The volcano Kilauea (Hawaii), the most active volcano in the world, erupts several times over a fortnight, and continues to erupt at irregular intervals over the next 12 years. 1977

Hawaii celebrates the bicentenary of Captain Cook's first landing. 1978

Four million tourists, more than four times the indigenous population, visit Hawaii. 1979

One of the largest infra-red telescopes is set up on Mauna Kea, the highest mountain of the Hawaii Islands.

The gross national product of the state of Hawaii is around 13 billion dollars; almost 24% (3.7 billion US dollars) of which is derived from tourism, but barely 2.5% (325 million US dollars) from the sugar industry which continues to decline in importance. 1981

History

1983   The population tops one million for the first time; two thirds of the population live in Honolulu.

1986   A satellite town is planned to be built on the virtually uninhabited west coast of Oahu to relieve Honolulu. Seven Japanese financed hotels are also planned.

1987   Total agricultural production amounts to 609 million US dollars. With an increase of 9% compared with 1982 agricultural production cannot keep pace with the steep price increases on the islands.

1988   With an occupancy rate of 78.5% Hawaii leads other US states. Honolulu is even higher with 85%, but the price level in general is very high.

1989   Life on Hawaii is expensive: the cost of living is on average 28.7% higher than in the US mainland states, yet the average income of the Hawaiians is the same.
     On June 1st the areas around Hilo, Puna and the Volcanoes National Park on Hawaii are shaken by two earthquakes.

1990   The construction of the first geothermal power station begins in the rainforest region of Puna. It is to provide 20% of the island's electricity requirements from the earth's heat. This expensive major project is indeed controversial, as it is neither ecologically nor economically defensible. The government plans to found an ensemble to perform Hawaiian dance and music in the United States and abroad in order to revitalise tourism.
     At the end of May the coastal town of Kalapana in the south of Hawaii Island is completely destroyed by a new eruption of the Kilauea volcano.

1991   On July 11th the volcanic peaks of Hawaii and Maui Islands are the best observation points of a total eclipse of the sun, an unusual astronomical spectacle visible from the Hawaiian Islands to North Brazil.

1992   On September 11th/12th hurricane Iniki sweeps across Kauai Island at speeds of up to 174mph/280kph, leaving enormous devastation in its wake.

Famous People

The following alphabetically arranged list includes people who were either born or died in Hawaii or else visited Hawaii and had some lasting influence and have achieved national or even international recognition.

Note

Born in Durham, Connecticut, USA the theologian and doctor arrived in Honolulu in 1831 aboard the fourth missionary ship. He was first stationed in Waimea (Hawaii) and was a practising priest and doctor. In the Baldwin Home Museum his living rooms and doctor's practice can be visited (see A–Z, Maui). He translated several chapters of the New Testament into Hawaiian. He spent the last years of his life in Honolulu. Among his eight childen his son Henry. P. Baldwin became a successful sugar farmer. With his brother-in-law Samuel T. Alexander he founded the firm Alexander & Baldwin, which is still one of the largest companies in Hawaii today.

Dwight Baldwin
Theologian
(1798–1886)

Born in Bennington, Vermont, USA Bingham studied at Middlebury College and at Andover Theological Seminary. He was ordained in 1818 in Boston and selected for the first mission to Hawaii in 1820. He was a priest in the first church in Hawaii, the Mokuaikaua Church. During his twenty years as a missionary his strict sense of morality often brought him into conflict with the whalers landing at Lahaina (Maui) who in his opinion were bringing immorality to Lahaina. He made an outstanding contribution to creating a written Hawaiian language. Active cooperation in codifying the Hawaiian alphabet and translation of large parts of the New Testament into the Hawaiian language count among his achievements. He died in New England, to where the family had returned in 1840 concerned about the poor health of his wife.

Hiram Bingham
Theologian
(1789–1869)

Princess Pauahi, granddaughter of King Kamehameha the Great, married the banker Charles Reed Bishop and was to succeed the heirless King Kamehameha V as Queen of Hawaii. Following the death of her cousin Ruth Keelikolani (1826–83) she became the main heiress of the Kamehameha estate (Bishop Estate), at that time encompassed 9% of the total area of the islands. She was unable to enjoy her wealth for long as she died almost a year after her cousin. In her will she bequeathed the establishment of the Kamehameha School in Honolulu for the children of Hawaiian descent, nowadays the most important school in Hawaii.

Bernice Pauahi
Bishop
Landowner
(1831–84)

Bishop, who originated from Glen Falls in New York state, arrived in Hawaii in 1846 from Oregon and married Princess Bernice Pauahi. Within a few years he became director of the customs office, founded the trading company Alrich & Bishop in 1858 and shortly afterwards the first Hawaiian bank, Bank of Bishop & Co, Ltd, today the First Hawaiian Bank. He was able to take early retirement from business life owing to the handsome profits from the expanding sugar cane industry and his wife's inheritance. He was nominated a life member of the Hawaiian Parliament and served as adviser to four kings as well as the last queen. In 1889 he opened the Bernice P. Bishop Museum in Honolulu (See A–Z, Oahu) in memory of his wife. The Bishop Trust Corporation, which he set up and is today still an important land estate firm, provided funds for the anthropological museum. Bishop died in 1915 in San Francisco.

Charles Reed
Bishop
Banker
(1822–1915)

Famous People

James Cook

King David Kalakaua

Queen Liliuokalani

Henry Augustus P. Carter Industrialist Diplomat (1837–91)	Henry Augustus Carter was born in Honolulu and began his successful business career at the early age of 19. Just six years later he was partner in the firm Charles Brewer & Co., which still exists today. He also made a fortune from the expanding sugar industry. In 1875 he negotiated a mutual trade agreement with the United States of America and was then sent by King David Kalakaua to London, Paris and Berlin to explain the significance of the treaty to their governments. In 1883 he was appointed Presidential Minister in Washington. With the extension of the mutual trade agreement in 1887, in which Carter was again influential, the United States were granted permission to establish a naval support base at Pearl Harbor.
James Cook Seafarer (1728–79)	Captain James Cook, the English circumnavigator, was the last great discoverer of maritime regions. During his three journeys (1768 to 1779) he discovered the East coast of Australia, New Zealand and numerous groups of islands in the Pacific. On his last journey, when he landed on Hawaii for the first time, he was looking for the northern passage from the Pacific to the Atlantic. Both his ships "Resolution" and "Discovery" sailed by Kauai, finally casting anchor in Kealakekua Bay, and were greeted with warmth and curiosity by the natives. Cook's arrival was understood to be the return of the god "lomo" and accordingly he was received with great reverence. Cook named the islands the Sandwich Islands in honour of his patron, Lord Sandwich. His second landing in Hawaii was not so fortunate. Cook had to return prematurely to Hawaii because of storm damage. This time his reception was not so friendly with tensions rising on both sides. When a kedge from the "Discovery" was stolen by the Hawaiians Cook went ashore to resolve the matter. There was a fight in which Cook was killed. Both ships returned to Great Britain with the remains of Cook's body.
Joseph Damien de Veuster Priest (1840–89)	Born in Tremeloo, Belgium this priest came to Hawaii in 1864 as a Heart of Jesus missionary and was ordained in Honolulu. In accordance with his own wishes he was sent to the leper colony on Molokai and devotedly tended those suffering from leprosy for many years. He contacted the then fatal disease himself and died of it years later. Damien became well known after his death through an open letter which the poet Robert Louis Stevenson, staying in Kalaupapa, sent to an opponent of the priest. Father Charles McEwen Hyde had attempted to belittle Damien's work with the lepers. His importance to Hawaii can also be seen in Washington where there are two Hawaiian statues by the sculptor Marisol, one is of Damien, the other is of King Kamehameha I.

Born in Boston and a graduate of Harvard University Dole arrived in Hawaii shortly before the turn of the century and became a succesful businessman establishing the pineapple industry. Founded by him in 1901 the Hawaiian Pineapple Corporation in Wahiawa (Oahu) harvested its first crop after only two years. Not long afterwards he built one of the largest pineapple canning factories in the world for its time on Oahu. He was president of the firm until 1932 and chairman of the board for another 16 years. In 1922 the company acquired the entire island of Lanai for 1.1 million US dollars. The largest pineapple plantation in the world was established on this land. A harbour was excavated for the shipment of the fruit and Lanai City built for the employees. From 1933 to 1958 Dole lived in Washington and San Francisco then returned to Hawaii and died shortly afterwards.

Today Lanai Island and the Dole Corporation, which has become a synonym for pineapple production, belong to the company Castle & Cooke.

James D. Dole
Industrialist
(1877–1958)

Sanford B. Dole, a distant relative of James D. Dole was born in Honolulu, the son of Daniel Dole, the founder of the Punahou School. He studied on the mainland, became a lawyer and returned to Honolulu at the end of the Sixties. In 1884 he was elected to parliament and appointed judge at the Supreme Court two years later. In 1893 he played a decisive role in the overthrow of the monarchy and in the same year was elected President of the provisional government remaining in office as President of the Republic of Hawaii until the Hawaiian Islands were declared US territory. He was the first governor from 1900 to 1903 and US district judge until 1916. His "Memoirs of the Hawaiian Revolution", published posthumously in 1936 in Honolulu, are an important if rather one-sided source of information about a crucial period in Hawaii's history.

Sanford Ballard
Dole
President of the
Hawaiian Republic
(1844–1926)

Born in Schenectady, New York State, John Owen Dominis came to Hawaii with his parents at the age of eight. After a few years of commercial activity before he had reached 30 he was appointed personal secretary and chief court adviser. In 1868 he was installed as governor of Oahu, a post which he retained for 19 years. In 1862 he married Lydia Kamakaeha Kaolaamali Liliuokalani, the sister of David Kalakaua, the seventh king of Hawaii, who named her as his successor. The couple lived in Dominis' house "Washington Palace", the present residence of the governor of Hawaii. When Liliuokalani became queen at the beginning of 1891, Dominis, now Prince Regent, had only seven months to live.

John Owen
Dominis
Governor
Prince regent
(1832–91)

Queen Emma was a great granddaughter of Kamehameha I and married King Kamehameha IV in 1856, a year after he came to the throne. Her maiden name was Kalanikaumakeamano and following the death of her husband she took the name Kalleonalani. She played a major part in founding the largest hospital of Hawaii, as it still is today, the Queen's Hospital and the episcopal religious community in Hawaii. When King Lunalilo (Kamehameha IV) died in 1874 after barely a year as regent and a successor had to be found she stood for the highest office in the country, but only received six out of 39 votes, being beaten by David Kalakaua. Her supporters instigated discontent towards the new ruler, but Emma recognised Kalakaua as the rightful successor. Her summer palace, situated close to Honolulu, still attracts visitors today.

Queen Emma
Wife of
Kamehameha IV
(1836–85)

Gibson, of English parentage, was born on board ship between London and Spain. He came in 1861 as a Mormon missionary and remained while the majority of the Mormons were recalled to Utah. When they returned to Hawaii several years later they discovered that Gibson had used church finances to acquire half of Lanai Island and

Walter Murray
Gibson
Theologian
Politician
(1822–88)

register it in his own name, and for this he was excommunicated. Two years later he became mayor of Hawaii and in 1872 became involved in politics. He bought the leading newspaper, "Pacific Commercial Advertiser" (now "Honolulu Advertiser") and was appointed Prime Minister and Foreign Minister of Hawaii by King Kalakaua in 1882. Corruption flourished under his period in office as never before. During this time he developed the idea of forming a federation of all the Polynesian islands which were not yet European colonies. He envisaged Kalakaua being the "Emperor of the Pacific". However, it soon became apparent that the island kingdoms concerned were not interested in such a plan. The day before Kalakaua signed the so-called Bayonet Constitution imposed by the revolutionaries Gibson was deported to the mainland. He spent his final year in San Francisco.

Hewahewa
last high priest
(died 1837)

The last high priest under the old "kapu" system supported King Kamehameha II and the regent Kaahumanu to demystify and abolish the ancient Hawaiian gods. More than 100 heathen symbolic figures are said to have been destroyed by him. He was converted to Christianity and became a zealous churchgoer in a parish in Waialua (Oahu). In his last years he ran a farm between Waialua and Waikiki.

Daniel K. Inouye
US senator
(born 1924)

Daniel K. Inouye, born 1924 in Honolulu, is one of the first Hawaiians of Japanese descent to play a significant role in Hawaiian politics. He studied at the University of Hawaii and the George Washington Law School in St Louis, fought in the Second World War in Europe and after the war settled down as a lawyer in Honolulu. From 1955 to 1959 he belonged to the Hawaiian Parliament and as a result of this was elected to Congress and has been a US senator since 1962. As such he distinguished himself as joint chairman in the Iran-Contra investigation in 1987/88.

Kaahumanu
Queen
Regent
(1768–1832)

Born in Hana (Maui) the daughter and sister of powerful chiefs she became one of the wives of King Kamehameha the Great. As the stepmother of Kamehameha II she became joint ruler and the first regent ("kuhina nui") after the death of Kamehameha I. In 1821 she married King Kaumualii of Kaui who had been brought to Honolulu as a hostage for resisting the unification of Hawaii, together with his heir Kealiiahonui. She took a leading role in abolishing the "kapu" systems and was converted to Christianity in 1825 in the church of pastor Hiram Baldwin in Kona. The missionaries' teachings served her in the introduction of laws which prescribed severe punishment for murder, theft and non-observance of Sunday peace. Shortly before her death in Honolulu she received the first translation of the New Testament into Hawaiian from pastor Bingham.

Duke Paoa
Kahanamoku
Swimmer, surfer
(1890–1968)

Born in Haleakala (Mauai), several times Olympic champion, he was the first Hawaiian sportsman of international renown. From being a schoolboy at the Kamehameha School in Honolulu he was one of the best surfers with his 50kg surfboard measuring 5m in length. At the age of 20 he developed the famous swimming style the "Hawaiian Crawl", later to be known as "American Crawl". At the 1912 Olympic Games in Stockholm he gained several gold medals and set a world record in 100m swimming which he broke soon afterwards in Hamburg. At the 1920 Olympic Games in Antwerp – he was already 30 years old – he set a new world record of 60 seconds in the 100m freestyle. In 1924 he lost his world championship title to Johnny Weissmüller who swam the distance in 59 seconds. Again in Amsterdam in 1928 he won medals, if not gold, and in 1932 in Los Angeles, now 42 years old, he belonged to the American water polo team. During the Twenties he worked on several films but with no lasting fame. Professionally he was only ever employed in unskilled jobs, checking water-meters, caretaker of Honolulu town hall and working at a petrol station until he was awarded the honorary post of sheriff by the people of Honolulu. In his final years he received prominent guests as the city's head of protocol.

David Kalakaua was born the descendant of the tribal chiefs of Hawaii Island in Honolulu. In 1874 he was chosen to succeed the heirless King Lunalilo and reigned for seventeen years. He was called the "Happy King" who promoted the Arts, travelled widely, whose court life resembled that of a European monarch and was only remotely interested in government affairs, leaving them to his officials. It was the first time a Hawaiian king had visited the United States and visited European capitals to meet other kings and emperors. He loved splendour, as was shown, for example, by both he and his wife, Queen Kapiolani, wearing diamond-studded crowns. His inability to stand up to the increasingly more powerful interest groups and to act against the widespread corruption stimulated the anti-monarchist atmosphere in Hawaii and forced him to sign the so-called Bayonet Constitution, which removed much of his power. He died in San Francisco, where he had gone to improve his weakened health.

David Kalakaua
Seventh king
of Hawaii
(1836–91)

Kamehameha I, also known as "the Great", is the founder of the Hawaiian monarchy and introduced the period of the Kamehameha dynasty, whose rule lasted from 1795 to 1872. His birthplace was North Kohala on the north coast of Hawaii. He witnessed the landing of Cook's expedition in Kauai in 1778 and was himself injured by cannon fire when the Hawaiians killed Captain Cook near the place now called Captain Cook at Kealakekua Bay, in the south-west of Hawaii Island. After ten years of war Kamehameha succeeded, with the help of allies, in consolidating his rule over Hawaii Island and in conquering Maui and Lanai. Molokai was the next island to come under his rule, followed by Oahu in 1795. During this year he formed his kingdom, which was formed from six of the eight Hawaiian Islands. Kauai and Niihau became part of the kingdom through an agreement with King Kaumualii of Kauai. Kamehameha I opened up Hawaii to the outside world. Trade with other countries flourished; the main goods traded were pigs, sweet potatoes and valuable sandalwood which has now completely disappeared from Hawaii. Kamehameha I died in Kailua-Kona (Hawaii), probably on the spot of the present-day Hotel Kamehameha. His remains were hidden in a secret cave or else a human victim would have had to be sacrificed. His death signalled the end of an era for Old Hawaii.

Kamehameha I
First king
of Hawaii
(1758?–1819)

Liholiho, the eldest son and successor of Kamehameha I and his "holy wife" Keopuolani, had to accept joint regency with Kaahumanu, the first king's favourite wife. Both women persuaded him to break the old "kapu" system – his natural mother was the first member of the Royal Family to be converted to Christianity on her death bed in Lahaina in 1823. His reign was characterised on the one hand by the loss of old values and on the other by new influences both from the missionaries and new contacts from abroad becoming more significant. The continual trade in sandalwood and Hawaii's development as a whaling station benefited the wealth of the Royal family rather than the people and the country. To gain the favour of Great Britain Kamehameha II went with his wife on board a British whaling ship in 1823 on the arduous journey to Great Britain. They died in London within six days of measles. Their bodies were returned to Honolulu on board a gunboat under the command of Lord George A. Byron.

Kamehameha II
Second king
of Hawaii
(1796–1824)

Kauikeaouli, the younger brother of King Kamehameha II, was only eleven years old when he became heir to the throne. However, it was a long time before he had any political influence, for Kaahumanu, favourite wife of Kamehameha I, continued to be regent until her death in 1832. When the older half-sister Kinau (1805–39) of Kamehameha III

Kamehameha III
Third king
of Hawaii
(1813–54)

was to take over the role of the deceased queen there was constant friction between the two. Kamehameha III, who had an extravagant lifestyle, was opposed to the puritanical rules of the missionaries, which Kinau wanted to apply strictly to Hawaiian society. The change from a kingdom into a constitutional monarchy took place gradually. The proclamation of Hawaiian rights in 1839 was followed one year later by the passing of the first constitution. A sharp division of crown and government property along with tax reform were carried through. As a next step a government was formed from five ministers and finally the "Great Mahele" proclaimed, a legal document for land distribution (1846) wherby every Hawaiian was able to own land for the first time. During the reign of Kamehameha III the great powers were making their claims to power evident. The king had to avert attempts by the French and British to make Hawaii one of their colonies – in fact in 1843 a British squadron had annexed Hawaii for five months – and at the beginning of the Fifties it was necessary to combat similar attempts by the USA. When he died in 1854 the Hawaiian economy was stronger than ever before.

Kamehameha IV
Fourth king
of Hawaii
(1834–63)

Alexander Liholiho, the son of Kinau and grandson of Kamehameha I was named as his successor by Kamehameha III. He had visited Paris, London, New York and parts of the United States with his brother when he was young. His reign is characterised by two developments: a gradual dissociation from the United States together with a strengthening of British influence. Furthermore he had to take measures to combat the constant fall in the Hawaiian population owing to illness, which led to the founding of the first Hawaiian hospital (Queen's Hospital in Honolulu). He died following a severe asthma attack at the age of 29.

Kamehameha V
Fifth king
of Hawaii
(1830–72)

The reign of Lot Kapulaiwa Kamehameha (Kamehameha V) was short. Over these nine years he tried to strengthen the monarchy, often by despotic means, which finally weakened it. "He dresses simply", Mark Twain, who travelled to Hawaii in 1866, said of him. "Day and night he can be seen unaccompanied on his old horse in Honolulu. He is popular, admired, even well-liked." In 1864 he wrote a new constitution himself, which remained in force for 23 years. Under this constitution he awarded himself and his cabinet considerable rights and restricted the citizens' right to vote. He was the only member of the Kamehameha dynasty not to marry, and as he died without designating a successor the next king was to be chosen by parliament as stipulated in the constitution.

Liliuokalani
last queen
of Hawaii
(1839–1917)

Lydia Kamekaeha Kaolamalii (Liliuokalani), two years younger than her brother David Kalakaua, was proclaimed the new ruler of Hawaii after his death. She married Owen Dominis, her brother's private secretary, in 1862 shortly before he was nominated governor of Oahu. She had already acted as regent during her brother's many trips abroad. When she came to the throne in 1891 she sought to regain the privileges of the monarchy and Hawaiian people that had been lost in the Bayonet Constitution, but this led to her fall in 1893. She was placed under house arrest in her Washington Palace home in Honolulu and was forced to sign a declaration of abdication. When the First World War broke out she swore allegiance to the United States of America. She is also the author of numerous Hawaiian songs, among them the well known "Aloha'ae".

Lunalilo
Sixth king
of Hawaii
(1833–74)

William Charles Lunalilo was the first elected king of Hawaii. As the grandson of a half-brother of Kamehameha I he was one of the last descendants of the ruling family. In the election he easily beat his only adversary David Kalakaua. As he was opposed to the constitution written by Kamehameha V in 1864 he suggested several amendments;

in particular he rejected land ownership as a precondition for having the right to vote. During his one-year reign there was a rebellion of bodyguards against their officers. He solved this problem by disbanding them later on the grounds of cost and being superfluous. Most of his life he was in poor health and finally died from the effects of alcohol and tuberculosis.

Part of his wealth went towards founding the Lunalilo home "for poor, ill and frail Hawaiians with preference given to the elderly".

Born in Honolulu and coming into contact with music at an early age John A. Noble wrote about 300 hit melodies, a good many with a definite Hawaiian sound. From 1922 he led the band of the Moana Hotel in Waikiki and created new musical variations of Hawaiian rhythms and jazz. Later he led the first ensemble which made recordings of Hawaiian music. Many of his own compostions have become Hawaiian evergreens.

John Avery Noble
Composer of hit songs
(1892–1944)

As a child Opukahaia had to witness his parents and brother killed in a tribal feud in his home town on Hawaii Island. An uncle in Napoopoo on the south-west coast adopted him but at the age of seven he left Hawaii and signed on as a member of the crew on a ship headed for New England. There he came into contact with students from Yale College and Andover Seminary, became converted to Christianity – the first Hawaiian Christian – and took the name Henry Obookiah. He was influential in the Foreign Mission's decision in Boston to send missionaries to the Sandwich Islands as Hawaii was then known. He was to have accompanied the mission but died of typhoid before departure of the two-master "Taddeus".

Henry Opukahaia
First Hawaiian Christian
(1792–1818)

John Waihee, the present governor of the Hawaiian government, is the first politician of Hawaiian descent to be elected to this high office. In 1986 he entered the election as a candidate of the Democratic party. His political career began earlier: for four years, 1982–86, he was deputy governor after having been a representative in the Hawaiian parliament. After being awarded his doctorate in law from the University of Hawaii he worked in several state departments and as a lawyer in Honolulu. He comes from Honokaa, a village on the north coast of Hawaii Island.

John Waihee
Governor
(born 1946)

Born the son of a missionary in Waimea (Kauai) he was sent to New England to be educated, but because of partial hearing loss, was unable to continue an academic career and instead learned the printing trade. In 1849 Whitney returned to Hawaii, established the first post office on the islands and until 1886 was director of Hawaiian postal services, for which he printed the first stamps. He opened his own printworks where all the missionaries' publications were published. In 1856 he founded the "Pacific Commercial Advertiser" as a weekly (now the daily "Honolulu Advertiser") and four years later the Hawaiian newspaper "Ka Nupepa Kuokoa". Having sold the "Advertiser" in 1870 he bought it back again 18 years later and was director until 1894. From 1873 to 1891 he was a member of the Hawaiian state council.

Henry Martyn Whitney
Printer
(1824–1904)

Culture

Hawaiian language

General

Hawaiian is a Polynesian language which has been passed on orally from generation to generation. This expressive and melodic idiom is peculiar to Hawaii and, as a result of a renaissance of Hawaiian culture, today is recognised as the official language alongside American English.

The Hawaiian language spoken by the natives, when the first missionaries set foot on the islands in 1820, is not the same as present-day Hawaiian.

First knowledge of the Hawaiian language

Captain James Cook, the discoverer of the islands, was the first to inform the world of the existence of a Hawaiian language. In 1785 he reproduced 200–300 words transcribed in English in his posthumously published book "A voyage to the Pacific Ocean".

The German poet and natural historian Adalbert von Chamisso, who in both 1816 and 1817 spent a month on Hawaii as a member of the Russian expedition led by Otto von Kotzebue, published a Hawaiian grammar a year before his death in 1837. Von Kotzebue, who visited Hawaii a second time on his journey around the world from 1823–26, wrote in the second volume of the English edition "O Wahi" for Hawaii, "Hanaruro" for Honolulu, "Tameamea" for Kamehameha, "Wahu" for Oahu, "Muwe" for Maui, etc. At that time there was no standard written language.

Written language

One year before von Kotzebue's book appeared the missionaries were trying to establish a standard written language. They decided upon an alphabet containing only twelve letters: seven consonants (h, k, l, m, n, p and w) and five vowels (a, e, i, o and u). The Hawaiian language had to be forced into this linguistic framework.

The first Hawaiian-English dictionary appeared in 1836 and it was another nine years before the English-Hawaiian edition appeared. More than a century later the first comprehensive Hawaiian-English dictionary by Mary Kawena Pukui and Samuel H. Elbert appeared, followed by the English-Hawaiian version in 1964. The second single-volume edition contains about 25,000 Hawaiian words.

Revival

Today Hawaiian is threatened with decline. Apart from the 250 inhabitants of Niihau only a few, mostly old Hawaiians, speak this language.

For some years efforts have been made to revive the language and rediscover the Hawaiian culture which is handed down in songs, stories and myths.

Although Hawaiian is taught in schools it is hardly ever used by Hawaiian families at home.

At the University of Hawaii in Honolulu, where courses in Hawaiian are on offer, the academics argue about the meaning of particular Hawaiian words and linguistic details rather than promoting the widespread revival of Hawaiian.

A tourist only comes across the Hawaiian language in a few situations. Some words have been absorbed into colloquial American, but the majority of Hawaiian concepts have been preserved in place and street names. The pleasant sound of the language can be heard in Hawaiian songs.

The best place to listen to Hawaiian is in the Kawaiahao Church in Honolulu where the services are held in Hawaiian every Sunday.

In the Practical Information section there is a Hawaiian-English dictionary along with an introduction to the Hawaiian language.

Music and dance

Traditional forms

Hawaiian music has its roots in the worship of the gods and was
presented in the form of religious songs, called "mele". The "mele"
were simple melodies with constantly repetitive sounds in which the
meaning of the words was more important than the music itself. The
songs, which were sung by the "kahunas", the priests, were in praise
of the land, the chiefs and kings or of the romantic side of life. The
oral handing-down of historic events was another purpose of the "meme".

Songs with rhythmic accompaniment were usually associated with
the hula dance. Instruments included drums, pumpkin rattles decorated with feathers, bamboo sticks and castanets made from pebbles.
Rhythmic stamping and hand-clapping reinforced the background
music.

The hula dance goes back to early Hawaiian history. It was a dance of
worship performed by the men. It was only over a period of time that it

Hula dancers, with musical instruments

was a source of entertainment and was learnt almost exclusively by women.

Presumably men were too concerned with wars and worries about earning a living to find time to dance. The men's hula dances were actually recorded by the artist John Webber, who accompanied Cook's first expedition.

Hula dancers were selected as children and educated in convent-like schools. Only after years of instruction did they become trained hula dancers.

In contrast with many dances of ethnic groups and primitive people the hula never had any sexual connotation.

Decline of
the hula dance

The arrival of the Calvinist missionaries signalled the temporary end of the "hula". The hula dance was seen as an obscene, heathen leftover that was irreconcilable with the Christian faith.

However, recognising the importance of music to the Hawaiians the missionaries founded church choirs and taught the Hawaiians the Christian beliefs through songs and hymns. The influence of choral music on Hawaiian music can still be recognised today.

Revival of the
hula dance

King David Kalakaua succeeded in rediscovering the hula dance in 1874. He founded a dance group and encouraged his subjects to learn the old styles of dancing. In the meantime some of the original dances had fallen into oblivion but some of the ancient styles were revamped.

Thanks to King Kalakauas efforts "hula halaus" (hula schools) were set up and are still in existence today.

Present-day
importance of
the hula dance

The "hula" has experienced a new lease of life with the revival of Hawaiian culture over the last decades. Various hula dancing schools train boys and girls in the traditional art of the hula dance.

To achieve professional skill years of training are necessary. Even if today "hula" is often performed for the tourists for commercial reasons, and the tourist is often made to join in, once some of the basic movements have been learnt, it is a rare pleasure to experience the high level of grace and elegance with which the professional dancers perform.

On watching a hula for the first time – at the Kodak Hula Show in Honolulu's Kapiolani Park, for example (See A–Z, Waikiki) – it may appear to be rather static as the dancers hardly seem to move their feet. It is the swaying body movements in tune to the rhythm of the music, the interplay of the raised hands and fingers and the changing expressions which create the fascination of this dance. For the outsider the symbolic hand movements are the most difficult to interpret, especially if the Hawaiian text of the accompanying singer is not understood. To add to this the dancers' own experiences find expression in their own individual styles of dancing.

Traditionally the hula is not danced in grass skirts. They were not common in Hawaii but came from the Gilbert Islands. Originally and occasionally today still the dancers wear skirts decorated with ti leaves, which always cover the knees. Traditional hula dancers also always kept their hips covered.

Despite the worldwide commercialisation of the hula dance it remains a symbol of Hawaii and still expresses Hawaiian art and life. Hula revues are often performed as evening entertainment in numerous hotels.

Influences of other cultures on Hawaiian music

Church music

The first period of Hawaiian music since the arrival of the missionaries is from 1820 to 1870. The Hawaiian conversion to Christianity was already completed in this period. It was the Calvinist hymns, with

Hawaiian texts translated from English by the priests, that attracted the Hawaiians in the service of worship, unlike the sermons which they found boring and difficult to understand.

The waves of immigrants, which were starting to arrive, brought differ-ent musical influences to Hawaii. The Portuguese brought their Fado songs with them to Hawaii, half sentimental, half sad songs, which were adopted into Hawaiian music.

Other influences

A small string instrument, the "ukulele", originated from Madeira. The guitar probably was brought by cowboys from Mexico and South America.

The second period, from 1870 to 1895, is characterised by the influence of the well-travelled King Kalakaua. The Hawaiian Royal Band, founded by his predecessor Kamehameha V in 1872, conducted by Heinrich Berger, became one of the leading European-style brass bands during his reign. Both Heinrich Berger and members of the Royal Family wrote lyrics and composed. With Berger as conductor the Hawaiian Royal Band gave over 15,000 concerts and became an established feature of Hawaiian light music.

Hawaiian Royal Band

After 1895 – the year in which Joe Kekuku introduced the Hawaiian steel guitar – an outstanding feature of Hawaiian music became its greater instrumental variety, for the new instrument soon found its place alongside the ukulele and the normal guitar.

New variety

From the mainland the influence of rag-time music, an early form of jazz, was noticable. Around the turn of the century the first Hawaiian songs with English words were composed. The "hapa haole" songs (half-white) became an essential part of Hawaiian music.

Around the turn of the century many Hawaiians emigrated to the mainland, among them Kekuku, not returning to Hawaii. There, they enthralled audiences with this new kind of Hawaiian music. Particu-larly successful were the revue performance of "Bird of Paradise" in 1904 and appearances at the Panama Pacific exhibition, held in San Francisco.

During the Twenties Hollywood entered the Hawaii-business. A series of South Sea films appeared commercialising the romance and atmosphere of Hawaii.

Influences from Hollywood

The result was that the music became almost completely "haole" (white): Broadway and Hollywood increasingly suppressed the real Hawaiian music with mainland fashions in light music dominating the Hawaiian music scene.

In the Sixties, when mass tourism began, rock music was prevalent with traditional music almost forgotten and seldom heard.

In the Seventies traditional Hawaiian music came back into favour again, but the sweetened versions by Bing Crosby and the Royal Hawaiian Seranaders no longer had an audience. Almost simulta-neously new groups arose, who combined jazz and rock influences with traditional harmonies and rhythms. With the Kalama Quartett, for example, the typical falsetto voice of the leading tenor can be heard.

Seventies

A range of traditional instruments were rediscovered, which were chiefly used to accompany the hula dance, such as the "ili'ili" (stone castanets), the "pahu" (drum covered in sharkskin), the "ipu" (gourd-pumpkin drum) and the "uli uli" (hollowed-out coconut filled with small stones or shells).

The following important Hawaiian musicians with their ensembles, who play both in Waikiki and occasionally in hotels on the other islands, should be mentioned here: Don Ho, who is responsible for the revival of Hawaiian music, the Cazimero Brothers, Henry Kapomo, the Peter Moon Band and the Makaha Sons of Nihau.

Music groups

Perhaps the most well known of the Hawaiian musicians is Al

Harrington, but his style is closer to the sentimental hit music of the mainland (Sinatra and Bing Crosby) and cannot be described as true Hawaiian.

In Honolulu the radio station KCCN (1420 AM frequency) broadcasts Hawaiian music of every description throughout the day and night. Music is still an important and ubiquitous part of Hawaiian life.

Music on the radio

Flower garlands (leis)

The tying and wearing of a flower garland, called a "lei" in Hawaii, is an expression of Hawaiian zest for life and closeness to nature. Leis are presents of love and symbols of beauty.

Significance

There is always good cause to give and wear a "lei": someone arriving or departing, at weddings, school-leaving parties and funerals. Sometimes several are worn on top of each other – and when there is no more room around the neck they are laid around the arms. It is tradition to kiss the person receiving the "lei".

"Leis" are works of art which require specialist knowledge about the various blooms and plants. The blossoms and leaves are carefully collected, arranged and processed according to methods which have been passed down from generation to generation.

Originally garlands of this type were made as presents for the goddess Laka (or Hiiaka), the goddess of mercy and protection. The lei chains were worn during religious dances and still have symbolic meaning in the hula dance.

Tradition

Initially the foliage of the Maile tree growing in the mountains was used for the "leis". Nowadays they are made primarily from blossoms that have a fragrant if not intense perfume, such as plumeria, pikake, carnations, orchids, hyacinths and others.

Blossoms

There are many types of "leis". In Honolulu, especially in Chinatown, the women can be observed weaving the different chains:

Manufacture

"Kui" is the commonest and cheapest type of lei chain. The blossoms are tied at the end or in the centre and stretched over a band. The blossoms of the "humuhumu" are worked into a flat "lei" and sewn onto a banana or ti leaf. They are best suited as headbands. "Wili" are lei chains which are made from leaves, fern and flowers up to the size of a bunch of flowers. "Hili" are plaited from scented leaves and ferns; combined with blossoms they form "haku", the most difficult, beautiful and expensive "lei" made from plants.

The materials are not always plants and blossoms. Kuikui nuts, small shells and colourful feathers are also used, for example. These "leis" are very rare and nowadays extremely expensive. In the past "leis" made from feathers were reserved for nobility.

Each island has its own "leis". On Kauai, the oldest of the main islands, the fruits of the mokihana tree, which smell of aniseed and keep their special scent for months, are used. On Maui the "lokelai" or "roselani" are garlands made from rose blossoms. On Molokai "leis" are made from leaves, blossoms and nuts of the kukui tree, whilst the white or orange coloured blossoms of the lehua tree are used on Hawaii. Rather unusual are the "leis" from Niihau made from tiny little shells. Prices vary according to the rarity, colour and quality of the shells and the length of the garland from 1000 US dollars upwards.

"Leis" typical of each island

◄ *"The Lei maker" in Honolulu Academy of Arts*

Hawaii in Quotations

David Samwell

"We found all the Women of these Islands but little influenced by interested motives in their intercourse with us, as they would almost use violence to force you into their Embrace regardless whether we gave them any thing or not, and in general they were as fine girls as any we had seen in the south Sea Islands."
Journal, January 31st 1778

James King

"But a diversion the most common is upon the Water, where there is a very great Sea and surf breaking upon the Shore. The Men, sometimes 20 or 30 go without the Swell of the Surf, & lay themselves flat upon an oval piece of plank about their size and breadth, they keep their legs close on the top of it & their arms are us'd to guide the plank, they wait the time for the greatest Swell that sets on shore, & altogether push forward with their Arms to keep on its top, it then sends them in with a most astonishing Velocity, & the great art is to guide the plank so as always to keep in a proper direction. If the Swell drives him close to the rocks before he is overtaken by its break, he is much praised. On first seeing this very dangerous diversion I did not conceive it possible but that some of them must be dashed to mummy against the sharp rocks, but just before they reach the shore, if they are very near, they quit the plank, & dive under till the Surf is broke, when the piece of plank is sent many yards by the force of the Surf from the beach."
Journal, March 1779

Mark Twain
(1835–1910)

Kaelakekua Bay
"The setting sun was flaming upon it, a Summer shower was falling, and it was spanned by two magnificent rainbows. Two men who were in advance of us rode through these and for a moment their garments shone with a more than regal splendour. Why did not Captain Cook have taste enough to call his great discovery the Rainbow Islands? These charming spectacles are visible to you at every turn; they are common in all the islands; they are visible every day and frequently at night also – not the silvery bow we see once in an age in the States by moonlight, but barred with all bright and beautiful colours, like the children of the sun and rain. . . . What the sailors call 'rain dogs' – little patches of rainbow – are often seen drifting about in these latitudes like stained cathedral windows."

Kilaurea Crater
"Here was a vast perpendicular-walled cellar, nine hundred feet deep in some places, thirteen hundred in others, level-floored, and ten miles in circumference! . . . There was a heavy fog over the crater and it was splendidly illuminated by the glare from the fires below. The illumination was two miles wide and a mile high perhaps; and if you ever, on a dark night and at a distance, beheld the light from thirty or forty blocks of distant buildings all on fire at once, reflected strongly against overhanging clouds, you can form a fair idea of what this looked like. . . .

"The 'cellar' was tolerably well lighted up. For a mile and a half in front of us, and half a mile on either side, the floor of the abyss was magnificently illuminated; beyond these limits the mists hung down their gauzy curtains and cast a deceptive gloom over all that made the twinkling fires in the remote corners of the crater seem countless leagues removed – made them seem like the camp-fires of a great army far away. You could not compass it, it was the idea of eternity made tangible, and the longest end of it made visible to the naked eye. . . .

"The greater part of the vast floor of the desert under us was as black as ink, and apparently smooth and level; but over a mile square of it was ringed and streaked and striped with a thousand branching streams of liquid and gorgeously brilliant fire! It looked like a colossal railroad map of the State of Massachusetts done in chain lightning upon a midnight sky."
Roughing It, 1872

"No alien land in all the world has any deep, strong charm for me, but that one; no other land could so longingly and beseechingly haunt my sleeping and waking, through half a lifetime, as that one has done. Other things leave me, but it abides."
Speech in New York, April 4th 1889

"The Sandwich Islands remain my idea of the perfect thing in the matter of tropical islands. I would add another storey to Mauna Loa's 16,000 feet if I could, and make it particularly bold and steep and craggy and forbidding and snowy; and I would make that volcano spout its lava-floods out of its summit instead of its sides; but aside from these non-essentials I have no corrections to suggest. I hope these will be attended to; I do not wish to have to speak of it again."
More Tramps Abroad, 1897

"O, how my spirit languishes
To step ashore in the Sanguishes. . . ."
Letter to Sidney Colvin, October 16th 1888

Robert Louis
Stevenson
(1850–94)

Molokai
"The place as regards scenery, is grand, gloomy, and bleak. Mighty mountain walls descending sheer along the whole face of the island into a sea unusually deep; the front of the mountain ivied and furred with clinging forest, one viridescent cliff: about halfway from east to west, the low, bare stony promontory edged in between the cliff and ocean; the two little towns (Kalawao and Kalaupapa) seated on either side of it, as bare almost as bathing machines upon a beach; and the population – gorgons and chimeras dire."
Letter to Sidney Colvin June 1889

"The Sandwich Islands do not interest us very much; we live here, oppressed with civilisation, and look for good things in the future."
Letter to Mrs. Adelaide Boodle, April 6th 1889

"In what other land save this one is the commonest form of greeting not 'Good day,' nor 'How d'ye do,'but 'Love'? That greeting is *Aloha* – love, I love you, my love to you. . . . It is a positive affirmation of the warmth of one's own heart-giving."

Jack London
(1876–1916)

"Hawaii is a paradise – and I never cease proclaiming it; but I must append one word of qualification: Hawaii is a paradise for the well-to-do. It is not a paradise for the unskilled labourer from the mainland, nor for the person without capital from the mainland. It must be remembered that Hawaii is very old, comparatively. When California was a huge cattle ranch, for hides and tallow, Hawaii was publishing newspapers and boasting schools of higher learning. . . . The shoe-string days are past. The land and industries of Hawaii are owned by old families and large corporations, and Hawaii is only so large."
My Hawaiian Aloha, 1916

Suggested Routes

Note

The following suggested routes are intended to encourage the visitor to experience the Hawaiian Islands in a variety of ways. They have been selected to incorporate a pleasant combination of scenery, bathing and culture emphasising the diversity of the individual islands.

As most visitors to Hawaii will probably tour in a hired car the routes all begin at the airport of the island capital.

The distances refer to the total distance for round trips (including diversions to the sights en route), but just the outward journey for the others.

Towns and regions which are described under an entry in the A–Z section are printed in bold type; descriptions of other places can be found by referring to the index.

1: **Hawaii Island** The Big Island

Tour of the north of the island (about 258 miles/415km)

General

This tour along the northeastern and northwestern coast of Hawaii island takes in the variety and lushness of the vegetation of this island. The return journey through the interior of the island provides a stark contrast: long stretches of almost barren upland areas of volcanic origin convey a picture of a strange yet fascinating landscape.

Culture is not far away from this captivating creation of nature: the museums in Waimea and ancient Hawaiian cultural sites on the northern part of the west coast are an essential element of this trip.

This tour can take place either in one day (early start) or two, staying overnight in Kailua Kona.

Hamakua coast

Leave Hilo heading north on road 19 which soon passes the town of Pepeekeo – past thick tropical vegetation and sugar cane fields on the left, the Hamaku coast on the right – and reach Honokaa. There road 240 turns off to the Waipio Valley Lookout. A visit to the **Waipio Valley** will necessitate booking overnight accommodation as the excursion down into the valley will take up the rest of the day.

Waipio Valley

Lookout

Waimea

Returning to Honokaa continue along road 19 to **Waimea (Kamuela)**, to see the Parker Ranch Museum in the large shopping centre of Waimea and the Kamuela Museum at the end of the town. The huge estates of the **Parker Ranch** stretch around Waimea to the coast.

Parker Ranch

Kapaau

Continue through the Kohala mountains on road 250 to the most northerly point of Hawaii Island. In the small town of Hawi, formerly important for sugar, turn off on road 220 and come to **Kapaau**, the birthplace of Kamehameha I, whose statue can be visited. The road terminates at Pololu Lookout. Return on road 270 to **Lapakahi State Historical Park** where a visit is recommended.

Lapkahi State
Historical Park

Puukohola Heiau
Kailua Kona

Follow the Kawaihae coast south to the open country of the **Puukohola Heiau**. Drive along the coast towards **Kailua Kona**, past many coves which are inviting for a swim. The journey could be broken staying the night at Kailua Kona.

Saddle Road

Leave Kailua Kona on road 190 in the direction of Waimea. If there is still enough time before nightfall and the driver is experienced and has the stamina, the return journey to Hilo on the Saddle Road (road 200) through the magnificent volcanic landscape is impressive. This lonely mountain road is badly made and the drive requires a lot of time. However, it is well worth the effort as the volcanic landscape along the route is a memorable experience. Past the turn-offs to **Mauna Kea** (day trip on foot possible) and to Mauna Loa the tour returns to more populated area around **Hilo**. Should this part of the tour be too strenuous then carry on from Waimea on road 19 along the coast back to Hilo.

2: **Hawaii Island** Big Island

Volcano route from Hilo to Kailua Kona (about 155 miles/250km)

This tour takes in the south of the island. The scenic highlight of this drive are the young volcanic landscapes which are still changing because of the constant eruptions. The following stretch along the Kona coast passes one of the most important Hawaiian cities of refuge, which, rebuilt in its original form, gives a clear insight today into the religious life of the Hawaiians.
    If this is a one-day tour staying in Kailua Kona is recommended. As a two-day tour part of the north island tour (route 1) could be added.

General

Leave **Hilo** heading south on road 11. The first part of this drive is along the picturesque fields of orchids of Hawaii Island. Just past the small town of Volcano the **Hawaii Volcanoes National Park** begins. On the left the Crater Rim Road branches off, a ring road which circles the caldera of the Kilauea volcano. It is possible to stop to enjoy the view or walk through the extraordinary volcanic countryside.

Hilo

Kilauea caldera

Proceed along road 11 to the southernmost point of the Hawaiian Islands, to Ka Lae. Shortly after **Naalehu**, at the end of the district Waiohinu a small road on the right leads to Ka Lae (about 10 miles/15km) with beautiful sea views and the surf splashing on the lava rocks. Back on road 11 continue along the bare slopes of **Mauna Loa** in the direction of the Kona coast.

Naalehu
Ka Lae

Continue along the Kona coast heading north. The well known **Puuhonua o Honaunau (City of Refuge)** can be reached by turning off towards the coast at Honaunau Bay and should not be missed. The interior of **St Benedict's Church (Painted Church)** should also be included in this tour.

Puuhonua o Honaunau
St Benedict's Church

Not far from the settlement **Captain Cook** in Kealakekua Bay stands the Captain Cook monument commemorating the seafarer's violent death. Only a few kilometres further on is Kailua Kona, the day's destination.

Captain Cook

Kailua Kona

Return the next day either via Waimea and coastal road 19 or on the Saddle Road (road 200; see route 1 for description).

Return journey

3: **Kauai Island**

Sights in the north and south

Kauai Island is almost circular, but owing to its remote northwest coast (Na Pali Coast), it is not possible to drive all round the island. The interior of the island is also practically inaccessible, so that sightseeing is quite restricted. Therefore a northern tour and a southern tour are suggested.

General

Suggested Routes

3a: North to Haena (about 46 miles/75km)

Lihue Wailua Kapaa Kilauea	From **Lihue** take road 56 travelling north to **Wailua** where Fern Grotto, Wailua waterfall and Coconut Grove can be seen. After this first interlude follow the coast to **Kapaa** and the north coast to **Kilauea**. A detour should be taken here to the **Kilauea Lighthouse** on the coast.
	This is where the tourist stretch of the north coast starts. First there is **Princeville** with its fine golf course, then **Hanalei** Bay with the town of the same name. The view into the Hanalei valley just before reaching Hanalei is not to be missed. It is a good idea to stop here and take a short walk in the valley. There is a wide choice of idyllic beaches in Hanalei Bay and the adjoining bays for those who would rather go for a swim.
Haena State Park Na Pali Coast	To see the spectacular cliffs of the **Na Pali Coast** drive to the end of road 56. As well as visiting the wet and dry caves a walk along the Kalalau path to the Hanakapiai beach (2 miles/3km) begins here. Remember that it is necessary to walk back again! On this walk the visitor gets a definite impression of the scenery and vegetation of this part of the island.
Return journey	As there is no alternative the return journey is back along the same route.

3b: South to the Waimea Canyon (about 50 miles/80km)

Lihue Poipu	To reach the south of the island leave **Lihue** on road 50 in the direction of Puhi and after a few miles take road 520 to make a detour to **Poipu**. Passing through the Tunnel of the Trees the road first comes to Koloa, a recently restored sugar town and finally to Poipu, a town popular with tourists. To the west of Poipu the Spouting Horn, a noisy natural spectacle, is worth a visit. There are several beautiful beaches in this region to stop and swim.
Lawai	From Koloa turn off towards Lawai on road 530. Here are two botanical gardens in close proximity: the **Pacific Tropical Botanical Garden** (branch road from Lawai) and the Olu Pua Botanical Gardens near Kalaheo. The tour continues to **Hanapepe**, a town with a special character.
Kalaheo Hanapepe	
	Follow road 50 to **Waimea**, the town which is of historical importance as the place where Captain Cook landed. After visiting **Fort Elizabeth** and the Captain Cook Monument, in fine weather drive into the mountains (road 550) to the Kalalau viewing point. The magnificent view down to the **Na Pali coast** easily compensates for the arduous, twisting drive. The views on the way down into the **Waimea Canyon Park** are also impressive. If time allows there are relaxing walks in the Kokee State Park. It would be convenient to stay overnight at the Kokee Lodge (advance booking necessary) and travel back the next day.

4: Maui Island

Wild countryside and beautiful beaches in the west. (about 65 miles/105km)

General	Discovering the west of Maui Island combines nature, beautiful beaches, many coastal views and inaccessible interiors as well as tourist comforts along the Kaanapali coast and ample opportunities to explore the historic town of Lahaina. Some of the roads in both the north and south of the island are in poor condition or are privately owned and closed to normal traffic.

Thus, at least at present it is not possible to make a circular tour of the island. Various excursions can be recommended instead.

Leave Kahului on express road 380 which later joins road 30 and leads to the coast. Proceed via Maalaea to **Olowalu**, where there are beautiful rock drawings. From here it is not far to **Lahaina**, the well known whaling town which demands a longer stop and a walk through the historic part of the town.

Kahului
Olowalu
Lahaina

The following stretch runs along sugar cane fields to the developed tourist coastal strip near **Kaanapali**. The long sandy beach and a considerable number of luxury hotels create an exquisite atmosphere. Somewhat further north lies Kapalua, with similar excellent bathing beaches but not so built-up as Kaanapali.

Kaanapali

Kapalua

There is no link road from Kihei to **Haleakala National Park**. Access to the latter is via Kahului, Pukalani and Haleakala. Road 377 then leads to the entry kiosk of the National Park. Inclusive of the return journey to Kihei this round trip will cover some 44 miles/70km.

Haleakala Volcano

5: Molokai Island

Fish ponds and forgotten valleys in the east (about 47 miles/75km)

The stretch along the south coast is intended for those who want to explore the island on foot along the way. Stout walking shoes are necessary.

General

From Hoolehua airport take road 460 towards **Kaunakakai** stopping at Kapuaiwa Grove, the large coconut grove. Continue through Kaunakakai, the main town on the island, and along the flat south coast (road 450) of Molokai. Visible all along the coast the offshore reefs of the **Royal Fish Ponds** made them the ideal place to berth. The next stop is Kamalo to visit **St Joseph's Church**. Follow the coastline to just before Pukoo; the road to **Illiopae Pukoo Heiau** branches off (advance warning!). Walkers can follow part of the **Wailau Trails** in the direction of Wailau Valley.

Kaunakakai

It is also possible to continue to the end of the unmetalled road. The drive is time-consuming but is worthwhile because of the wonderful scenery and the view into the **Halawa Valley** at the end of the road. From here the visitor can walk down into the valley, visit the Moaula Falls and bathe at the beach in Halawa Bay. Remember to leave sufficient time for the long return journey.

Halawa Valley

6: Oahu Island

Round tour with a taste of pineapples – and wind (about 93 miles/150km)

This tour traverses the different landscapes of Oahu: first driving past the suburbs of Honolulu into the intensive agricultural plain (Schofield Plateau), which is enclosed by both mountain ranges, the Koolau Range and Waianae Mountains, then visiting both part of the leeward coast (west coast) and almost all the windward coast (east coast).
    The tour can be divided into two parts involving staying overnight on the west coast or returning along the same route after visiting Waimea Falls Park. A separate visit is necessary to do justice to the extensive programme of the Polynesian Cultural Center.

General

The first part of the tour is completely devoted to pineapples. Leave **Honolulu** in a northwesterly direction on Lunalilo Highway (H1), which

Honolulu

Pearl City
Wahiawa

becomes part of the Kamehameha Highway, past Foster Village and Pearl City. Turn off to the north on Highway 2 (H2); skirting past Mililani Town and into the agricultural centre of Oahu, Wahiawa. The **Wahiawa Botanic Garden** is worth a visit.

From the edge of the town the pineapples lure the visitor. Both the major pineapple companies are represented here; in the Dole Pineapple Pavilion and in the Del Monte Variety Garden (both situated outside the town) there is everything that can be be learnt about pineapple growing, types of pineapples and processing. Return along road 99 past pineapple and sugar cane fields, where the newly acquired knowledge can be put straight into practice.

Haleiwa

Having crossed the Schofield Plateau the tour comes to Haleiwa on the windfacing coast of Oahu. There are many opportunities to stop and swim either here or along the coastal road heading north (road 83).

Waimea Bay is not far away with several places of interest; one not to be missed is the **Puu O Mahuka Heiau**. Turn off down into valley of the Waimea River and arrive at the **Waimea Falls Park**, famous for its waterfalls, beautiful plants and an interesting programme of Hawaiian cultural events.

Waimea Falls Park

Honolulu

The tour can stop here returning to **Honolulu** on the described route.

Lee side

The second part of the tour continues along road 83 around the northern point of Oahu. It passes the beaches preferred by expert surfers (Waimea Beach Park, Sunset Beach), who display their skill, especially in winter when the waves are highest and at their most beautiful. Continue past the idyllically situated Turtle Bay Hilton luxury hotel and via Kahuku with its sugar mill, which is open to visitors, to Laie, the centre of the Mormons. Sights include the **Mormon Temple** and the **Polynesian Cultural Center**.

Laie

Windward side

The following section (continue on road 83) follows along the windward side of Oahu with the steep mountain slopes and small green valleys of the Koolau range on the right.

Sacred Falls

Time permitting stop and walk (2 miles/3km) to the **Sacred Falls** to admire the beautiful countryside of this island.

Proceed along the coast to Kualoa National Park with panoramic views of Mokolii Island, also vividly described as the **Chinaman's Hat**. Close by is a Hawaiian fish pond (Molii Fishpond), a water pool separated from the sea by coral reefs.

Kaneohe
Honolulu

The final stretch is to Kaneohe and back on road 63 (Likilike Highway) or road 61 (Pali Highway) with the Nuuanu Pali Lookout to **Honolulu**.

7: **Oahu Island**

Craters, beaches and temples in the south-east (about 62 miles/100km)

General

This tour on well constructed and open roads takes in the diverse aspects of Oahu – and all quite close to Waikiki. It is possible to do this tour in an afternoon if the stops at the various sights are not very long. However, it is more relaxing to take the whole day. A separate visit is suggested to Sea Life Park in order to see everything.

Honolulu

Diamond Head

Turn off the Lunalilo Freeway (H1) in Waikiki, leaving Honolulu on Kalakaua Avenue in a southeasterly direction, passing Kapiolani Park on the left and arrive at the first destination, the Diamond Head Crater. It is possible to drive through a tunnel into the caldera of the crater, which is on the north side of the Diamond Head.

The tour continues through the exclusive suburb of Kahala (possible to visit the Kahala Hilton hotel grounds) to highway 72 (Kalanianaole

Highway), which follows the coast to the astoundingly beautiful
Hanauma Bay. This is ideal for swimming or snorkelling or a walk in the
Koko Head Regional Park.

Road 72 past Coco Crater leads to the **Sea Life Park**, where there is an
extensive programme of shows, events and exhibits. The daredevil
hang-gliders diving off the cliffs at Makapuu Point provide an interesting distraction.

Sea Life Park

The **Haiku Gardens** provide a welcome contrast to these many attractions with quiet gardens where the visitor can contemplate and relax.
   They can be reached by continuing towards Kaneohe (roads 72, 61,
83). Another detour into the Valley of the Temples to the **Byodo-In
Temple** could be included.

Haiku Gardens

Byodo-In Temple

If visibility is good then stopping at the Nuuanu Pali Lookout is recommended, from where the whole tour can be seen from above and the
best views of Honolulu are to be had. Proceed down through the
mountains along the Nuuanu Valley (possible detour to Queen
Emma's Summer Palace), through the exclusive suburbs of Honolulu
back to Downtown. At the end of the Pali Highway follow the signs to
Honolulu International Airport.

Nuuanu Pali
Lookout

Hawaii from A to Z

In this section the eight main islands of the State of Hawaii are introduced alphabetically: Hawaii, Kahoolawe, Kauai, Lanai, Maui, Molokai, Nihau and Oahu. The places of interest to be found on these islands are also set out alphabetically here.

Hawaii Island – Big Island

Area: 4035sq.miles/10,454sq.km
County: Hawaii
Population: 122,300
Main town: Hilo

The Island of Hawaii, commonly known as Big Island, lies furthest south-east in the archipelago. Its area of 4035sq.miles/10,454sq.km makes it the largest of the Hawaiian islands. Measuring 93 miles/150km long and 76 miles/122km wide, Hawaii is more than twice the size of all the other islands put together.

    Geologically speaking Hawaii is the youngest island in the archipelago and the only one which, as a result of sustained volcanic activity, is contin-uing to grow. Five volcanoes originally created Hawaii's land mass. The two largest volcanoes are called Mauna Loa (13,676ft/4167m) and Mauna Kea (13,800ft/4205m) which together comprise 73% of the island's surface. Mauna Kea, an extinct volcano, is the highest mountain (13,800ft/4205m) in the Pacific Basin. Add to that its enormous mass underwater – it descends to a depth of 18,051ft/5500m – and it becomes the highest mountain in the world. Mauna Kea has been inactive for thousands of years but Mauna Loa still occasionally erupts. Kilauea, one of Mauna Loa's neighbouring volca-noes, is the most active in the world. Its countless eruptions occur inde-pendently of Mauna Loa's. During the last century, new volcanic eruptions have taken place on average every eleven months.

A further geographical feature distinguishes the island – Ka Lae is the most southerly point of the United States.

Location and history

Hawaii's rich and varied landscape is dominated by its enormous volca-noes. Tall volcanic craters, their peaks covered by snow in winter, wide expanses of lava in the south of the island and extinct volcanic mountains, with deep ravines and sheer cliffs, characterise the scenery. Although Hawaii has relatively few beaches, they are particularly charming because of the coloured sand which can be white, green or black.

Nature

The meaning of the name "Hawaii" is unknown but it is clearly of Poly-nesian origin because it is used on several Polynesian islands in varying forms. In New Zealand it is known as "Hawaiki", on the Cook Islands it is called "Awaiki" and in Samoa "Savai'i" – the variations can be traced back to different alphabets which do not always recognise the same consonants. Actually, Hawaii should really be written as Hawai'i to pronounce it cor-rectly but this is not generally done.

    So as not to confuse the Island of Hawaii with the State of Hawaii, a string of other names exists for the island, of which Big Island is most frequently used. "Orchid Island" or "Volcano Island" capture the flavour of Hawaii but are not acceptable as names for the island.

Name

◀ *Burning lava from Kilauea falls into the sea*

Climate and vegetation

The climate does not differ particularly from that of the rest of the island, but, because of the high volcanic mountains, it is more extreme in many ways. The east coast, particularly Hilo and its surroundings, has much rain, with an almost tropical climate. Short, very heavy rain showers usually fall in quick succession. In contrast, the area around Kailua-Koa on the west coast is very dry.

Vegetation on the island is accordingly varied. While rain forests with tropical vegetation grow on the east coast, there is only desert on the west coast, particularly around Kau.

Population

The population of the Island of Hawaii has increased in leaps and bounds in the last century. At the beginning of the 1970s, 63,000 people lived on the island. This number rose to 93,000 at the beginning of the 1980s and stands today at 112,000. Estimates as to the population of the island by the year 2005 range from 173,000 to 258,000 inhabitants.

Hilo, the island's principal town with some 40,000 inhabitants, is by far the largest town, followed by Karluna-Kona with just under 6000. Only nine other towns on the island have between 1000 and 2000 inhabitants. Whites make up the largest part of its population (34%), followed by Japanese (27%), Hawaiians and part-Hawaiians (19%), Filipinos (14%), Chinese (2%)

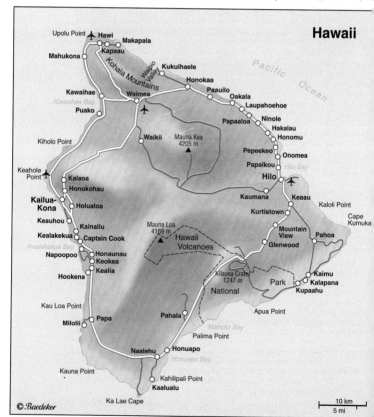

and other nationalities (4%). In the Hawaiian Parliament, the Island of Hawaii is not very strongly represented. Of the 25 senators in the State Parliament, only three are allotted to Big Island; of the 51 seats in the House of Representatives, only four are taken by members from the island.

Farming on Big Island plays a greater role than on the other Hawaiian islands even though about two-thirds of the land is unsuitable for agriculture because of a thick top layer of lava. Forty per cent of the total sugar cane harvest is given to the state. About 16 million kg of the most expensive nuts in the world, macadamia nuts, are produced each year and the most sought-after and very expensive Kona coffee is harvested. The Parker Ranch (see entry), the largest family-owned ranch in the United States, is responsible for cattle breeding in Hawaii. It produces two-thirds of the beef requirement of the whole state. A further source of income is flower growing which is carried out on around 300 farms.

Farming

The Island of Hawaii relies on growing numbers of tourists and therefore plans rapid development of accommodation. There are proposals for no fewer than 30 hotels along the west coast, which is particularly attractive to tourists because of its sunny weather and fine beaches. The number of available hotel rooms will climb from the current 5000 to 21,000 if these schemes go ahead. This figure does not include plans for accommodation in apartments and holiday homes. As yet, problems of street building, water supply and waste disposal, which would arise as a result of such rapid development, have not been solved.

Tourism

A settlement was probably first founded on the Island of Hawaii in the 7th c. at Ka Lae, both the most southerly point of the island and the closest arrival place of the Polynesian islands.

History

The custom of offering up human sacrifices, which spread throughout all the islands, is said to have started in Hawaii and particularly in the southern-lying Wahaula Heiau (today a part of the Hawaii Volcanoes National Park, see entry). Thought to have begun with a Tahitian priest named Paao, it continued until the reign of Kamehameha I.

The fate of Kamehameha I is tightly interwoven with that of the Island of Hawaii. He was born in 1753 (or 1758 – the exact date is unknown) in the district of Kohala to the north-west of the island. With his birth the legend grew up that shortly before his mother Kekuiapoiwa's confinement, a priest predicted that the expected child would grow into "an exterminator of the chiefs". As a result, several chiefs decided to kill the child but Kekuiapoiwa outwitted them by giving birth in a Hawaiian temple and handing him over to a servant, who took him to the rugged coastal area of Kapaau on the northern point of the island, where the child grew up. The prophecy was nevertheless fulfilled by Kamehameha's conquering troops and the subsequent founding of the first Hawaiian kingdom (see Famous People).

Hawaii was also the starting place for the first wave of missionaries. On April 20th 1820 the first Christian missionaries landed in Kailua-Kona, only a few months after Kamehameha II had put an end to Hawaiian religion by lifting the *kapus* and destroying the wooden and stone images of gods found everywhere on the island.

In the following period the island lost its supremacy; first Lahaina (Maui) became capital city of the group of islands and soon after Honolulu. Only with the development of mass tourism did Big Island regain some of its historical position. Today it stands undoubtedly at a turning point in its development.

Captain Cook   K 7

Captain Cook village, situated on the Kona coast near Kealakekua Bay, is named after the British seafarer and discoverer of the Island of Hawaii,

Village

Captain James Cook (see Famous People). The village has no tourist attractions but is recognised nowadays as the centre of Kona coffee production.

Royal Coffee
Mill Museum

On the way to Kealakekua Bay a visit can be paid to the coffee museum. Here it is possible to find out everything about the growing and processing of the very fine blend of Kona coffee cultivated in this area.

Captain Cook
Monument

Looking out from Kealakekua Bay a small white monument can be seen in the distance, protruding from the water. It marks the place where Captain James Cook met his death. The granite obelisk can only be reached by boat.

Captain Cook's
death

When Captain James Cook landed in Waimea (Kauai) on January 20th 1778, he and his companions were greeted with great honour by the Hawaiians because they were the first white men they had ever seen. Almost a year to the day later, returning from Alaska, he dropped anchor in Kealakekua Bay. When he first arrived, the Hawaiians were celebrating the festival of *Makahaki*, which honoured Lono, god of harvest and fertility. The customary *kapus* had been lifted. According to Hawaiian legend, during one such festival Lono would return to Earth and, when Cook arrived with his ships, he was taken for the god and his ships for travelling temples. He was treated as a god and the Hawaiians did their best to supply his ships with provisions. After Cook and his companions had spent a month there, one of the sailors died and the Hawaiians concluded that the sailors were not gods but mere mortals. The ships left the bay on February 4th but turned back nine days later because one was damaged during a fierce storm.

The natives grew more and more hostile towards the white men. After all manner of incidents matters finally came to a head when a cutter was stolen by the Hawaiians. Cook ordered that reprisals be taken and, when a chief was killed, an angry crowd attacked the Englishmen with clubs. Cook was hit over the head and his men opened fire. Cook is said to have killed

Coffee Museum . . .

. . . and Kona Coffee

two Hawaiians but he was injured slightly, thrown into the water and drowned – a terrible death for a sailor who could not swim. The Hawaiians carried his body away and, a few days later, returned the flesh having cooked it in an *imu*, according to their custom. The enraged sailors opened fire and wounded countless Hawaiians, including the future King Kamehameha I. Several days later, Cook's bones were handed over and his funeral took place at sea. The English finally weighed anchor on February 22nd 1779 and returned home.

★★Hawaii Volcanoes National Park   K/L 6/7

Among the many places of interest that the Hawaiian Islands, and in particular Big Island, have to offer, the Hawaii Volcanoes National Park is undoubtedly the most important. Here in the Halemaumau crater on the southern side of Kilauea is the home of the fire goddess Pele. According to Hawaiian legend, a volcano will erupt if she gets in a bad temper. Since July 1986 a new series of eruptions has spewed enormous quantities of lava up on to the surface. The island has grown by about 358,800sq.yd/ 300,000sq.m. Kilauea is one of the most impressive volcanoes in the world and

General information

its activities can be observed everywhere in the national park. Witnessing a fire-spitting eruption, however, would prove highly unlikely as these occur, on average, only once every eleven months.

The Hawaii Volcanoes National Park lies to the south-east of the Island of Hawaii and was founded in 1916. It includes a large part of Mauna Loa, all of Kilauea, including its eastern and southern sides, as well as the Puna Coast – in all, a considerable area of 21sq.miles/54sq.km.
   The most accessible part of the national park is the Kilauea Caldera region which is signposted off Road 11 when travelling from either Hona or Hilo. To reach the park from the coast take the coastal road out of Hilo and approach the mountains along Chain of Craters Road through an impressive volcanic landscape. This route is more difficult and dangerous as the road is often blocked by new flows of lava.

Size and situation

The Kilauea Visitor Centre lies on the edge of Kilauea Caldera, 550yd/500m to the left of the entry kiosk to the Hawaii Volcanoes National Park. It is open daily from 9am–5pm. In addition to general information packs and maps, suggested routes for walks are available here. There is also a film about the history and development of the volcano and its most recent eruptions.

Information centres

The last violent eruptions of the Kilauea crater occurred in 1790 and 1924, since when it has not appeared active. However, the neighbouring Halemaumau crater in the middle of Kilhauea Caldera, is more active. Eruptions on the slopes and in the thick forests are described only as flank eruptions, which are not as spectacular as summit eruptions as they usually bring only lava and are not accompanied by rivers of fire.

Kilauea's most recent eruptions

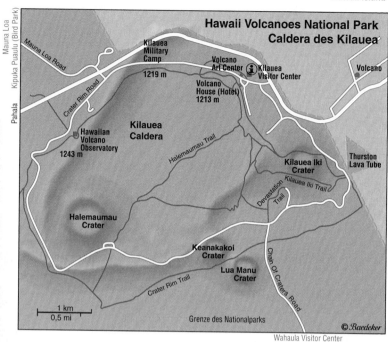

Wahaula Visitor Center

Lava flows have caused permanent changes to the landscape around Kilauea. Red-glowing magma, reaching temperatures of some 2200°F/1200°C, forces its way almost constantly through lateral channels to the outside, streams out of holes down the sides of the volcano and leaks out of weak spots known as fissures. One of these stretches out from the crater in a southerly direction as far as Ka'u, another east-north-east via Puna to the sea.

Lava sometimes flows through small valleys, which become filled in, and can destroy entire forests. But at the same time a new floor forms on which vegetation can grow, as demonstrated by the Destruction Trail in the National Park (see below).

Lava masses bring great destruction – time and again houses are buried and roads made impassable. In April 1990 all the houses in the coastal village of Kalapana and the greater part of the world-famous Kaimu Black Sand Beach were destroyed. Since then road 130 between Kupaahu and Kalapana has also been partly destroyed. Only one of the village's two churches, the Star of the Sea Painted Church, could be successfully dismantled before the lava reached it; it was later rebuilt on stilts near the end of the road.

Despite all this the recent eruptions are considered mild compared with earlier ones. It was reported in 1790 that Keoua, a Hawaiian island chief and opponent of Kamehameha I, was resting with his troops near Kilauea when they were surprised by an eruption. The majority of the army died, leaving Kamehameha's troops little difficulty in defeating the remainder.

Current methods of assessing natural phenomena such as volcanoes and earthquakes have prevented any loss of life through volcanic eruptions on Hawaii in recent times.

Places of interest along Crater Rim Road

What must definitely be seen in the national park? Planning depends on time available as well as the weather, which, unfortunately, does not enjoy what might be considered typically Hawaiian sunshine because of the park's proximity to the east coast – it often falls victim to sudden heavy rain. Volcano House, the only hotel in the park, is recommended for overnight stays. Advance booking is essential, especially in high season.

Planning

First drive along Crater Rim Road, which circles Kilauea Caldera. Starting from the information centre, the drive measures 11 miles/17.5km but stopping off at lush rainforests, craters and devastated areas makes the journey longer than expected. Along the route there are several viewing points from which the volcanic landscape can be observed.

Crater Rim Road

Somewhat remote yet within reach of Mauna Loa Road, which branches off from Crater Rim Road just before the Volcano Observatory, is the Bird Park (Kipuka Puaula).

Bird Park

Comprising about 99 acres/40ha this park, made an island by recent lava flows, is an ideal location for different species of endemic plants and trees, including koa, kolea and mamani trees. Rare Hawaiian birds can also be spotted here. A 1094yd/1km path leads through meadows and forests and offers ample opportunity to experience Hawaii's unique plant world. A brochure detailing everything of interest in the Bird Park can be obtained at the entrance.

View into the Kilauea Iki crater

Mauna Loa Road continues for 10 miles/16km to a 6564ft/2000m high viewing platform complete with car park. If the weather is good, panoramic views can be enjoyed.

A path leads on further to Mokuaweoweo crater at the summit of Mauna Loa (13,676ft/4167m). This 19 miles/30km walk, climbing to a height of 6564ft/2000m, although not difficult, requires two days to complete.

Devastation Trail

Along the south-east stretch of Crater Rim Road, a 1 mile/1.6km long, recently tarred road leads to a 10ft/3m thick recent lava layer known as Devastation Trail, from either side of which a weird lunar landscape reveals itself. Devastation Trail was formed in 1959 as a result of an eruption from the small Iki crater. Only bare ohia trees remained; however, it was not long before fresh flowers and saplings began to grow. A fine view of the Iki crater (*Iki* is Hawaiian for small) can be gained at the end of Devastation Trail.

Thurston Lava Tube

From the eastern section of Crater Rim Road a trail branches off to Thurston Lava Tube, invisible from the road. Leading through a forest with enormous ferns and trees, it reaches a lava tunnel measuring 492ft/150m long and 20ft/6m high, which was formed by chunks of lava cooling at different rates. The exterior of the lava cooled rapidly while the magma inside continued to pour through it, thus forming a hollow tunnel. The path through the tunnel is illuminated.

Halemaumau crater

Continue in a south-westerly direction around Crater Rim Road to the very active Halemaumau crater, an enormous fiery hole, spanning 2625ft/800m and inhabited, according to legend by the Hawaiian goddess of fire, Pele. It was filled until 1924 with a bubbling sea of lava but this eventually sank with a mighty roar beneath the floor of the volcano and the lava flowed away. The hole filled up again in the 1960s but soon sank again. Halemaumau is monitored regularly but forecasts of its future activities are difficult to make.

Scientific reports accurately reflect the enormous number of lava flows from Hawaiian craters. When Mauna Loa remained active for 23 days in 1950, it alone spewed up 2354 million cu.ft/600 million cu.m. During the course of a century four thousand million cubic metres of magma was pushed to the surface, together with enormous lumps of rock. When Halemaumau erupted in 1924, seismologists estimated these to weigh 14 tons.

Jagger Museum

Further information about recent volcanic activity is available in the Jagger Museum next to the Volcano Observatory, situated along Crater Rim Road. As well as offering a basic introduction to volcanoes, the scientists here put much emphasis on showing a connection between the Hawaiian legends and natural phenomena.

The films and slide shows about various eruptions give the visitor a clear impression of the incredibly powerful forces of nature at work here.

Volcano Art Center

A visit to the Volcano Art Center, situated near the entrance to the national park, is also recommended. It occupies the old Volcano Hotel, built in 1877 but subsequently rebuilt on the opposite side of Crater Rim Road.

Advice

In recent years lava flows have made many coastal roads impassable, including road 130 to the east of Wahaula. It will take some time before they are operational again so observe warning signs when approaching a prohibited area.

★Hilo

L 6

Hilo lies on the east coast of the Island of Hawaii in the heart of Hilo Bay, whose crescent shape has earned it the name "Crescentmoon Bay".

The settlement of Hilo was founded in the same year that Captain Cook arrived at the Hawaiian islands (1778). Its population of 43,500 makes Hilo the second largest town in the State of Hawaii. One third of Big Island's inhabitants live here. Hilo is Big Island's main town and an important centre of agriculture (sugar cane and flowers), as well as a significant port.

Two disastrous *tsunamis* (spring tides) in 1946 and 1960 destroyed great parts of the town. Most of the government offices, which were situated near the coast, were rebuilt in safer parts of Hilo. As coastal protection, several grassed areas for walking and leisure activities were laid in their place.

Destruction by
Tsunamis

Hilo's rainy climate does not make it a particularly favourite haunt for tourists. However, its well-preserved Old Town, with buildings dating from 1870, is well worth exploring. Thanks to the heavy levels of rainfall a unique display of flowers, particularly orchids and anthurias, can be admired in the gardens and surroundings of Hilo.

Tourism

Hilo is a suitable starting point for exploring the various places of interest nearby such as the Hawaii Volcanoes National Park (see entry), only 32 miles/50km away, several waterfalls and tropical rainforests.

The town cannot be recommended to those seeking a bathing resort. The few beaches are mainly man-made beach parks which cannot be compared to the natural sandy beaches found elsewhere on the island.

Places of interest in Hilo and the surrounding area

Banyan Drive

Banyan Drive circles the Waiakea Peninsula which protrudes into Hilo Bay. This wide coastal road is planted on either side with many overhanging banyan trees which form an archway above it. Most of Hilo's hotels are here and it is well worth a stroll along this unique street, even for those visitors who are not staying here.

Banyan Drive borders, on one side, the fine, green Banyan Golf Course and, on the other, Liliuokalani Garden (see entry).

Coconut Island

This islet can be reached via a footbridge from the Hilo Hawaiian Hotel. Clear weather permits a particularly fine view of the Pacific or – if the weather conditions are right – the snow-covered summit of Mauna Kea.

Hawaii Tropical Botanical Gardens

In the Hawaii Tropical Botanical gardens visitors can enjoy over 1800 different species of native plants, many flowers including orchids (Hilo is the orchid-growing centre of Hawaii), shrubs, palms and trees. A trip along 4-Mile Scenic Drive is a beautiful experience; the drive branches off from road 19 4 miles/6km beyond Papikou and returns to the same spot.

Location
Street 19,
7½ miles/12km
north-west of
Banyan Drive
Tel. 964–5233

About 10 miles/16km north of Hilo, road 220 branches off from road 19 and leads to Akaka Falls. From the car park there is a beautiful short walk leading through rich countryside to the Akaka Falls and thence to the Kahuna Falls.

Akaka Falls

Kalakaua

This small park lies in the middle of Hilo's Old Town between Waianuenue Avenue and Kalakaua Street, Kinoole and Keawe Street.

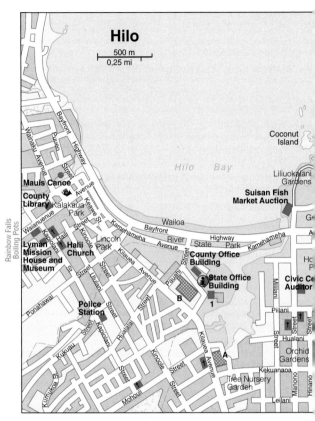

Several of the trees in the park are said to have been planted during the reign of the Hawaiian King David Kalakaua who was a frequent visitor to Hilo and after whom the park is named. A bronze statue of King Kalakaua stands in the middle of the park.

Kalakaua Park provides an ideal starting point for a stroll through the Old Town. The Federal Building is situated directly opposite the northern end of the park and only a stone's throw away on Kalakaua Street is the old police station, which now houses the East Hawaii Cultural Center. Old houses interspersed with cafés and restaurants surround the park and exude a very special charm.

Liliuokalani Gardens

Bearing the name of the last king of Hawaii, this park lies at the end of Banyan Drive and is laid out in the style of a Japanese garden. A Japanese tea house stands in the middle in which the Japanese tea ceremony regularly takes place. Pagodas and stone lanterns lining the paths, and delicate half-moon bridges crossing small ponds, give the park a truly oriental flavour.

Panaewa Zoo

Kong's Floral Garden

Keaukaha Beach Park

Avenue

Kalanianaole

Drive

Kapili Avenue

Pakele

Kauhane Avenue

Silva Street

View

Ocean

Avenue

Kalanianaole

Bay Park

King

Avenue

amehameha Avenue

Kuhio Bay

Puhi Bay

Ocean

tic

la
ula

Hilo International Airport

General Lyman Field

Terminal

Hawaii National Guard

Kekuanaoa Street

Leilani Street

Hotels	Shopping Centers
1 Hilo Lagoon	A Hilo S.C.
2 Hilo Hawaiian	B Kaikoo Mall S.C.
3 Hilo Bay	C Waiakea Square S.C.
4 Naniloa Surf	
5 Country Club Villa	© *Baedeker*
6 Hilo Hukilau	

Mau Gardens,

★Lyman House Memorial Museum

This restored house dates from 1839 and is considered to be the oldest wooden house on the island. It was built by the missionaries David and Sarah Lyman, who lived there with their family. Until the 1920s it was owned by the Grunder family, but in 1932 it became a museum detailing the lives of the first missionaries in Hawaii. The furniture is of that period, mainly made from ohia wood, with the floor and doors made from koa wood. One of the rooms was originally used as a school room while those on the upper floor served as bedrooms for the Lyman's eight children.

A modern two-storey extension to the museum has been built. The ground floor contains the Island Heritage Gallery, the upper floor the Earth Heritage Gallery. Both show the history of the Hawaiian islands and their inhabitants by means of artefacts, pictures and photographs. On view here are a Hawaiian grass hut, tools used by the Hawaiians, stone lamps, mortars and *iomi-iomi* sticks, which were used for massage. A large collection of minerals has been assembled in the Earth Heritage Gallery as well as shellfish, fossils embedded in wood and examples of the endemic animals and plant life of the Hawaiian islands. A library of 26,000 books and photographs will answer any relevant questions.

Location
276 Hall Street, corner of Kapiolani Street
Tel. 935–5021

75

Coconut Island

Mauna Loa Macadamia Nut Co.

Location
Street 11,
about
5½ miles/9km
south of the town.
Follow signs.
Tel. 966–9301

The Island of Hawaii, including Hilo, blessed with its heavy rainfall, tropical sun and lava-covered land, is one of the centres specialising in the growth of macadamia nuts. These originated in Australia and were introduced here as recently as 120 years ago.

The Mauna Loa Company began by planting trees, harvesting the first crop eight years later. With its 800,000 trees, the Mauna Loa Macadamia Nut Mill rates today as one of the world's largest producers of these very tasty, yet very fatty, nuts. The production of macadamia confectionery, cakes, biscuits and other items is demonstrated in the visitor centre and all these goods can be bought in the shops on the island.

Naha Stone

In front of Hilo's town library in Waianuenue Avenue, between Ululani and Kapiolani Street and only a short distance from the Lyman House Memorial Museum, stand two great rocks. The larger one, called the Naha Stone, is a 7056lb/3200kg monolith from Kauai. The smaller one is said to come from Heiau. A legend surrounds the Naha Stone stating that whoever could stand this giant stone on its end with their bare hands would become the first King of Hawaii. King Kamehameha accomplished this feat allegedly with help from the gods.

Nani Mau Gardens

Location
421 Makalika,
5 miles/8km along
Street 11.
Tel. 959–3541

Located just outside Hilo in the rich Panaewa Rainforest, the park contains the largest orchid collection on the Island of Hawaii. It is an ideal place to learn about orchid growing and the numerous varieties of anthuria. One of Hawaii's rare fern gardens, a water lily pond and a Japanese pavilion can also be enjoyed here.

Huge banyan trees along Banyan Drive

Rainbow Falls

A short walk from Waianeuneu Avenue the waterfall forms part of Wailuku River State Park in the west of Hilo. The approximately 98ft/30m high waterfall can be viewed from various vantage points. It looks particularly lovely when the sun shines on the water and creates a rainbow – hence the name, Rainbow Falls. Pee-Pee Waterfall is 2 miles/3km further along Waianeuneu Avenue.

A little further up the river valley a small circular pond called Boiling Points is reached. (**Warning:** dangerous currents!)

Suisan Fish Market

A lively fish auction takes place daily from 7.30am near Banyan Drive. Fishermen sell mahimahi, okakapa, tuna and other seafood to wholesalers. The dealing can prove difficult to follow as English, Japanese and Hawaiian are used – and sometimes a mixture of all three! It resembles pidgin English, a language which originated in China to aid dialogue with the people of the Pacific (it is said that the word "pidgin" comes from the way the Chinese pronounced "business").

Location
Corner of Banyan Drive and Lihiwai Street

Tsunami Memorial

Surrounding the Wailoa Information Center car park, reached via Kamehameha Avenue and Pauahi Street, runs a memorial to the countless victims of the spring tides (*Tsunamis*), which last flooded Hilo in 1946 and 1960. A curved wall of volcanic rock, it is an abstract, symbolic representation of a flood wave.

Town plan

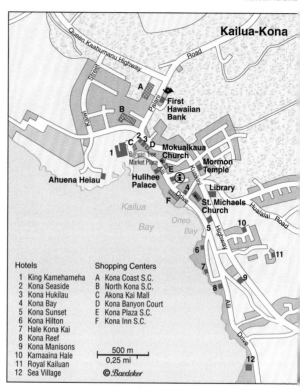

Kailua-Kona

First Hawaiian Bank

Mokuaikaua Church

Mormon Temple

Banyan Tree Market Place

Hulihee Palace

Library

Ahuena Heiau

St. Michaels Church

Kailua Bay

Oneo Bay

Hotels

1 King Kamehameha
2 Kona Seaside
3 Kona Hukilau
4 Kona Bay
5 Kona Sunset
6 Kona Hilton
7 Hale Kona Kai
8 Kona Reef
9 Kona Manisons
10 Kamaaina Hale
11 Royal Kailuan
12 Sea Village

Shopping Centers

A Kona Coast S.C.
B North Kona S.C.
C Akona Kai Mall
D Kona Banyon Court
E Kona Plaza S.C.
F Kona Inn S.C.

500 m
0,25 mi

© *Baedeker*

★Kailua-Kona

K 6

General information	The area known as Kailua-Kona comprises a string of neighbouring villages along the west coast of Hawaii. The word *kona* means "won from the wind" and, for this reason, several villages on the leeward side of the islands bear this name (Kauai, Molokai, Oahu and Nihau). To avoid confusion, the hyphenated name Kailua-Kona was adopted on the Island of Hawaii. The oldest Hawaiian village, the history of Kailua-Kona is tightly interwoven with that of Big Island. This historically important area has a great deal to offer the tourist.
How to get there	Previously it was only possible to reach Kailua-Kona via Hilo's airport, the busiest on the island, about 97 miles/156km away. Although the number of flights to and from the Hawaiian islands has decreased, it is now possible to fly directly from the American mainland to Keahole Airport, some 7½ miles/12km from Kailua-Kona. To explore fully Big Island, it is advisable to spend time both on the east coast (Hilo) and the west coast (Kailua-Kona).
Tourism	South Kona, Kona, Kailua and North Kona rank among the most visited parts of the Island of Hawaii. This has much to do with the consistently good weather. Kailua-Kona lies in the rain shadow of high mountains

(Mauna Loa and Mauna Kea) and it is said that the sun shines here 344 days a year, hence the region's other name – the Golden Coast.

The Kona coast has everything – luxury hotels or simple ones, interesting shops and a wide range of places to visit. An abundance of bouganvillea, jasmine and plumeria blooms throughout the year and there is a rich choice of fine beaches. If lazing on the beach offers insufficient stimulus, Kailua-Kona can easily be explored on foot.

Places of interest in Kailua-Kona

★Ahuena Heiau

This fully-restored temple, directly behind the Kamehameha Hotel, is possibly the best example of a Hawaiian place of sacrifice. Ahuena Heiau, in which human sacrifice also took place, was built by Kamehameha I on Kamakahonu Beach and dedicated to the god Lona.

Kamehameha I spent the last years of his life at Ahuena Heiau, possibly dying here – not too far from his birthplace, Kapaau (see entry). According to Hawaiian custom, his bones were removed from his corpse on a stone platform in the temple and taken north, possibly to Wawahiwa Point, where they were left at a secret location.

His son and successor, Kamehameha II, grew up here and this area became central to the abolition of the *tabus* and the destruction of heathen idols and temples during his reign (see Facts and Figures, dissolution of Hawaiian religion). Further measures to abolish the old religion were then implemented from Lahaina (see entry), the seat of government. Restoration of Ahuena Heiau was supervised by the Bishop Museum in Honolulu, but only about one third of the temple has been rebuilt (free entry).

Ahuena Heiau

Alii Drive

Hotels, shops, boutiques, restaurants, cafés and historical monuments line this lively shopping street and beach promenade running along Kailua Bay. It is a good place to begin a walk round the town and to enjoy the colourful atmosphere.

Hulihee Palace

Location
Alii Drive
Tel. 329–1877

Built in 1838 by Kuakini, governor of the island and brother of the late Queen of Hawaii, this building is on the site where King Kamehameha I's original palace once stood. Princess Ruth, half-sister of Kings Kamehameha IV and V, then the richest woman on the island and – at 331lb/150kg – the heaviest, lived here for a while. King Kalakaua had it converted into a summer palace for the Hawaiian monarchy. Prince Kuhio, who inherited it, for some reason sold off all its furniture. The organisation called Daughters of Hawaii was able to buy much of the furniture so that most of it is authentic. The museum contains a portrait gallery, featuring the Hawaiian kings, as well as a collection of spears said to have belonged to Kamehameha I. Photography is not allowed inside the museum.

Kailua Pier

Kailua Pier lies opposite Ahuena Heiau in the north-west of Kailua-Kona. It is a centre for pleasure cruises and the departure point for deep water fishing trips as well as the commercial fishing industry, which is so prevalent around Kona. Snorkelling equipment and underwater cameras can be rented. Marine traffic dominates the scene here almost all day long (see Practical Information, Tours of the Island and Sport).

Hulihee Palace

Keauhou Bay

This bay at the end of Alii Drive is characterised by a series of historical sites and the remains of several temples (a map showing most of the places of interest is available from the Keauhou Bay Hotel). Also here is the Kona Surf Hotel, whose beautiful gardens containing 30,000 plants, flowers, fruits, shrubs and trees from the South Sea Islands are well worth a visit. The nearby Kona flea market opens on Saturdays only between 7.30am and 2.30pm.

Mokuaikaua Church

Opposite Hulihee Palace (see entry) stands the oldest church (1837) on the Hawaiian islands. The 108ft/33m-high tower is the tallest building and landmark in Kailua-Kona.

Location
Alii Drive
Tel. 329–1589

The land on which the 118ft/36m-long and 46ft/14m-wide Mokuaikaua Church stands was given to the first missionaries on Hawaii in 1820 by King Kamehameha II. A model of the three-master "Thaddeus" from Boston (on which the missionaries arrived after several months of travelling in Hawaii) is on display inside.

Designed by its first priest, Asa Thurston, the walls of the church are constructed from lava, plastered with ground coral and bonded with oils from kukui nuts. The cornerstones are supposed to have come from a temple. The pillars and the balcony inside are carved from natural ohia wood while koa wood was used for the chancel and the pews. Services are held on Sundays at 10.30am and Wednesdays at 7pm.

Kamuela

See Waimea

Kapaau   K 5

Kapaau is known as the birthplace of King Kamehameha I as was that of the Hawaiian monarchy. Nowadays a sleepy village with about 600 inhabitants, near to the northern point of Big Island and reached by Road 270, Kapaau's one claim to fame is its original statue of Kamehameha I. Originally destined for Honolulu (see Honolulu, Aliiolani Hale), it was lost during transportation. It is worth seeing this original statue because it is far more true to life than the copy in Honolulu. Wind and weather take their toll on the statue so once a year, on the evening before Kamehameha Day (June 11th), its is given a fresh coat of paint.

Original statue of
Kamehameha I

Sugar production once made Hawi (reached via Roads 270 or 250 to Kapaau) a prosperous town. Today Hawi serves as an example of the effects of the decline in sugar production in this area. It has become a backwater with its abandoned Kohala Sugar Company works.

Hawi

A little further on from Kapaau the road ends at Poiolu Lookout from where the steep-sided Poiolu Valley can easily be viewed.

Poiolu Lookout

Lapakahi State Historical Park   K 5

Following the coast to Kapaau, the road passes Lapakahi State Historical Park. A small track leads from Road 270 through fields in a seaward direction to the park, Hawaii's largest excavation site. Among the remains of a 600-year-old Hawaiian fishing village, visitors can get a taste of daily life in those times.

Lava Tree State Park   M 7

Half way between Kilauea crater and the sea, about 2 miles/3km from the sea amid a devastated volcanic landscape, is one of Hawaii's most unusual natural phenomena – ohia trees encased in lava.

The Lava Tree State Park was formed in 1790 when a fast-flowing stream of lava engulfed a forest of ohia trees to a height of 13ft/4m. The lava cooled around the trees and formed a hard outer shell. At about the same time, fissures appeared underground, caused by several earth tremors, through which the still-liquid lava could drain away. Today fresh tall trees have grown up, providing a unique contrast to the petrified stumps which are the sole remnants of the old engulfed forest and making a visit to State Park a very worthwhile experience.

★Mauna Kea   K/L 6

Highest mountain

At 13,800ft/4205m Mauna Kea (White Mountain) is not only the highest mountain in the Hawaiian islands but in the whole of the Pacific region. Add to that the extra 18,050ft/5500m under the sea and it becomes the highest mountain in the world. In contrast to Mauna Loa, which is administered by the Hawaii Volcanoes National Park (see entry), Mauna Kea is governed directly by the State of Hawaii. Its summit covered by snow all year round, Mauna Kea is a popular skiing resort from December to May – a fact which often escapes visitors to Hawaii.

Saddle Road

An experienced driver using a four-wheel drive vehicle could reach the summit via Saddle Road (Road 200), a partly unsurfaced, narrow route along which there is no accommodation, no access to water and which is subject to rain, wind and hail. Saddle Road begins in Hilo and continues across the plateau between Mauna Kea and Mauna Loa to Waimea (see entry) and from there via Road 190 to Kona – the shortest route but one which, because of poor driving conditions, takes longer than following Road 19 along the coast.

Ascent

The ascent begins about 26 miles/42km out of Hilo at a turning off Saddle Road. Hale Pohaku is 4 miles/6km further, home to some of the Mauna Kea Observatory employees. After a short distance, at the Kilohana viewing point, the road forks, offering the choice of a 6 mile/9.6km trail or remaining on the road which leads to the observatory.

Trees soon give way to barren land covered with the remains of red lava. Those who undertake the ascent are rewarded with a fantastic view, provided the cloud cover is not too low. This route also passes Waiau (water whirlpool), which, at 12,143ft/3700m, is the third highest lake in the United States.

The summit is snow-covered for most of the year, offering an opportunity to go ski-ing in the Tropics!

The unusual height and thin air make the ascent very long and strenuous – care should be taken not to over-exert oneself.

Observatory

The position of the observatory, located near the summit, makes it one of the finest in the world. Maintained by NASA and the University of Hawaii as a research centre, it can be visited on certain weekends in May (telephone Hilo 935–3371). An accompanied tour of Mauna Kea in a four-wheel drive vehicle can be undertaken, departing from Kailua-Kona (telephone 775–7121).

Mauna Loa

See Hawaii Volcanoes National Park

Naalehu — K 7

Naalehu is the most southerly village in the USA. It has almost 1200 inhabitants comprising mostly Italians and Filipinos, who show little sign of their origins.

Most southerly point of the USA

Naalehu, located on Road 11, which runs south between Hilo and Kona, includes an area called Waiohinu, with giant trees, several churches, including Kauaha'ao Church (well worth visiting), and the only hotel in the region, the Shirakawa Hotel, built near a tree planted by Mark Twain on his visit to Hawaii almost 125 years ago.

Waiohinu

Not far from the village a rough path branches off to Ka Lae, about 10 miles/16km away, which is not only the most southerly point of the Hawaiian islands but of the whole of the USA. Ka Lae lies 497 miles/800km further south than Miami and 994 miles/1600km further south than Los Angeles.

Ka Lae

Ka Lae is uninhabited but, according to experts, it is here that Tahitians and other South Sea Islanders landed when they first arrived on Hawaii.

Painted Church – St Benedict's Church — K 7

This small Catholic wooden church stands not far from Puuhonua o Honau-hau National Historic Park and is well worth turning off Road 160 to look at, not only because of its lovely position but because of the original decoration of the interior. The Belgian priest, Jean Berchman Velghe, who built it at the turn of the century, used whitewash for painting the walls and

Painted decoration inside St Benedict's Church

added pictures of various biblical scenes and Hawaiian motifs which reveal an astonishing talent. Behind the altar he created an image in perspective based on Burgos Cathedral in Spain. The church columns are painted with Hawaiian motifs such as flowers and palms. Velghe, who was only in charge of this church for five years (1899–1904), also painted other church interiors in the South Seas.

★Parker Ranch K5

Largest ranch in the USA

The enormous estates of the Parker Ranch, which stretch from the north-west coast of Hawaii to the mountains of Kohala, give an unusual impression of the island. The Parker Ranch in Waimea (see entry), located on Road 19, has an area of 355sq.miles/920sq.km, about 9% of Hawaii's total area. From small beginnings in 1847, it has grown to become the largest cattle ranch in the United States. It is now run by the sixth generation of the Parker family.

Since the 1960s, particularly in areas of the estate close to the coast where land is not rich enough to support cattle rearing, tourism and shopping have been developed. A considerable number of hotels, including luxury hotels (such as the Mauna Kea Beach Hotel, the Sheraton Royal Waikola and the Mauna Lani Bay Hotel), and apartment buildings have been constructed here.

Beginnings of cattle rearing

Towards the end of the 18th c. the first cattle were brought to Hawaii by the British seafarer George Vancouver as a present for King Kamehameha I. They were kept in the wild and quickly established themselves, breeding rapidly. The king commissioned his friend John Parker, who came to Hawaii in 1809 from Massachusetts and who married a woman from the island's ruling classes, to capture and tame the cattle. In doing so, he was to

Cattle grazing at Parker Ranch

select the best for his own herd. Thus began Parker cattle rearing. Only with the law of 1847, which apportioned land (the "Large Mahele"), did Parker receive a small piece of grazing land on Mauna Kea's north-eastern slopes. In addition, his wife, Kelii-Kipikane-O-Kolakala, a cousin of one of Kamehameha I's wives, was entitled to 1sq.mile/2.5sq.km of land. Parker bought a considerable amount of land and this formed the basis of his ranch. The current owner of the ranch and its stock (50,000 cattle, 1000 horses) is Richard Smart, great-great-great-grandson of the founder.

Some of the Hawaiian cowboys, who still work today on the Parker Ranch, are direct descendants of the *vaqueros* brought over by Parker from Mexico in 1830 to help capture the wild cattle. As there was no Hawaiian equivalent, they became known as *paniolos* after the word *espanol* (meaning Spanish). Rodeos and other events take place here on Kamehameha Day (June 11th) and on American Independence Day (July 4th) as well as at other times.

Paniolos

Since 1988, the whole ranch has been open to visitors, who can enjoy a four-hour or a half-hour tour. The tour includes a visit to the family cemetery, the Puukalani stables (where lunch is served on the longer tour), John Parker's house (reconstructed by Smart with its original furniture from the second half of the 19th c.) and the elegant modern house, Puuopelu, which houses Smart's considerable collection of French and Venetian art, pieces of Chinese jade and rare glassware. About 100 paintings are also on display here, including works by Degas, Renoir, Pissarro, de Vlaminck and Dufy.

Visits to the ranch

John Palmer Parker Museum

Much of the Parker family history is covered in the John Palmer Parker Museum whose exhibits include family portraits, old Bibles, antique clothes, implements, weapons, a printing press and much more. One room is devoted to the career of Duke Kahanamoku (see Famous People) who enjoyed several Olympic successes in swimming.

An extension to the museum houses a small cinema in which a four-hour film is shown, depicting the history and projected future of the Parker Ranch.

Location
Parker Ranch
Shopping
Center, Waimea
Tel. 885–7655

★★Puuhonua o Honaunau National Historic Park   K 7

The present temple site was restored by the national park authorities and is a replica of the original which dates from the end of the 18th c.. The division of the temple site by means of a 10ft/3m-high, 16ft/5m-wide wall into the City of Refuge area and the Palace Grounds can be seen today. The thick wall between the former palace and the sanctuary has been preserved over the centuries, with repair work being carried out in 1902 and 1963–64.

Using information gleaned from pictures, replica koa wood carvings of temple gods have been placed in their original positions.

There is more to be seen on the 952sq.yd/800sq.m estate and a free map is available at the visitor centre. Attractions include the landing place of the royal canoes (*"keone'ele"*), the stones on which the royal family played a type of Hawaiian nine men's morris (*"konane"*), the Kuuhumanu Stone (behind which the Queen hid from Kamehameha's henchmen but was discovered when her dog began to bark), a royal fishpond (*"he-lei-palalu"*), the Keoua Stone (supposedly the favourite place of Keoua, King of Kona), burial vaults, rock carvings (petroglyphs) and models of houses belonging to the priests and inhabitants of the City of Refuge.

When the whole temple has been reconstructed, Hawaiian history will come to life in a vivid and varied way. Nowhere else in Hawaii – with the possible exception of the Bishop Museum (see entry) in Honolulu – can so much be learned about island traditions.

Location
11 Honaunau
Street.
Turn off at
milestones 104
or 103
Tel. 328–2326

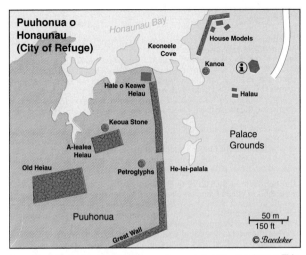

Inside map:

Puuhonua o Honaunau (City of Refuge)

Honaunau Bay

Keoneele Cove

House Models

Kanoa   ⓘ

Hale o Keawe Heiau

Halau

Keoua Stone

Palace Grounds

A-lealea Heiau

Old Heiau

Petroglyphs   He-lei-palala

Puuhonua

Great Wall

50 m
150 ft

© Baedeker

Communal life in the Hawaii of the past was defined by the *kapus*. This system of rules governing behaviour and actions dictated many areas of daily life and was applied to land ownership, eating customs, conduct between the sexes, the role of women and even to people's sex lives. Members of the royal family (*ali'i*) ensured that the *kapus* system was adhered to. According to Hawaiian belief, the *kapus* originated from the gods so every violation was a challenge to the gods and had to be punished with death. The only escape was to attempt an extremely difficult flight into a sanctuary.

Kapus – the rule of life

On the Island of Hawaii there were six sanctuaries, of which Puuhonua o Honaunau (the Sanctuary of Honaunau) was the most important and holy. Immediately next to it stood the ancestral home of the kings of Hawaii.

To understand the significance of these places it is necessary to examine the relationship between religion and the Hawaiian monarchy. The Hawaiians believed strongly in the godly charisma (*mana*) of their kings, which started at their skeletons after death. The places in which their skeletons were hidden (mostly *heiaus*) were also filled with holiness because of this. Under the protection of *mana*, these temples became a safe place of refuge for those who had broken the *kapus*. After an "absolution ceremony" had been conducted by a priest (*kahuna*), the "criminal" could return home safely and without punishment.

Protection through mana

The construction of Puuhonua o Honaunau is thought to have been started in 1550. The sanctuary was dedicated to the ruler of Kona at that time, Keawe-Ku-I-Ke-Kaai, who had risen to the status of a god. After his death, a temple (Hale-O-Keawe heiau) was built for him in which his bones were interred. During the next two-and-a-half centuries, a further 22 rulers of Kona were buried here. The holiness of this place increased as the number grew because their skeletons produced *mana*. The last member of the royal family to be buried here was a son of Kamehameha I who died in 1818. After the abolition of Hawaiian religion and of the *kapus* system, this holy place was one of the last to be destroyed. The remains of kings buried here were moved to secret locations.

Building of the sanctuary

◀ *Koa-wood idols on the beach of Puuhonua o Honaunau*

★Puukohola Heiau

K 5

Location
Take Road 19 from
Waimea to Kona,
then Road 270.
Tel. 882–7218

This temple is the last great *heiau* remaining on the Hawaiian islands. It was built on the orders of Kamehameha I between 1790 and 1791 at a time when he had not yet managed to establish a united Hawaii and monarchy. Puukohola Heiau is built on the remains of a previous temple, at least 200 years old. In the 223ft/68m × 98ft/30m grounds are the remains of three temples. Puukohola Heiau, with its enormous sacrificial platform, is particularly impressive. Nearby are the remains of a smaller temple, Maiklekini Heiau, and those of a third, Haleokapuni Heiau, lie some 98ft/30m under the sea.

The piece of land on which John Young, a close employee of Kamehameha, built his house, borders the site of the temple. A British seafarer who arrived in Hawaii in 1790, he adopted the name Olahana and governed the island from 1802 to 1812. From his house at the northern end of the *heiau* site, on the other side of Road 270, there is not much more to be seen.

The temple was built to fulfil a prophecy of a priest called Kapuokahi, according to which Kamehameha would inherit all the islands if he built a temple in honour of the god of a war, Kukailimoku, on Puukohola Hill near to Kawaihae. Puukohola means "angry water" – in this very dry region the Hawaiians used to argue about water.

When the temple was completed, Kamehameha invited his cousin Keoua Kuahuula, his only serious adversary on the Island of Hawaii, to its consecration on the pretext of wanting to make peace with him. Hardly had Keoua stepped out of his canoe with his entourage when they were massacred by waiting troops. Keoua's corpse was carried to the *heiau* as a sacrifice to the god of war.

In this vigorous manner Kamehameha helped fulfil the prophecy. Keoua's death brought an end to opposition and in 1794 Kamehameha reinherited the islands of Lanai, Molokai and Maui, which he had once owned but subsequently lost. With the conquest of the Island of Oahu in the following year Kamehameha could claim sovereignty of Hawaii. He gained control of Kauai only through an agreement with its king.

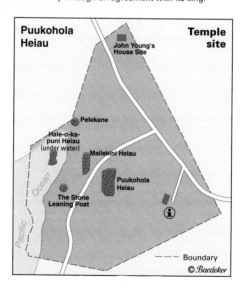

Waikoloa petroglyphs

After 1819 Puukohola Heiau, together with all remaining *heiaus*, was destroyed as part of the dissolution of Hawaiian religion, although its founda-
tions even withstood earthquakes. In 1928 a Hawaiian organisation built a
path and steps to the *heiau*. In 1972 the area was declared a National
Historic Site and given into the care of the National Park Service in Washington, which is gradually repairing the damage.

Destruction and
reconstruction

Waikoloa petroglyphs

Follow Road 19 along the coast in a southerly direction to the Waikoloa rock
carvings located not far from Puako. The two rock carving areas can be
reached by following a narrow footpath on the edge of the village. The
variety of motifs is most impressive, being very well preserved in the black
lava rock.

Rainbow Falls

See Hilo

Saddle Road

See Mauna Kea

Waimea – Kamuela   K 5

Waimea ("red water") is located in the north-west of the island and can be
reached from Hilo via Road 19 and from Kailua-Kona via Roads 19 and 190.

Centre of cattle
rearing

Continue from Hawi on Road 250 to the northern point of the island. All roads in the north of the island meet in Waimea (population about 1500) and it is well connected to the other centres on the Island of Hawaii (Hilo, Kailua-Kona). The development of Waimea is closely linked to the important Parker Ranch (see entry), thanks to which Waimea has become the main centre of Hawaiian cattle rearing.

Kamuela

As Waimea is a place name on Kauai and Oahu, as well as on Hawaii, the post office has introduced the name Kamuela, the Hawaiian spelling of Samuel. Whether this honours the former postmaster, Samuel Spencer, or Samuel Parker, the son of the ranch's founder, remains unknown.

Tour of the village

For such a small place Waimea has an unusually large shopping centre, the Parker Shopping Center (along with the Parker Museum, see entry), a multi-purpose auditorium and far more restaurants than might be expected. Imiola Church is also an unexpected find; built by Lorenzo Lyons in 1857 in the style of churches in New England, it has white-painted wood and a pointed tower. The priest learnt the Hawaiian language and translated English hymns into Hawaiian as well as old Hawaiian songs into English. A simple memorial to him stands in front of the church.

Kamuela Museum

Location
West of Waimea
where Roads 19
and
250 cross
Tel. 885–4724

Waimea has its own museum, Kamuela Museum, which originated from a collection of assorted Hawaiian artefacts put together by Albert Salomon, a policeman in Honolulu, and his wife Harriet, granddaughter of John Palmer Parker. The collection was started more than 50 years ago.

It is almost impossible to describe all that is on display here – Mrs Parker usually takes visitors under her wing and directs them to those exhibits she considers most important. If time permits, visitors should look round the house which is filled with the results of a passion for collecting and does not include solely Hawaiian objects.

Kahua Ranch

Half way between Waimea and Kapaau on Road 250, which passes through the Kohala Mountains, stands the Kahua cattle farm, second in importance to the Parker Ranch (see entry). The owner of this ranch has expanded his business by means of alternative energy supplies, using the wind to generate electricity. The steel wind wheels at first appear somewhat alien to the Hawaiian landscape but they are nevertheless a means of achieving environmentally-friendly energy.

Waipio Valley   K 5

Unspoilt Hawaii

This valley on the north-eastern coast of Big Island, about 50 miles/80km north of Hilo, has often been described as a sort of "Shangri La" – a timeless place cut off from the outside world.

The valley, about 1 mile/1.5km wide, dissects the Kohala Mountains and is difficult to reach because of the steep cliffs on the three landward sides. Strong waves make it equally unapproachable from the sea.

Bananas, papayas, mangoes, avocados and grapefruit grow on the fertile valley floor and colourful ginger trees, orchids and hibiscus decorate the landscape.

View of Waipio Bay and Waipio Valley

Waipio, with its various streams and branches, is fed by the 985ft/300m Hiilawe Falls. This double waterfall is one of the highest in the world but in the dry season has very little water nowadays because it is used to irrigate the land above the valley.

Hiilaw Falls

Waipio Valley ("winding water") understandably plays a large part in Hawaiian mythology. The grandfather of all the Hawaiian islands is said to have lived in this valley from choice and the two head gods, Kana and Kanaloa, were also here and are reputed to have become intoxicated on awa. The demi-god Maui is supposed to have died here when he tried to steal a baked banana from these two gods.

Hawaiian mythology

Waipio Valley is also known as the "Valley of the Kings", from where Hawaiian chiefs ruled over their people. Traditional songs tell how this once densely-populated valley used to be the political and cultural centre of Old Hawaii. Along with bananas and sugar cane, taro is the main crop grown on the floor of the valley. After the arrival of the white men, the population here declined rapidly. Only 1500 people were thought to have lived here 150 years ago.

"Valley of the Kings"

A new wave of settlers arrived at the beginning of this century, when Japanese and Chinese came to the valley, planted rice and taro, built houses and formed a community. A new migration occurred following the *tsunamis* of 1946, which not only caused great damage to Hilo, but which flooded this whole valley and forced the few survivors to leave. At the beginning of the 1970s some returned but a second spring flood in 1979 drove them away once more.
    Today 50–100 people (mainly Filipinos) lead a very secluded and simple life here, fishing and growing taro.

New settlement

Waipio Valley
Lookout

No visitor should leave Hawaii without experiencing this lovely view. Leaving Hilo on Road 19 proceed in a northerly direction until Road 240 branches off just before Hilo. Follow this road until it ends in Kukuihaele. From here, gaze down into Waipio Valley, 985ft/300m below, and drink in its beauty.

Excursions to the valley

The road leading from the lookout down into the valley is steep, stony and narrow, totally unsuitable for cars and should only be attempted by experienced drivers of four-wheel drive vehicles. One way of visiting the valley is to walk, provided that plenty of time is allowed for this. Another way is to travel by mule train or by four-wheel drive vehicle from Kukuihaele through the valley, a service offered by Waipio Valley Wagon Tours (Tel. 775–9518) or Waipio Valley Shuttle (Tel. 775–7121). Both companies require reservations, preferably on the day before the planned trip.

There is a small eight-roomed hotel (Tel. 775–0368) in the valley, built years ago for members of the American Peace Corps, who trained volunteers for action in South East Asia. Provisions must be taken as there is no restaurant in the valley.

Waipio Valley offers the opportunity to experience a "natural Hawaii", an opportunity long since lost on the other islands.

Kahoolawe Island

Area: 47sq.miles/121sq.km
No inhabitants

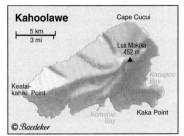

Kahoolawe, only 7 miles/ 11km off the south coast of the Island of Maui, can easily be seen from both there and Lanai. The island has few trees and lies in the rain shadow of Maui's Haleakala crater and consequently experiences little rain. Daytime temperatures are high while the nights are cold. Excess grazing by goats and the lack of water have resulted in widespread wind erosion which has worn away the topsoil and left a bare surface. Politically speaking, for 50 years the island occupied a special position in Hawaii. It belonged to the State of Hawaii, but after the attack on Pearl Harbor in 1941 the US military took possession of the island and used it for military exercises and for testing bombs and grenades. Following massive protests by peace campaigners such tests were discontinued in 1991. Today the island is uninhabited except for wild goats; however, it is dangerous to walk here because of the risk of unexploded ammunition.

General information

The Hawaiians consider Kahoolawe a holy island. A group called Protect Kahoolawe Ohana has existed since 1976 with the aim of returning the 10½ miles/17km-long, 6 miles/10km-wide island to the Hawaiians. When the US discontinued using it for military manoeuvres in 1991 this aim was finally achieved and since then the members of Ohana can officially again set foot on the island and celebrate religious feasts.

Holy island

Today interested visitors are welcome. The Protect Kahoolawe Ohana group will provide information about the history, importance and long abuse of the island. Precise details can be obtained from Ohana, P.O. Box 62012, Honolulu, HI 96839.

Kahoolawe is said to have been named after Kanalda, one of the four main Hawaiian gods, who was banned from Heaven by Kane, the chief god and comparable to Lucifer. From Kahoolawe, Kanaloa is reputed to have ruled over all poisonous things and the dead.

Myths

Apparently the island was only inhabited by Hawaiians until the 13th c. when, owing to a continuing drought, they migrated to other islands which had more water. For almost 600 years, Kahoolawe remained uninhabited. In the 1830s a penal colony was set up there but soon abandoned.

History

In the 1870s various attempts were made to rear cattle on the island but only Angus MacPhee, who leased the island for 200 US dollars a year, succeeded in developing a profitable ranch. Ohia trees, cotton and tobacco grew wild on the island. MacPhee planted eucalyptus trees and grass to try to prevent soil erosion and he began to raise cattle successfully. Although the leasing contract with the government of Hawaii lasted until 1954, MacPhee in 1939 offered the US Army a narrow strip along the south coast of the island as a shooting range. After the Japanese attack on Pearl Harbor, 105 miles/170km away, the US Marines took possession of the whole island.

For several decades the island, today regarded by the Hawaiians as a living reminder of their history and religion, enjoyed the dubious label of "the most bombed piece of land in the world", although the American government placed the island on its register of historic places.

Kauai Island

Area: 552sq.miles/1431sq.km
County: Kauai. Population: 50,700. Main town: Lihue

Location and development

Kauai, the most north-easterly of the inhabited islands in the archipelago, is also the fourth largest. Its 25 miles/40km width and 33 miles/53km length make Kauai almost circular in shape. With an estimated age of 3.8 and 5.6 million years, it is the oldest inhabited island. It was formed by an eruption from a single volcano. While Kauai, together with its satellite island, Niihau, were in the process of evolving, the other Hawaiian islands, lying some 1367 miles/2200km further north, were already largely eroded, flooded or remained as coral atolls. Today, Kauai is shrinking – its north–south diameter had decreased from 30 miles/48km to 25 miles/40km, while the east–west diameter measures about 33 miles/53km.

Nature

Kauai offers the most impressive natural scenery in the Hawaiian islands. Topographical features of the island include the mountain Waialeale (from which rain water flows into the 30sq.miles/78sq.km Alakai Swamp), Waimea Canyon (which runs in a north–south direction and is 3545ft/1080m deep) and the Na Pali coast along the north-west edge of the island (with its 3983ft/1200m fissured cliffs, which can only be seen at their best from the air). The inaccessibility of the inland area protects the island's unique character and confined any colonisation to the coastal land.

Name

William Bligh, later renowned as captain of the Bounty, belonged to Cook's expedition of 1778, which first landed on Kauai. He drew a map of the island and labelled Kauai "Atooi" because the Tahitian "t" still existed in the islands at that time. The meaning of the name Kauai remains unknown but it is called "Garden Island" because of its rich vegetation.

Climate and vegetation

Water shapes Kauai in different ways. The only navigable river on the Hawaiian islands is in Kauia – Wailua River (see entry), but even better known is the weather station at the top of the 5238ft/1569m Waialeale Mountain. It is regarded as the rainiest place not only in the Hawaiian

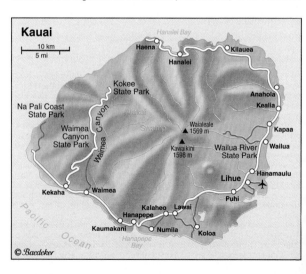

islands but in the whole world. Its north-westerly location makes Kauai particularly exposed to stormy cold air masses. In November 1982, when Orkan Iwa raged, wind strengths of up to 171 miles/275km an hour were measured on Kauai, making the storm there the most powerful in Hawaii.

Despite these extremes the climate on Kauai hardly differs from that on the other islands. The average temperature fluctuates between 26° and 29°C, the average lowest temperature between 15° and 21°C. Tourists need not fear record rainfall measurements since it is possible to stay in the dry area of the south-west part of the island.

As a result of heavy rainfall, from which only the south coast is spared, Kauai possesses unusually rich and unique vegetation. Since large areas of the island are almost completely impenetrable, many endemic plants have developed here and survive today.

Population

As on the other Hawaiian islands, Kauai has a mixed population – every ethnic group is represented in a small way. Whites (28.5%) are the most numerous followed by Filipinos (26.2%), Japanese (25%), Hawaiians (14.6%) and Chinese (1.3%).

People live in small towns – the largest settlements are Kapaa, Lihue, Kekaha and Waimea.

Farming

Although Kauai was the first island on which sugar cane was grown (in 1835), the present area of land used for this purpose has been strongly decimated and takes second place to the cultivation of taro. The present yield from farming on Kauai is relatively unimportant.

Tourism

With the onset of mass tourism in the 1960s, Kauai also became a centre for tourism. The first large hotel to be built, the Coco Palms Hotel in Wailua, was followed by several more in Princeville and Poipu, where the building boom has been particularly intense. The area around Lihue has most recently been overtaken by development and the luxury complex Westin Kauai (now under Japanese ownership) was the largest hotel on the island for several years. The focal points of tourism today are Princeville and Hanalei in the north, Kapaa, Waipulu and Wailua in the east, Hanamaulu, Lihue, Nawiliwili and Puhi in the south-east (with luxury hotels such as the Westin Kauai and the Kauai Hilton) and Poipu in the south, which has developed the most rapidly and which has the most luxury hotels. The west of the island remains free of tourism and the interior is practically uninhabited.

History

The history of the settlement of the Hawaiian islands, including the Island of Kauai, is tightly bound up with the development of the South Sea Islands. In about 200 b.c. the Polynesians settled on the Marquesas Islands and the Company Islands, from where Hawaii was reached for the first time. The exact date of the colonisation is not known but it is assumed that the Polynesians from the Island of Hawaii located the other Hawaiian islands.

The modern history of the Hawaiian islands began on Kauai, for it was here in Waimea that Captain Cook and his companions first set foot on Hawaiian soil on January 21st 1778, the day on which Hawaii was discovered.

Kauai was the island which withstood occupation by Kamehameha the longest. Twice, in the years 1796 and 1804, Kamehameha tried to conquer Kauai by armed force. The first time he failed because of a fierce storm, the second time his troops were badly weakened by a sudden illness, probably cholera. Finally, after Kamehameha had conquered all the other islands and in 1805 had given himself the title of king of his new kingdom, King Kaumualii of Kauai gave way to him. Kamehameha designated him as governor of Kauai – in this way Kaumaualii saved the island from becoming part of the Hawaiian Kingdom through war. After Kamehameha's death in 1819, his widow, Kaahumanu, sent the new king to Kauai to kidnap

Kaumualii and take him to Oahu. Kaumualii was forced to marry Kaahumanu, who saw this as a way of strengthening the bond between Kauai and the other islands.

The death of Kaumualii in 1824 caused a period of uncertainty for Kauai. In increasing numbers, missionaries and, after 1835, owners of sugar plantations, gained influence. Koloa, near the south coast, became the most important settlement on the island through its role as a port and centre of sugar cane and taro cultivation.

Lihue was first founded in 1837 in the middle of sugar cane fields. The development of Kauai was tied to sugar during the following period. A deficiency in the sugar production workforce first brought Chinese, then Portuguese, Japanese, Puerto Ricans, Koreans, Spaniards, Germans and ultimately a large number of Filipinos to the island. Today, the sugar cane industry on Kauai is increasingly eclipsed by tourism.

In September 1992 hurricane "Iniki" caused widespread devastation on the island. Since then however the land has largely recovered from the damage caused, although some signs of it can still be seen here and there.

Hollywood quickly discovered that the relatively undisturbed and unique nature of Kauai provided an ideal South Sea location for countless films. Kahalahala Bay served as a setting for part of "South Pacific". An even more famous film, "Blue Hawaii" with Elvis Presley, was shot on Kauai, as was "Donovan's Reef" starring John Wayne. Huleia National Wildlife Refuge on Kauai's south coast was used to represent Vietnamese jungle in the film "Uncommon Valor".

Kauai as a film location

Coconut Grove

See Waimea

Fern Grotto

See Waimea

Fort Elizabeth

B 2

Above the place where Captain James Cook landed in Waimea (see entry), the remains of a fort can be seen on Road 50. The German doctor and adventurer, Dr Georg Anton Scheffer, apparently built it in 1817 on behalf of the Russian tsar Alexander I and for several months the Russian flag flew here.

Initially the fort was built according to a star-shaped ground plan but in 1864 it was extensively taken apart. The walls of the fort were built without mortar to a height of 13ft/4m but are today only a single pile of rocks. The 38 guns, which were later removed, were trained on the Pacific and the mouth of the Wailue River. Evidence of the men's and the officers' quarters can still be seen. The fort is to be rebuilt in the future.

Dr Scheffer built another fort in Honolulu, on the site where the Aloha Tower (see entry) now stands, but this was never finished. Only the name Fort Street bears witness to the construction. In Hanalei Valley (see entry) he began another defensive wall but this work also remained incomplete because Scheffer had to flee from the king's troops and leave Hawaii.

◀ *The Wailua Falls on Kauai Island*

Hanalei

Location

Hanalei, a village with only about 500 inhabitants, lies in Hanalei Bay on the north coast of Kauai. The village, which is blessed with a fine sandy beach, is at the same time a gateway to the scenic and delightful Hanalei Valley.

A museum and a host of good restaurants invite the tourist to linger.

Waioli Mission House

Waioli Mission House, built in 1841 and located on Route 56 on the edge of the village, is one of Hawaii's best-preserved mission houses and therefore well worth visiting. While most mission houses are built in the New England style (including the interiors), the exterior of this house shows a definite influence of the Southern States. This can be attributed to the fact that the missionary William P. Alexander came to Kauai from Kentucky. Five years later, the Wilcox family, who were also missionaries, moved in. The rooms have been kept as far as possible in their original state and show the Hawaiian style of home decoration of the *malihin* (non-natives). A large part of the missionary Abner Wilcox's library can still be seen in his study including some of the earlier schoolbooks printed in Honolulu.

On the left-hand side of the street is the old Waioli Huila Church, with its roof of green shingles and stained-glass windows. It is now a community centre, where Hawaiian hymns can occasionally be heard on Sundays (10–11.30am).

Hanalei Museum

The private Hanalei Museum on the Kuhio Highway accommodates a local history collection and examples of Hawaiian handiwork. However, it was badly damaged by hurricane "Iniki" in 1992. There are plans to rebuild it.

For further information about the particularly fine beaches in and around Hanalei (Hanalei Beach, Lumahai Beach and Kee Beach) see Practical Information, Beaches.

Taro fields in the Hanalei Valley

Haena State Park

Caves

Leaving Hanalei Road 56 continues about 6 miles/10km further to the north-western part of the Na Pali Coast (see entry). Within Haena State Park, to the left of the roadside, are several caves, including Dry Cave near the coast and Waikanaloa Wet Cave and Waikopaloe Wet Cave which are reached by climbing about 427ft/130m up the hill from the road.

Nearby are the remains of two Hawaiian temples (Kaula Paoa Heiau and Kaula o Laka Heiau).

Hanalei Valley

The finest view of Hanalei Valley is experienced from Hanalei Lookout, on Road 56, which is indicated by one of the customary Kamehameha signs. Hanalei River flows like a silver thread through the whole valley, which is a patchwork of sugar cane and taro fields. Mountains, 3938ft/1200m to 4923ft/1500m high, form a backdrop.

It is possible to drive down into the valley. Crossing a bridge built in 1912 and fortified after a strong *tsunamis* in 1957, a road is reached which follows the river as far as the entrance to the Hanalei National Wildlife Refuge, from where it is possible to continue on foot.

Hanapepe   B 2

Artists' village

Hanapepe is situated on Kauai's south-west coast on the route to Waimea (see entry). From here, as in Hanalei, a fine view is afforded of the Hanalei Valley. This is mostly planted with taro, the tuberous crop from which Hawaiians prepare their national dish, called *poi*. Today, Kauai is the main centre of taro growing and exportation to the other Hawaiian islands.

A boutique in Hapapepe

Hanapepe is reminiscent of a pioneering town and appears somewhat neglected. Today many artists have settled here and interesting shops and an orchid garden, designed by a Japanese, are worth visiting.

Salt ponds

On the western edge of Hanapepe a marked path leads to Salt Pond County Beach Park. Salt is still harvested from these ponds in the traditional Hawaiian way. Sea water is diverted into the ponds and left to evaporate slowly. The salt remains as a crust at the bottom of the pond. Salt production in the Hanapepe Salt Ponds is described as far back as in James Cook's diaries.

Olu Pua Botanical
Gardens

Following Road 50 to Hanapepe a detour can be made on the edge of Kaheheo village to Olu Pua Botanical Gardens (turn right into Mehana Road). The site of about 12 acres/5ha is planted with a variety of orchids and hibiscus plants with variegated leaves, as well as many tropical trees and plants.

Kapaa   C 1

Kapaa, the most heavily populated town on Kauai, lies on the east coast, north of Lihue. In the centre of the town is a large workers' housing estate, some hotels and restaurants. Tourists interested in Hawaiian church decoration should visit the Catholic St Catherine's Church in Kealia, 1½ miles/2–3km to the north. The church's walls were painted by Hawaiian artists.

Near to Kapaa is Nonou, the "Sleeping Giant", a mountain ridge which resembles the face of such a sleeping monster. Legend has it that the giant overate at a Luau banquet and fell into eternal sleep.

Kilauea   C 1

Plantation
settlement

On Kauai's north coast Kilauea can be reached via Road 56. The village began life as a plantation settlement for people working in the neighbouring sugar cane fields, although sugar production here ceased years ago.

Kilhauea
Lighthouse

It is worthwhile making a short diversion to the coast, where Kilhauea Lighthouse, probably the tallest in Hawaii, was built in 1913 on a steep rock. Having ceased to function as a lighthouse it is now used as a weather station. Unfortunately, it cannot be climbed; access to it is via a 2 mile/3km path which leads off Highway 56 at an acute angle.

Kilhauea Point is the northernmost point of Kauai Island and is a nature reserve. Here live and nest various species of birds, including terns, storm petrels and albatrosses. A walk around this small peninsula offers the opportunity to learn much about the plants and birds of the Hawaiian islands. The National Wildlife Refuge is open Sun.–Fri. (closed Sat.), noon–4pm (tel. 828–14 13; parts of it are closed because of hurricane damage).

St Sylvester
Church

St Sylvester Church, built of coral c. 1880, is also worth a visit. The life of Jesus is portrayed in the small stained-glass windows.

Kalihiwai

Contemporary art is on display in the Hawaiian Art Museum in the nearby town of Kalihiwai.

Kokee State Park

See Waimea Canyon

Lihue

C 2

Lihue is the main town of the County of Kauai (to which the neighbouring "forbidden island", Nihau, belongs) and is, with the exception of Molokai, the smallest of the Hawaiian island counties.

Only about 4000 people live in Lihue of whom a large number are state and county officials and their families. The airport, only a few kilometres away from Lihue, is becoming increasingly important as a source of income.

Lihue is also a junction for island traffic as both Road 50 and Road 56, which circle most of the island, meet here.

Nawiliwili Harbour is Kauai's main port and can accommodate offshore vessels.

Lihue was originally in the midst of fields of sugar cane – both of the Lihue Sugar Company's chimneys still stand tall in the centre of the town and bear witness to the importance of the sugar industry to Lihue. The town offers the tourist the advantage of being only a few minutes by car away from several good beaches (see Practical Information, Beaches).

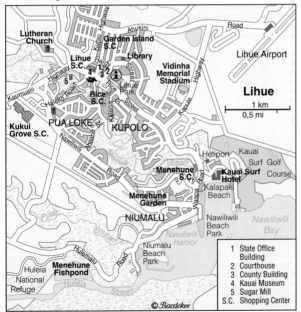

1	State Office Building
2	Courthouse
3	County Building
4	Kauai Museum
5	Sugar Mill
S.C.	Shopping Center

Places of interest in and around Lihue

Grove Farm Homestead Museum

Location
Nawiliwili Road
Tel. 245–3202

Grove Farm began life in 1864 as a sugar plantation run by George Wilcox. The main building, having been enlarged several times, now serves as a museum and can be visited – together with the remaining huts, workplaces and flower and vegetable gardens – during a two-hour tour. These guided tours are on Mon., Wed. and Thurs. at 10am and 1pm; the museum stays closed on rainy days. Grove Farm remains as an example of the age when Kauai had sugar plantations and, because it has not been worked for a long time, it retains an authentic atmosphere. The different buildings, as well as the furnishings and the surrounding land, belong to what is one of the oldest, almost unchanged sugar plantations. Visiting here, the tourist is confronted by a living piece of Kauai's past, which can hardly be found anywhere else on the islands.

★Kauai Museum

Location
4428 Rice Street
Tel. 245–6931

Located in a building dating from 1924, which originally housed Kauai Public Library, the museum offers a comprehensive account of Kauai's history and culture. Visitors can learn about its geology, flora, ethnology and history (open: Mon.–Fri. 9.30am–4.30pm, Sat. 9am–1pm). Kauai's main events are portrayed – its evolution, its discovery by James Cook in 1778, the attempted Russian expansion on the island after 1815, the arrival of the missionaries and the changes which they effected, life on a plantation during the 19th c. and the immigration of different ethnic groups from Europe and Asia.

A model of an old Hawaiian village is displayed on the ground floor, as well as photographs of Kauai from the turn of the century, furniture which belonged to missionaries and examples of Kauai's natural history. Exhibits on display upstairs include photographs of missionaries and a large shell collection.

An aerial film of Kauai's more inaccessible areas, above all the Na Pali Coast (see entry) and the interior of the Waimea Canyon (see entry), is shown at regular intervals – it is a pity that it does not last longer than six minutes. The visitor is finally introduced to the world of the legendary Menehune (see Menehune Fish Ponds).

Old Lutheran Church

Location
Hoomana Road

Hawaii's oldest Protestant church was built in 1885. A hurricane destroyed it in 1982, but it has been faithfully rebuilt. Its nave is shaped like the ship in which German immigrants and missionaries came to Kauai.

Nearby lies a sugar-mill; Wailua Falls (see Wailua) are just 4 miles/6.5km away.

Kilohana Plantation

Location
Street 50, some
2 miles/3km
south-west of Lihue
Tel. 245–5608

Kilohana Plantation is similar to Grove Farm (see entry) in that it is a contemporary witness to Kauai's era of plantations. Its founder, Gaylord Park Wilcox, the nephew of Grove Farm's founder, promoted the house as a focal point of Kauai's society and culture. To this end he named the house "Kilohana", Hawaiian for "the best". Until 1970, the farm was under family ownership but was then closed and reopened for a short time as a school. It was redeveloped some years ago and today it houses a museum, shopping centre, restaurant and fruit and vegetable garden (open: daily 9.30am–9pm; Sun. to 5pm). Shops now occupy what were previously the children's rooms, bedrooms, library, a dressing room and various guest houses in the grounds. The range of goods for sale is of high quality and

The Menehune Fish Pond

quite expensive, which is also true of the Gaylord Restaurant. The plantation can be explored either on foot or by carriage.

Menehune Fish Pond and Alakoko

Only a few kilometres away from Lihue on Road 51 – the continuation of Waapa Road and Hulemalu Road – a vantage point is reached near Nui-malu, from which the Menehune Fish Pond, also known as Alakoko Pond, can be seen. The vantage point affords a wonderful view of the Huleia River, Nawiliwili Port, with the 2297ft/700m-high Haupu in the background and further elevations of the Hoary Head Range. The pond, whose stone edging is in many places up to 10ft/3m high and 31in/80cm thick, was used originally for the breeding of fish. Now part of it is used as an oyster-bed.

The Menehune are reputed to have built the 886ft/270m-long fish pond for a Hawaiian royal couple. The edge was built from stones which the Menehune transported across a distance of 25 miles/40km by standing in a line and passing them from hand to hand. According to legend, they insisted that no one watched them carrying out the work – but the prince and princess climbed the mountainside overlooking the pond and secretly watched them. However, the Menehune spotted the royal couple and changed them into pillars of rock, which can still be seen above the south side of the pond. The Menehune, legendary builders of temples and fish ponds, are seen as the original inhabitants of Hawaii. They are supposed to have lived on the Hawaiian islands and, above all on Kauai, even before the first Polynesians. Dwarf-like people, somewhat like goblins or gnomes, the Hawaiians called them *keiki o ka'aina,* which roughly means "children of the country". One of their characteristics was that they were only active at night.

Many Hawaiians still believe in their existence today. In the 18th c. King Kaumualii of Kauai reported that 65 Menehune were to be found in his kingdom, apparently living in Wainiha Valley on the north coast of Kauai. Their size was given as between 2ft/60cm and 2ft 7½in/80cm, their bodies were very muscular and hairy. They could not speak but could only make sounds which resembled barking dogs. Excellent stonemasons, they built temples and moats overnight and disappeared before daybreak.

Other South Sea Islands know similar beings to the Hawaiian Menehune by such names as Manahune, Manahua or Makahua (this word is said to be of Tahitian origin) and even the Maoris in New Zealand have similar night creatures which they call Patupai-arehe. The similarity of such legends owes much to the relationship of the Hawaiians with the other Polynesian tribes.

Menehune Gardens

Location
Near Street 58
Tel. 245–2660

Menehune Gardens are located near Nawiliwili Road (Road 58) shortly after it crosses Niumalu Road. These gardens have a particularly peaceful and lovely atmosphere. All the plants are clearly labelled. Especially worth mentioning is the extensive collection of herbs as well as an enormous banyan tree. With luck, visitors will be surprised after their tour by the singing of Hawaiian songs.

Menehune Ditch

See Waimea

★ Na Pali Coast   B 1

Inaccessible coast

The Na Pali Coast in the north-west of the island is one of the most inaccessible parts of the Island of Kauai. The chain of mountains, climbing in places to 3938ft/1200m, forms steep cliffs plunging into the sea, whose beauty can only be appreciated from the water or from the air. Steep valleys on the landward side divide the mountain crests. All attempts, until now, to create a road along the coast have had to be abandoned. Thanks to this seclusion, a unique variety of vegetation has been able to survive here, which, together with the high, steep cliffs, offers a fascinating view of nature. The bizarre shapes of the weathered volcanic mountains with caves and water courses, forming waterfalls, the intense greenery of the thick layer of vegetation and the hidden sandy beaches at the foot of the mountains are all worth experiencing.

Excursions

It is easiest to survey this part of the coast by boat or helicopter (see Practical Information, Tours of the island), from which a good view of these impressive cliffs can be gained. Those who want to spend more time here and who are not afraid of strenuous exercise can explore part of the Na Pali Coast on foot.

Kalalau Trail

Kalalau Trail is an 11 miles/17.5km path originally made and used by the early Hawaiians. This path is difficult and taxing, even for experienced walkers. The climb begins at Haena State Park (see entry) in the north and ends after almost 11½ miles/18km in Kalalau Valley. To gain an impression of the landscape and vegetation, it is enough to cover the first 2 miles/3km as far as Hanakapiai Beach. This stretch is easier to walk, although after rain it can be slippery – good footwear is needed at all times.

Those who want to tackle the whole walk must take a tent and food with them and stay overnight before returning as two to three days should be allowed to complete the 22 miles/35km round distance. The path beyond Hanakapiai is steep, stony and not without danger. At the right time of the year it is possible to sample wild fruits such as mangoes, bananas, guava and apples, which grow beside the path. Campers need permission from the Division of State Parks (3060 Eiwa Street, Lihue. Tel. 245–4444).

The Na Pai Coast

★ Pacific Tropical Botanical Garden   B 2

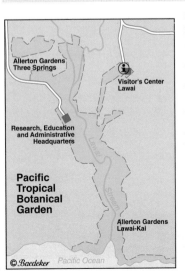

Allerton Gardens
Three Springs

Visitor's Center
Lawai

Research, Education
and Administrative
Headquarters

**Pacific
Tropical
Botanical
Garden**

Allerton Gardens
Lawai-Kai

© *Baedeker*   Pacific Ocean

Developed about 20 years
ago, the Botanical Garden
is combined with a
research station for tropical
plants. It is the only garden
of its type in the USA and is
recognised, according to a
charter of the US Congress,
as a public institution. However, it is funded privately.
The Botanical Garden can
only be visited as part of a
tour, part of which is undertaken by vehicle. As a
result, no more than 15
people can join the tour at
any one time. It is imperative to book a day ahead of
a planned visit.

The long, narrow garden,
which covers just under
½ sq.mile/1 sq.km, stretches
to the Pacific. The Lawai, a
small river, bisects the garden. As both endangered
and useful tropical plants

Location
Lawai, leave Lihue
on Roads 56, 50,
530 and Hailima
Road
Tel. 332–7361
(Telephone
bookings
required)

105

are grown here, there are a considerable number of plant varieties on view. Only part of the extensive selection can be mentioned here – about 800 types of palm; about 60 different banana plants; coconut trees, a large number of ginger bushes with different coloured flowers; herbs such as cardamom from Southern India; cloves from the Spice Islands; Jamaican pepper and other spices; native bread fruit trees; Java plums; the similarly native taro and countless tropical flowers with anthuria. Above all, the garden includes water lilies with their large, round leaves, one of which, it is claimed, could bear the weight of a small child – namely the Victoria Amazonica from Brazil.

Leaving the Botanical Garden the visitor enters the Allerton Garden, begun by Chicago baker Robert Allerton and developed further by his son, Gregg Allerton. This land originally belonged to Queen Emma, the wife of King Kamehameha IV, whose summer house still remains today.

Poipu   C 2

Poipu lies on the particularly warm and sunny south coast of Kauai where the island's finest beaches are to be found.

Until the tourism boom sugar was the main source of income for Poipu and its surrounding area. The development of tourism started relatively late here and consequently it was far more intense than in other places. Now, Poipu possesses Kauai's largest number of luxury hotels and holiday homes. An urban development regulation permits buildings to be no more than three storeys high so that Poipu can protect its rural character.

Its favourable location near Lihue Airport (only 14 miles/22km away and easy to reach), together with its pleasant climate and excellent watersports

"Spouting Horn"

opportunities, have helped Poipu to become one of Kauai's most popular resorts. The long, white, sandy beach and the clear, blue water are an invitation to swim and surf – Poipu's favourite watersports.

A stroll around Poipu's large number of inviting shops and boutiques will reveal high quality goods with prices to match.

Do not forget to visit Kiahuna Gardens. Built before 1930, the centre of the garden is occupied by a house that used to be inhabited by the "sugar baron" of Poipu – today, it accommodates the Plantation Gardens Restaurant.

Spouting Horn

Spouting Horn is a jet of water which can be seen shooting up from the sea like a geyser. The pressure of the rising wave pushes water through channels in the volcanic rock and it escapes upwards out of the holes as fountains. A gurgling and groaning noise accompanies this display. If there are strong breakers, it is possible to watch the waves break on the black rock along the coast.

Koloa

Head inland from Poipu to reach Koloa or Old Koloa Town, as it is often known nowadays. Koloa was the first place in Hawaii where sugar production was developed on a large scale (about 1835). Today, Koloa's 1500-plus inhabitants retain their sugar cane fields in the immediate vicinity of the town. From 1845 to 1870 Koloa was Kauai's largest settlement and also possessed the island's only harbour. Koloa's decline began after the Second World War but Poipu's increasing popularity soon became of benefit to the town. Between 1983 and 1986 a large part of the town was restored so that today Koloa, with its old wooden houses, presents a picturesque face – its many old churches and temples are particularly attractive. St Rafael's Church, the oldest Catholic church on Kauai, dates from 1854. Five years later the Protestant Koloa Church was built in a New England style, followed in 1910 by both the first Buddhist Hongwanji Temple and the Jodo Mission and, finally, in 1985, a larger Japanese temple was built.
Kauai's first sugar-mill, built in 1835, is now only a ruin.

Old Koloa Town

Waita Reservoir, which supplies the region with its water, is located immediately north-east of Koloa. Built in 1906, its area of 695sq.miles/1800sq.km makes it the largest lake in the Hawaiian islands.

Waita Reservoir

Princeville   C 1

Princeville, on Kauai's north coast, does not enjoy such a settled climate as the south coast, but has nevertheless been able to develop into a popular holiday resort. The name Princeville arose from a visit there by King Kamehameha IV, his wife, Emma, and their two-year-old son, Albert. The Scottish doctor, Robert Crichton Wyllie, who later became foreign minister under Kamehameha IV and Kamehameha V, was then running a sugar cane and coffee plantation. Dr Wyllie's enthusiasm for the little prince led him to name his plantation Princeville in honour of him.
The coffee plantation was later abandoned and Dr Wyllie sold the sugar cane plantation. Until 1968, cattle rearing became the main source of income.
Since 1969, Princeville has been developed into a holiday resort. Today, the place is well-known for its particularly fine golf course. Luxury hotels

offer the tourist every kind of comfort and there is also plenty of sport on offer. The two available beaches are, however, relatively small.

Wailua   C1

The area around Waimea and the mouth of the river which bears the same name was colonised by native inhabitants many years ago. Before the Polynesians settled here this region was said to have been inhabited by the legendary Mu, a tribe of dwarf-like people similar to the Menehune, who aparently developed their own strange physical characteristics as a result of their centuries of isolation. Very few of the hundreds of *heiaus* which were built in this area remain. Near the Coco Palms Hotel Pohaku-hoo Hanau remains standing from ancient Hawaiian times. Noblewomen gave birth to their children on this birth stone. The babies' umbilical cords were hidden in the crevices to protect them as they grew up. Wailua River, which flows into the sea on the edge of the village, is the only navigable river in Hawaii. Its lower reaches are called the "Kingly Way".

South of the mouth of the river lies Lydgate State Park, containing remains of a Hawaiian temple of refuge.
Wailua (meaning "two waters", doubtless referring to the sea and the river) is a well spread-out village on Road 56 with about 1600 inhabitants.

★Fern Grotto

Wailua's greatest attraction is Fern Grotto, which extends along the 3 miles/5km river to its source and can be reached by boat (Smith's Motor Boat Service, tel. 822–4111 or 822–5213 and Waialeale Boat Tour, tel.

A trip on the Wailua River to Fern Grotto

822–3467, 9am–2.30pm, every 30 minutes). Both boats depart from Wailua Marina.

The grotto is an enormous amphitheatre made of rock in which, thanks to the constantly-damp atmosphere, conditions are ideal for bracken to grow. It is also a popular place for weddings – they take place here almost daily. The boat's crew sing a Hawaiian wedding song for tourists while a commentary is given over a megaphone.

★Wailua Falls

Between Lihue and Hanamaulu Road 583 branches off Road 56 and winds its way for a few kilometres to a waterfall. This is less than ¾ mile/1km away from Fern Grotto but cannot be reached directly from there. A double waterfall can be found at the end of Road 583. This falls 27ft/25m down a rockface.

Legend has it that the chiefs of old Hawaii had to take the risk of jumping from the top of this waterfall to prove their strength and courage.

Those who relish the thought of a refreshing shower can climb down to the bottom of the waterfall along a very steep path.

Coconut Grove

A few kilometres along Road 56 north of Wailua, standing directly on the side of the road, is Coconut Grove one of the Hawaiian islands' largest plantations. The trees were planted in the 19th c. by a German immigrant, William Lindemann. He wanted to process the flesh of the coconut (the copra), which contains up to 65% fat, into oil and flakes. His project came to nothing, however.

The coconut trees remained and are today an attraction not only for tourists but also for film makers. Scenes from the films "South Pacific" and "Blue Hawaii" were shot here. A marriage chapel was even built here for a Rita Hayworth film, in which more that 2000 weddings have since taken place. This area is really beautiful and exudes that romantic aura expected of Hawaii but no longer found everywhere on the islands.

In the very middle of this area is Coco Palms Resort, for those tourists with sophisticated tastes. The Market Place at Coconut Plantation is dominated by an enormous shopping centre where a local display, including a Hula Show, is performed.

Smith's Tropical Paradise Park

This beautiful garden is reached by turning left before the bridge over Wailua River and following a narrow path along the river's edge. Its 30 acres/12ha (which can also be viewed from a small train) are divided into various sections including an orchid garden, a Japanese garden and primeval forest vegetation. Various events take place here (musical, hula dancing and torch ceremonies).

Waimea

Hawaii's modern history began at Waimea on the south coast of Kauai. Captain James Cook and his expedition sailed into Waimea Bay on board the two ships "Resolution" and "Discovery" and dropped anchor. Today, a memorial honouring the discoverer of Hawaii marks almost the very spot where Cook first set foot on Hawaiian soil (it cannot be missed on Road 50, Waimea's Main Street). Present day Waimea is a large village of about 1600 inhabitants. Historically an important seat of government for the early kings (like Wailua on the east coast – see entry), it is also one of Kauai's three ports together with Hanalei and Poipu-Koloa (see entries).

Captain Cook's landing place

Hawaiian Church

The Hawaiian Church is worth visiting primarily because it is attended by the former inhabitants of Nihau Island, who have settled in Waimea. On Sundays, the service is regularly conducted in Hawaiian. A linguistic peculiarity is that these former inhabitants of Nihau speak the old Hawaiian language from the time of the missionaries. The church stands on Road 50 on the left bank of Waimea River when facing east.

Menehune Ditch

Immediately in front of the Hawaiian Church, Menehune Road bears left, ending at the famous Menehune Ditch, or what remains of it (more about the Menehune can be found under entries for Lihue and Menehune Fish Ponds). The ditch is considered their master work because they employed a building style not seen anywhere else in the Hawaiian archipelago – here and only here polished and cut stones are found. Today, only about 66ft/20m of the upper part of the ditch can be seen, as many stones were hacked out for use in building roads and houses.

When George Vancouver landed in Waimea in 1793, he described the wall of the ditch as projecting almost 26ft/8m out of the river and mentioned that it served as a tributary of Waimea River and, as such, must have been quite long. Today nothing is to be seen of it. According to his description, the uncut rock came from a quarry 7½ miles/12km away. It remains unknown how it was transported, for the Hawaiians had no knowledge of the wheel at that stage. No wonder the Menehune had problems explaining this piece of building work. In Hawaiian, it is called *kiki ola*, Ola's Waterfall (Ola was one of Kauai's principal chieftains).

East of here, built on a small hill, stands Fort Elizabeth (see entry) with its fine view over the Pacific and the mouth of Waimea River. Waimea means "reddish earth" in Hawaiian, a name which refers to the red earth carried along in the river.

Barking Sands

Drive further along the west coast on Road 50 to reach Barking Sands, a missile control station, which is a military prohibited area and cannot be visited.

★Waimea Canyon

B 1

Grand Canyon of the Pacific

Two roads lead from Road 50 to this work of nature called the "Grand Canyon of the Pacific", a 12 miles/19km-long, 2954ft/900m-deep canyon. It can be reached either via Waimea Canyon Road, a branch of Menehune Road, and only a few minutes' drive from Road 50, or via Road 550, which leaves Kehala a little further to the west. Both roads meet again after a few kilometres. It is between 20 miles/32km and 22 miles/35km to the 4122ft/1256m-high Kalalau vantage point at the end of the road. Enough time should be allowed for this journey (at least one day) in order to stop a few times and savour the unique nature of the canyon. Good walkers with time available could easily spend a week in the canyon.

★Views into the canyon

On the way up are a series of vantage points, all clearly marked, each with different views. There is Waimea Canyon Lookout, followed a few kilometres further by the 3610ft/1100m-high Puu Hinahina Lookout, and finally, at the end of the road, the aforementioned Kalalau Lookout. From there, an unmade road leads to Puu o Kilia vantage point, with its fine view over the Na Pali Coast. Moving inland, the enormous plateau of the Alahai Swamp emerges, a wooded marshy plateau, which is extremely boggy because of the high rainfall and consequently cannot be crossed by foot.

Waimea Canyon, as far as size is concerned, does not bear comparison with the Grand Canyon in Arizona/Utah. However, it is no less remarkable in its own way for it too is a work of nature.

From Waimea Canyon Lookout gaze down and enjoy the almost constantly changing colours of the gorge or admire the three smaller canyons, shaped by the tributaries of the Waimea, the Waialae, the Koale and the

Waimea Canyon

Poomau. In the distance, two powerful waterfalls, the Hihinui and the Waialae, are discernable.

From Kalalau Lookout look down on the Na Pali cliffs and Kalalau Valley (see Na Pali Coast), which cannot be reached from here by climbing down.

Depending on what time of day the top of the canyon is reached and what the weather conditions are like, the mood differs. It can rain heavily and frequently here (although mostly in short showers) which should not deter visitors (take waterproof clothing) because a few minutes later the sun will shine again, even if the climber is still in cloud. Experiencing the battle between the banks of low cloud and the sun is one of the greatest impressions to be taken away from Kauai and Hawaii. | Weather

The headquarters of Kokee State Park is reached about 1 mile/2km before the end of the road. They contain a small, free of charge, natural history museum containing information about the evolution of the canyon, its fauna and flora. From here a wide network of trails spreads out for over 43½ miles/70km in all directions. As well as a restaurant, overnight accommodation is available but this must be reserved for weekends and the high season (Tel. 335–6061, written applications should be sent to Kokee Lodge, Box 819, Waimea H196796 and must be accompanied by a pre-payment of 20 US dollars. Stays of up to five days are possible).

Looking down from the vantage points into the canyon, Kalalau Valley and along the Na Pali Coast, the meaning of the words of an old Hawaiian song becomes immediately clear. *"Maika'i Kauai hemolele i ka malie"* – "Kauai is beautiful and above all comparison". | Kauai is beautiful

111

Lanai Island

Area: 140sq.miles/363sq.km
County: Maui
Population: 2200
Main Town: Lanai City

Location and history

Lanai, the sixth largest island in the Hawaiian archipelago, covers an area of 140sq.miles/363sq.km (18 miles/29km long, 13 miles/21km wide) and measures only half the size of Molokai Island, its closest neighbour.

Other neighbouring islands lie not very far away. The west coast of Maui is a mere 7½ miles/11km away. The 7 miles/11km-wide Kalohi Channel separates Lanai from the south coast of Molokai. Kahoolawe Island lies only 15 miles/24km further south-east.
Lanai can be seen with the naked eye from both Maui and Molokai. Its shape makes it stand out like a long hump against the horizon.
Lanai evolved from a single dome-shaped volcano. The island's original shape has been exaggerated by erosion.

Geographical features

The major part of the island consists of a plateau about 1641ft/500m above sea level. The highest point is Lanaihale (3371ft/1027m) in the east of the island. The only crater basin, Palawai Beach, lies south of Lanai City.

Name

The Hawaiian word *lanai* means "day of conquest". Unfortunately, the background to this remains unclear. Today, Lanai is often called "Pineapple Island" after its main product, which covers most of the island.

Climate and vegetation

Lanai enjoys an even climate with an average temperature of 24°C and average rainfall of 29½in./750mm – on the whole drier than neighbouring islands. The natural vegetation remains only on parts of the island, particularly the deep valleys on the damp eastern side. The Norfolk pines, typical of Lanai, are grown from seed.

Population

Today about 2200 people live on Lanai, almost all in Lanai City, which was founded in the middle of the island as a settlement for plantation workers. Lanai's population reflects the ethnic mix found throughout the Hawaiian islands – Filipinos, Japanese, Chinese and whites. The one difference is that the Filipinos, who came here to work on the pineapple plantations, account for more than 50%. They are followed by the Japanese with 18%, the whites with 11% and the Hawaiians with 9%.

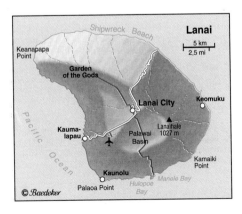

Lanai's economic fate was sealed when the island was bought by the Dole Company in 1922. Throughout the 19th c., attempts had been made to develop the sugar cane industry – with little success. Subsequent cattle ventures also did not survive for long. The new industry was to be pineapples.

Economy

The Dole Company had its initial experience of the pineapple industry on Oahu and was looking for new land in order to expand. It bought Lanai from the descendants of Dwight Baldwin, the missionary, for the ridiculously-low price of 1.1 million US dollars. Soon 90% of America's pineapples came from this island, about 50 million pineapples a year shipped to the world market via the purpose-built port of Kaumalapau in the south-west of the island. At the same time, workers had to be recruited and they were housed in Lanai City.

In 1966 the Dole Company was bought by Castle and Cooke Inc. Today, Lanai is the world's largest producer of pineapples. Despite this, a world-wide surplus has forced a reduction in the amount of land used for this purpose.

Tourism hardly existed on the island for many years. Until 1990, Lanai City possessed only one ten-roomed hotel – the Lanai Hotel. Castle and Cooke, or Dole, who originally grew pineapples on 25½sq.miles/66sq.km of land, has recently ventured into the tourism boom. Two luxury hotels have now been opened – the Manele Beach Resort (250 rooms) at Manele Bay in the south of the island and the Lodge at Koele in Lanai City (102 rooms). As well as the hotels leisure facilities have been developed, including a new 18-hole golf course.

Tourism

The legend grew up around Lanai that evil ghosts lived here. For this reason Lanai remained unpopulated until the 14th c. when Kaululaau, the nephew of the King of Maui, was exiled here and allegedly killed all the ghosts.

History

The first settlers established themselves along the eastern side of the island (facing Maui) where they planted taro and fished. Later cereal crops were cultivated inland.

The first description of the island came from a successor of James Cook, the first European to set foot on the island. Subsequent seafarers bypassed Lanai and only many years later did white people appear on the island again. The island's population declined rapidly, although the reason for this remains unknown. It is suspected that most of the inhabitants moved on to other islands. In 1854 Mormons arrived on the Hawaiian islands and decided to form a community on Lanai. After they had already bought land, internal arguments led them to leave the Hawaiian islands and move back to their original community in 1872. When they returned to Lanai two years later one of their followers, Walter Murray Gibson (see Famous People), had bought the estates. Gibson and his descendants grew sugar cane and raised cattle on Lanai until they finally sold the land in its entirety to the Dole Company in 1922. The Mormons founded a new community at Laie on the Island of Oahu.

Garden of the Gods   H 4

The Garden of the Gods lies in the north-west of the island and is quite difficult to reach. It is best to use a four-wheel drive vehicle as only a small part of the road is made up. The stretch of road along the Awalua Highway is not always easy to find. From Lanai City, proceed via Fraser Avenue to a crossroads. Carry straight on to a larger crossing. Turn right and continue along this narrowing road to the next crossing. Go straight across and the Garden of the Gods is soon reached.

This wonderful rock garden is a geological peculiarity. Unique lava formations and blocks of rock have arisen here through thousands of years of erosion. At sunset the red earth can glow a deep red, sometimes a golden yellow colour which casts its magic on the landscape.

From this, the strangest garden in Hawaii, many paths lead to the coast. One leads through wasteland to Kaena Point where steep cliffs descend to the sea (adulterous Hawaiian women were banished there). Another ends at Polihua Beach which has beautiful white sand.

Hulopoe Bay and Manele Bay   H 4

These adjoining bays in the south of Lanai are reached by leaving Lanai City on Road 441.

Lanai's most beautiful beach is to be found at Hulopoe Bay. A natural lava pool allows safe bathing.

Manele Bay has a harbour for small boats, in which yachts on day excursions from Lahaina (Maui) moor. From here there is a beautiful view across to Kahoolawe Island. In particularly clear conditions, the snow-covered summit of the Island of Hawaii can be seen. Hulopoe Bay's crystal-clear water is very soft and generally a few degrees warmer than the sea around the other Hawaiian islands.

Kaunolu   H 4

At the western end of the south coast lies Kaunolu, once a Hawaiian fishing village. The village enjoys particular fame as King Kamehameha I selected it for his summer residence and came here for the fishing. Today, little remains of the original Kaunolu. It has been uninhabited since about 1900, although the remains of 80 houses give the impression that it was once an important village. The large temple site Halulu Heiau and its rock drawings

The beach at Hulopoe Bay

emphasise the previous standing of this historic place. The remains of the temple are located on the southern tip of the island in the western part of the bay.

As its last inhabitant, Ohua, acting on instructions from Kamehameha V and regardless of the fact that Hawaiian religion had already been abolished some time earlier, hid the stone fish god Kunihi, which stood in the altar of a temple not far from Halulu Heiau. Ohua is said to have been put to death for damaging the stone idol, reputed to be buried in a ravine only about 328ft/100m from the temple.

Keomuku   H 4

Keomuku, on Lanai's eastern coast, is another village which has long been uninhabited. This plantation settlement lost its only source of income at the beginning of 1900 when the Maunalei Sugar Company's factory closed as a result of the unprofitable sugar cane industry in this area. Today, only a half-ruined church and a nearby small *heiau* remain, Keomuku's houses having been completely torn down in the 1970s. The stones from Kahea Heiau were used by the Maunalei Sugar Company to build a new short-lived railway. The Hawaiians saw this as the reason for the failure of the sugar business – in their opinion, the temple had been desecrated and a taboo broken. Only the ruins of the sugar company are to be seen.

Uninhabited village

Naha, another abandoned old Hawaiian village, lies 6 miles/10km further on. The road, which is difficult to drive along, ends here.

Naha

Lanai City   H 4

This settlement was established in the 1920s by the Dole Pineapple Company for its workers and today is inhabited by 98% of Lanai's population. The town stands about 1575ft/480m above sea level in the shadow of Lanaihale, Lanai's highest mountain. The Norfolk pines, planted by the New Zealander George Munro (who ran a ranch for a short time on Hawaii in the 19th c.), now give Lanai City an almost park-like appearance. The mostly uniform houses with their corrugated iron roofs are multi-coloured and surrounded by flower and vegetable gardens. The main street is Lanai Avenue which has roads leading off it numbered from three to thirteen (there is no one or two). In the north, on land once belonging to the Munro Ranch, is the excellent Cavendish Golf Course.

Munro Trail

From Lanai City, follow the Munro Trail to the summit of Lanaihale, at 3371ft/1027m Lanai's highest mountain. The trail can be covered either in a four-wheel drive vehicle (very bumpy and not recommended for those who suffer from back problems) or on foot. The route begins on Road 440 leading to Shipwreck Beach (see entry). After no more than 2 miles/3km turn right at the first big gravel path. About 1 mile/1.5km further on, turn left at the next crossing and continue to the next. Turn right along the main path, past several ravines, until the path ends at the summit. A fine view can be enjoyed here. Clear conditions, usually experienced in the morning, afford a view of all the large Hawaiian islands (with the exception of Kauai) and, above all, of Haleakala Crater on Maui.

Luahiwa Petroglyphs   H 4

The black Luahiwa rocks are difficult to reach. Follow Road 440 (Manele Road) from Lanai City in a southerly direction to Hoike Road, a gravel road.

Pass two moats and, after the second, turn left and continue along the right-hand side of the moat as far as a water pipe. Continue along this conduit to the third electricity mast (bearing a "No Trespassing" sign) and then turn left. The black rocks become visible from here. This part of the route is quite bumpy. Of the many rock drawings to be seen on Lanai, those at Luahiwa are not the most extensive but they do show nearly all the known forms and symbols – from circles and other symbols to human figures. It is possible to make out *kanus*, barking dogs, interspersed occasionally with men on horseback. This shows that the Hawaiians were still drawing these pictures after white men discovered Hawaii and introduced horses to the islands. The rock drawings are to be found, almost without exception, on the south-east of the rocks.

Shipwreck Beach   H 4

Lying on the windy north coast of Lanai, this beach owes its name to the wrecked ships and boats found there. The hull of a Liberty freighter from the Second World War is the largest wreck there. Strong winds pushed vessels on to the reef here, from which there was no escape.

Following Road 440 from Lanai City, this area is easy to find. Up until 1 mile/1.5km from the coast, the road is made up; along the coast is a sandy track not suitable for vehicles.

From here, walk for 8 miles/13km along the coast via the Garden of the Gods (see entry) to Polihua Beach. The sea is shallow but dangerous here (swimming is not recommended) and often throws up shells and interesting flotsam and jetsam, which can be found when walking on the beach.

Maui Island

Area: 694sq.miles/1887sq.km
County: Maui. Population: 88,100. Main town: Wailuku

Maui Island lies west of the Island of Hawaii and is separated from it by
the Alenuihaha Channel. Maui lies about 68 miles/110km from Oahu as
the crow flies. The second largest island in the Hawaiian archipelago,
Maui covers an area of 694sq.miles/1887sq.km with a coastline of
120 miles/193km.

Location and history

The island resembles Tahiti in shape. It evolved from two volcanoes –
first, West Maui with the 5789ft/1764m-high Puu Kukui and later East Maui
with the 10,026ft/3055m-high Haleakala. This latter volcano's crater, before
it became extinct centuries ago, threw up so much lava over its slopes that
a pass developed between the two parts of the island.

The western old part of the island consists of a rugged mountainous
landscape dissected by deep valleys. This area proves difficult to penetrate
and has only been opened up by the coast road. Separated by the isthmus
with its surrounding plains, the eastern part of the island joins it. This area,
twice the size of the west, is dominated by the powerful Haleakala volcano.

Geographical features

The origin of the nickname "Valley Island" remains unclear. One explanation refers to the isthmus as the valley between East and West Maui,
another links the name with the valleys of western Maui and especially with
Lao Valley.

Name

Maui's mountainous relief causes its weather to vary quite strongly but on
the whole it is relatively in line with the other Hawaiian islands. It enjoys
high temperatures of about 30°C and low temperatures of 15°C – apart from
Haleakala where a temperature of minus 11°C (a record for the Hawaiian
islands) was recorded in 1961. It seldom rains on Maui and the rainfall is
scattered very unevenly. While it generally rains more in East Maui than in
the west, Puu Kukui (with an average rainfall of 441in./1120cm a year)
counts as the wettest place on the island. The old coastal port of Lahaina
(only 6 miles/10km away as the crow flies) experiences only about
19½in./50cm of rain a year, with none falling between May and September.
In the impenetrable areas to the west of the island, some endemic plants
have survived. The fertile, weathered lava plains of the pass offer good
conditions for growing sugar cane and pineapples.

Climate and vegetation

With the exception of Nihau Island, which is populated entirely by
Hawaiians, the 15% of *Kamaainas* (natives) living on Maui make it the
island with the largest percentage of resident Hawaiians. The largest ethnic
group on the island is the whites (36%), followed by the Japanese (23%)
and the Filipinos (17%). The remaining 9% comprises several nationalities.

Population

The importance of farming on Maui grew during the course of the decline
of the whaling industry and was only superseded in the 1960s by tourism.
Today farming plays a secondary role on Maui. Together with sugar cane,
pineapples, flowers and *pakololo* (the Hawaiian word for marijuana) are
grown. Cattle are reared on the southern and western slopes of Haleakala,
where two large estates of 50sq.miles/130sq.km and 27sq.miles/70sq.km
respectively are located. *Pakololo* is cultivated on remote land in the
western mountains and along the Hana Coast – illegally, of course.

Farming

The development of mass air travel in the 1960s led to the onset of tourism
on Maui. Today, it is even possible to fly directly from the American
mainland to Kahului.

Following Oahu, Maui (with about two million tourists a year and with
more five-star hotels than any other island) is the most-visited island in the
Hawaiian archipelago. However, no intensive building has occurred on

Tourism

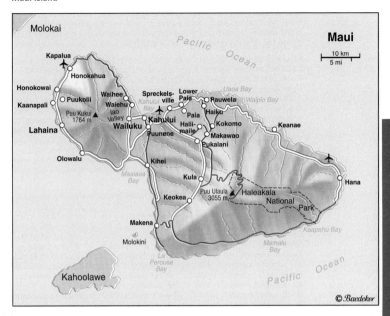

Maui in comparison to Honolulu or Waikiki. One reason lies in the tough building regulations of the County of Maui, another is that Maui's many beaches have made concentrated building unnecessary. In most cases, the hotel complexes (with the exception of Kihei) are fairly far apart. Many experts on Hawaii prefer Maui to the other islands. Maui itself is not modest – its motto is *Maui no ka oi* (Maui is the best).

The negative effects of the island's developing tourist trade have not yet appeared. At first sight the problems which confront Maui are not obvious to tourists because they concern the infrastructure – above all, refuse removal, sewerage and the water supply. In addition, the permanent presence of 500 building workers and the increase in hotel staff has led to a lack of accommodation and increased rents. This is true mainly of the town of Kihei. Here two large hotels (the Grand Hyatt with 815 rooms and the Four Seasons with 380 rooms) have been built and include their own golf courses and tennis courts. Wailea has four more hotels with a total of 1800 rooms and this allows the island's greatest concentration of tourism to be based here. The building of another hotel (Ritz-Carlton) in Honokahua, to the extreme north-west of the island, was delayed for several years following the protests of a Hawaiian organisation when it emerged that a mass grave from the early days of Polynesian migration (1000–2000 years old) was located beneath the building site on the beach.

The protest caused the proposed building's location to be moved further inland. The State of Hawaii won the rights to the burial land, which is being restored to its original condition. Excavation work has already begun and the first skeleton has been unearthed.

Effects of tourism

According to legend, Maui was created by the demi-god of the same name, honoured on almost all the Polynesian Islands, who fished the Hawaiian

Mythology

◀ *Maui: the cratered landscape of the Haleakala Volcano*

islands out of the sea with a large fishing hook. Other feats are ascribed to him – he is said to have captured the sun and kept it captive in Haleakala's crater until it promised to move more slowly across the mountains, thus giving the island's inhabitants more daylight.

History

Maui was the last big island to be discovered by Europeans in 1786. James Cook had already spotted it on November 26th 1778, before he landed on Kauai, but sailed past as he could not find a suitable landing place. A French expedition, led by Jaen La Perouse, was the first to land here on May 28th 1786 in a bay near Lanai, which was named after him. Around this time, Maui was ruled by a chief called Kahekili whose troops severely beat those of Kamehameha (who wanted to conquer Maui) in 1790 near Lao Needle. In 1802 Kamehameha stopped off at Lahaina with a large force and remained there for a whole year, before hitting back with a decisive attack against the then ruler of Maui, Kalankupule (the son of Kahekili), after having conquered Molokai shortly beforehand. Kamehameha made Lahaine his seat of government and later the Hawaiian capital. In 1843 Honolulu replaced Lahaina as the seat of government.

Protea

One plant has found particularly good living conditions on the slopes of Haleakala – the protea.

About 75 different species of this flower can be found on Maui. They grow at a height of 2133ft/650m to 4065ft/1300m because they need warm days and cool nights. Perhaps the most beautiful and best-loved of the proteas are the "King" and "Queen", which appear in different colours. They can be viewed at their best in the Hawaii Protea Cooperative (Road 377, shortly before it joins Road 378 to the Halaekala Crater), in Kula Botanical Garden (on Road 377, about 1 mile/1.6km away from the intersection with Road 37) and in the Upcountry Protea Farm (Upper Kimo Drive, a turning off Road 377). These flowers, which originally came from Australia and South Africa, were named by the Swedish natural scientist Carl Linné after the Greek God Proteus because of their many forms. According to legend, Proteus could alter his appearance at will. Protea seeds were only brought to Hawaii in great numbers 25 years ago when they were planted in the volcanic earth on the slopes of Haleakala and flourished. Altogether there are 140 varieties of this flower which distinguishes itself above all by its unusual strength and durability (it can survive intact for four days without water). It is very popular as a dried flower because the colour and shape of the petals change through drying.

Alexander and Baldwin Sugar Museum

See Kahului

★★Haleakala National Park   J 4

Legend

Hina, the mother of Maui the demi-god, complained to her son that she could not dry any of her leather clothing – the days were too short. As a result, Maui climbed the volcano, caught the sun with a rope and held it captive. When it promised to move across the mountains somewhat more slowly, he set it free. From then onwards,

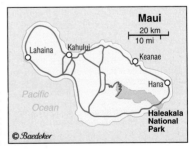

Maui

20 km
10 mi

Lahaina   Kahului   Keanae

Pacific
Ocean   Hana

Haleakala
National
Park

© Baedeker

Maui's inhabitants had more sunlight by which to carry out their work and the volcano has been called "House of the Sun" – Haleakala.

Haleakala Crater is one of the largest places of interest in the Hawaiian archipelago and without doubt Maui's principal attraction. The constantly-changing colours of the crater caused Mark Twain, who spent several months in Hawaii in 1866, to talk of the "most sublime of natural spectacles" which he had experienced. Today's tourists cannot experience it any other way, particularly when witnessing the sunset here. It is most easily reached from Kahului via Roads 37, 377 and 378, its 9846ft/3000m-plus height can be climbed in a car without difficulty. The journey there and back takes three hours. The national park land is divided into two parts which, although adjoining, are reached by two different routes which means that both parts cannot be visited on one day. One part includes the enormous region of the crater with its many paths, the other consists of the lower part of Kipahulu Valley, which stretches from here to the south-east coast. To be found here are the Seven Pools and the Waimoka Waterfall, both reached via Road 31 from Hana (see entry).

General information

Today Haleakala is a long-extinct clinker peak – its last eruption occurred in 1790 – whose interior is streaked red, yellow, grey and black, which illustrate the paths where lava, ashes and clinker once flowed.

Haleakala's evolution

Maui, one of the younger Hawaiian islands, may have evolved from two volcanoes on the sea bed which erupted frequently during millions of years while continuing to develop and which finally emerged from the sea. Lava, ashes and alluvial land joined the two volcanoes together and formed the Island of Maui. The larger eastern volcano, Haleakala, grew to 11,815ft/3600m (measuring 29,866ft/9100m from the sea bed) although it has since lost 1962ft/600m due to erosion. This erosion is essentially the result of heavy rainfall – streams of water running down the volcano created two large valleys near the summit which combined to form the present large crater.

The crater's current inactivity is explained by geologists as a result of the constant northerly movement of the Pacific Plate (see Number and Figures, Evolution of the Hawaiian islands). By the mid-18th c., Maui had moved several kilometres from the "hot spot". Although 200 years constitute a short time geologically speaking, a new eruption remains conceivable. Since 1790, two small streams of lava have flowed from the lower slopes of Haleakala's south-western side, entering the sea at Makena in the south-west of Maui. Occasional, weak earth tremors on Maui bear witness to the fact that the land has still not settled but there are no signs of volcanic activity on the island. Therefore Maui's evolution may have ceased while further south, Hawaii, due to continuing eruptions from its volcanoes, is still growing.

The headquarters of the national park, where general information, books, postcards and so on can be obtained, is situated about 1 mile/1.5km from the entrance to the park. The visitor centre, 10 miles/16km further on, at a height of about 9846ft/3000m, offers information about the crater's evolution illustrated with models and diagrams. The best view of the crater can be seen from here. The Puu Ulaula Observatory (*puu ulaula* means red hill) is located at the summit and offers a rewarding view of western Maui, Big Island, Lanai, Molokai and, in clear weather, Oahu.

Information

Telephone weather report
Tel. 572–9177

Haleakala offers a variety of walks. The Haleakala Trail, or Sliding Halemau Trail, is a two-day tour which leads to the crater and Holua Hut and back. The tour begins on a bend on the Haleakala Highway, some 2 miles/3.2km beyond the visitors' centre and the entry kiosk; it is suitable only for experienced walkers. The Polipoli Loop Trail is recommended for novice walkers; the 6 mile/10km walk takes about 3½ hours.

Walks

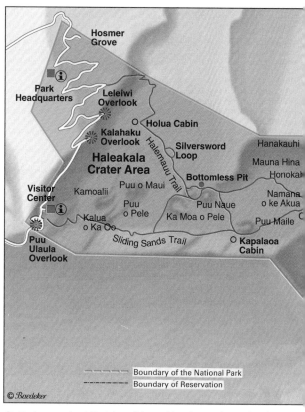

Hosmer Grove

Park Headquarters

Leleiwi Overlook

Holua Cabin

Kalahaku Overlook

Silversword Loop

Hanakauhi

Haleakala Crater Area

Halemauu Trail

Mauna Hina

Bottomless Pit

Honokah

Visitor Center

Kamoalii

Puu o Maui

Namana o ke Akua

Puu o Pele

Puu Naue

Ka Moa o Pele

Puu Maile

Kalua o Ka Oo

Puu Ulaula Overlook

Sliding Sands Trail

Kapalaoa Cabin

—————— Boundary of the National Park
—·—·—·— Boundary of the Reservation

© *Baedeker*

Changeable weather

Particular care should be taken of the sudden changes in weather that can occur on Haleakala. Near the summit, the temperature is about 20°C lower than in the valley, making warm clothing necessary. The summer is usually sunny and warm – it can even be hot in the crater – but a change to cold, wet and rainy weather, particularly in the afternoons, always remains a possibility and protection against the rain should always be taken. In the winter, it is always cold, foggy, rainy and windy (a north-east wind!) on Haleakala. Spring and autumn days can display all weather conditions. The lowest temperature ever experienced on the Hawaiian islands (–11°C) was recorded on Haleakala.

Flora and fauna

A number of endemic plants grow on Haleakala and its slopes and these cannot be found anywhere else on the islands. Particularly well-known and conspicuous is the silversword plant – called *ahinahina* in Hawaiian – which can be found on Haleakala at heights of more than 6564ft/2000m, mainly in the crater itself. This silver-leafed plant, which can grow to a height of 8ft/2.5m, lives for between five and 20 years. In the last year of its life, usually in May or June, 100–500 yellow-red flowers shoot from the plant and these are fully developed by July or August. Every flower produces hundreds of seeds and, while these ripen, the plant dies. By autumn

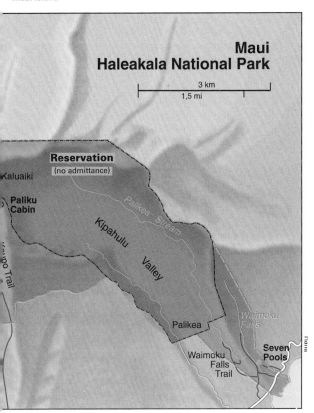

only a decaying skeleton remains. Tourists are fortunate to see this unusual plant, which is legally protected. Several silverswords have been planted along the road as a hedge around the Kahaluka Vantage Point.

Another flower which grows nowhere else on the Hawaiian islands except on the slopes of Haleakala is the protea. This originates from Australia and South Africa and grows in a number of shapes and colours.

Even some of the birds that are gradually disappearing from Hawaii can only be seen on Haleakala's slopes, including the state bird, the nene (Hawaiian goose) and the akohehohe, a particularly lovely bird. The nene, which was almost extinct and which is somewhat smaller than its relative, the Canada goose, today numbers several hundred. The nene is no longer a water bird as it has lost much of its once-webbed feet.

Hawaiians considered Haleakala a holy place for more than a thousand years. Today the remains of an old stone path can be seen in the crater which was laid in early times. Some time ago the National Park Service found the bones of Hawaiians who probably belonged to the families of chieftans. The bones had been hidden, according to custom, in an almost-impenetrable bed of lava. A further Hawaiian custom was to throw the umbilical cords of new-born babies into the crater. This was to ensure that the children grew up into strong and honourable adults. The remains of an

Haleakala
– holy place

123

Rare plants: Silversword and King Protea (see page 122)

old temple (*heiau*), complete with altars, can be found in the crater. Hawaiians sacrificed victims to the gods here.

★★ Hana and Hana Highway   J/K 4

Original Hawaii

Hana is a village of about 800 inhabitants in one of the most thinly-populated districts in the whole of Hawaii. Its isolated position has enabled it to maintain an image of the Hawaii that existed before the invasion of mass tourism – idyllic with lush fields and gardens, thanks to the plentiful rains, characteristic of the east coasts of all the Hawaiian islands.

History

Its proximity to Hawaii gave Hana great strategic importance during the battles for unification of the Hawaiian islands at the end of the 18th c. Kamehameha I used the village as a base for his decisive attack on the large neighbouring island. Queen Kaahumanu, King Kamehameha I's wife, was born in Hana in 1768. After Kamehameha's death she remained as the reigning monarch of Hawaii until 1832.

View

A particularly fine view of Hana and Hana Bay is gained from Lyon's Hill, a hill above village with memorial honouring the founder of Hana Ranch.

Wananalua Church

This church, built in 1838 from lava stone, is still used for services preached in the Hawaiian language.

Hana Cultural Center

Hana Cultural Center, a museum in the middle of the village, offers all sorts of interesting information about Hana's past and present, of which the many old photographs and the fantastic shells deserve special attention.

Hasegawa General Store

Hasegawa General Store is certainly one of the most interesting shops imaginable. Its small premises sell everything and anything – groceries, everyday commodities, souvenirs and so on. The store was completely burnt down on the night of August 5th 1990 but it has been rebuilt. Hasegawa also possesses the village's only petrol (gasoline) station – fill up here for the return journey as there are no petrol stations between Hana and Paia.

After a period of fairly unsuccessful sugar cane production, cattle rearing became an intensive industry in Hana again. Hana Ranch, with its considerable stock of cattle, has been economically successful since its founding by Paul Fagan and is a major employer of Hana's inhabitants.

Hana Ranch

Places of interest along Hana Highway

Although the road to Hana is not long, it is extremely difficult with no fewer than 617 bends and more than 50 narrow bridges along a stretch of about 52 miles/83km. Hana Highway is the name for Road 36 and Road 360 respectively which runs close to the airport at Kahului (see entry). From Huelo the road becomes narrower and there are many more bends. At weekends the traffic is very heavy. In all, some 3 to 4 hours should be allowed for the stretch from Kahului to Hana.

Road conditions

The return journey should be started fairly early to avoid having to drive back in darkness. The best thing is to arrange to stay overnight in Hana. Unfortunately, there are not many hotels to choose from; the best is the Hotel Hans-Maui, but it is also the most expensive in Hawaii. One far cheaper alternative is to rent a small holiday home (through Hana Bay Vacation Rentals, P.O. Box 318, Hana, HI 96713).

Anyone intending to travel all the way round the island should allow 2 to 3 hours to travel from Seven Pools (see below) to Ulupalakua Ranch; the road is not asphalted and is negotiable only with a four-wheel drive vehicle (hire cars not allowed).

If the car journey proves too strenuous, fly instead from Kahului to Hana's small airport, located in the immediate vicinity of Waianapanapa State Park. Aloha Island Air and Air Hana offer connections. The former has no fixed timetable – for information about Oahu, telephone 800/833–3219, for other islands, telephone 800/652–6541. Air Hana is a charter service offered by the Hotel Hana-Maui which began in 1989 and runs a twin Cessna 421 plane seating four passengers. For information, telephone 800/321–4262. The hotel offers a free shuttle service from the airport. The flight from Kahului to Hana lasts about fifteen minutes.

The road, which follows the rugged coastline in a westerly direction, passes through an unusually thickly overgrown, almost primeval area, with countless places where it is absolutely necessary to stop. Along the difficult route immediately after leaving Haiku, the vegetation becomes increasingly lush – guavas, many ginger bushes, coconut trees, slim bamboo plants and flowers almost all the colours of the rainbow are to be found here. This exotic world of plants and flowers proves a rich reward for the difficulties encountered in reaching it.

Flowering splendour

This twin waterfall (about halfway between Kahalui and Hana and a 5 minute journey on the Hana road) plunges down through dense undergrowth into a circular pool below.

Twin Falls

The road borders the coast for the first time at Honomanu Bay. Unfortunately, there is only a small parking area here from which the ocean can be viewed.

Honomanu Bay

Anyone interested in tropical vegetation should stop briefly at Keanae Arboretum (free entry), located on the landward side of the road not far back from Honomanu Bay. It is necessary to follow a climbing path to reach the two main areas – tropical plants and endemic Hawaiian plants.

Keanae Arboretum

Waterfalls . . .   *. . . the lava coast*

Wailua Lookout

From Wailua Lookout there is a beautiful view of Keanae Peninsula (formed from lava from Haleakala). The powerful Waikani Waterfall is also visible from here, one of the many (mostly nameless) waterfalls which appear along the road.

The villages of Keanae and Wailue, through which the road passes, have a combined population of no more than 250.

Puua Kaa State Park

As the best stopping-off point choose Puua Kaa State Park, where travellers can rest and picnic surrounded by banana and eucalyptus trees. It is located on the left-hand side of the road after a bridge.

More picnic places are available shortly before reaching Hana at Waianapanapa State Park. Camping is allowed here and cabins can be rented for overnight stays (for conditions, prices and essential advance booking, contact the Maui Division of State Parks, 54, High Street, Wailuku. Tel. 244–4354). The black lava beach at Paiola Bay in the state park is worth visiting but refrain from swimming in the strong waves.

Further on there is a pair of caves formed from black lava in which, according to legend, Chief Kaakea killed his wife, Popoalaea, because he suspected her of having an affair with her younger brother. In old Hawaii, incest was not taboo – to the contrary, it was believed that a relationship between siblings produced particularly strong offspring. As the death occurred in April, every year during that month the sea is said to turn red. There is, however, a more rational explanation for this – at that time of year there are many young red prawns in the water.

Hana lies 3 miles/5km further on. Shortly before reaching there, Road 360 splits but both branches continue to Hana and leave there as Road 31.

Seven Pools

Leaving Hana on the recently asphalted Road 31, continue to Kipahulu and the Seven Sacred Pools, which are often called the Seven Pools of Oheo

The Seven Pools, seen from the Oheo Bridge ▶

Ravine or the Seven Holy Ponds, although in fact they were simply given this name by a clever hotelier with the aim of making the region more interesting to tourists. From the car park, a ½ mile/1km path leads through grazing land past tumbledown houses and along the coast. The water coming down from the hills cascades through the deeply indented lava rock and finally into the sea. Bathing is permitted in the lower pools. The ocean here is not suitable for swimmers!

A path starts at the car park and leads through Oheo Ravine for ½ mile/1km to Makahika Waterfall. From here it joins the Waimoku Falls Trail; this leads, after 1½ miles/2.5km, to the impressive Waimoku Waterfalls. The first part of the walk is not too difficult; after 1 mile/1.6km the way crosses a bridge and proceeds uphill on the other side.

Palapala Hoomau Church, Charles Lindbergh

Beyond Kipahulu lies Palapala Hoomau Church, built in 1857, in the graveyard the famous Atlantic pilot Charles Lindbergh lies buried. In the "Spirit of St Louis" in 1927 he was the first to fly across the Atlantic. Lindbergh passed the last years of his life on Maui and died in 1974, having expressed the wish to be buried in the inaccessible solitude of this country churchyard. Nevertheless, the number of tourists wishing to visit his grave grows year by year.

From here onwards only four-wheeled vehicles are suitable (see under Road conditions above).

Iao Valley State Park   H/J 4

Popular for excursions

Iao Valley (*iao* is sometimes translated as "highest cloud" or "highest light") lies west of Wailuku on Road 32, the continuation of Main Street, and used to be one of the old Hawaiian holy valleys. Hawaiians would undertake pilgrimages to such places in honour of their gods.

Today, several well-maintained paths lead from the car park to this beautiful valley. It is a popular place for excursions.

★Iao Needle

In the middle of the valley stands Iao Needle, a pointed lump of basalt, reaching 2215ft/675m above sea level – a monolith standing alone in the eroded valley.

This unique overgrown rock was apparently used as an altar in prehistoric times. A legend surrounds Iao Needle's origin. It is said that the demi-god Maui took captive an unwanted suitor (the water sprite Puukamoua, comparable to Triton, son of the Greek god Poseidon) of his beautiful daughter, Iao, and wanted to kill him. But Pele, the fire goddess, ordered Maui to turn him to stone – hence the needle!

The valley is said to be full of *manas* – the ghosts of Hawaiian gods.

Kepaniwai Park Heritage Gardens

In Kepaniwai Park and Heritage Gardens (which will be passed on the return journey), buildings have been erected as a tribute to Hawaii's ethnic minorities. A Portuguese villa, a Hawaiian grass hut, a New England house, a Chinese pagoda and a Japanese tea house stand as symbols of Hawaii's united nationality.

Kepaniwai means water dam. The meaning can be drawn from early Hawaiian history when Kamehameha defeated the King of Maui's forces in a decisive battle and the Wailuka River was filled with the bodies of the dead soldiers.

Pali Ele'ele

Pali Ele'ele (a dark black cliff) will be passed on the left-hand side of the path to Iao Needle. In the 1960s, after the murder of President John F. Kennedy, it was thought that his profile could be seen in the cliffs.

The Iao Needle, a monolith in the Iao Valley ▶

★Kaanapali
H 4

Tourist centre

Kaanapali lies in western Maui and belongs to Lahaina (see entry). It is reached via Road 30. A superlative tourist centre has developed here since the 1960s in place of sugar cane and pineapple growing.

Ranged along the 4 miles/6km beach, Maui's finest, stand six luxury hotels of which the Hyatt Regency and the Sheraton Maui stand out, although the others – the Maui Marriott, the Westin Maui, the Kaanapali Beach and the Royal Lahaina – are among the best and most expensive hotels in the Hawaiian islands. In each of these hotels there are several restaurants to choose from. There are golf courses and tennis courts as well as one of Hawaii's finest shopping centres (The Whalers) with the Whalers Village Museum and its superb collection of memorabilia from Maui's whaling times such as models of ships, pieces of whaling equipment, carvings from whales' teeth and so on (free entry).

A small new airport guarantees quick connections to Kahului and to the other Hawaiian islands. The "Sugar Cane Train" railway line runs from Lahaina to Kaanapali and is used for excursions through the sugar cane fields which still remain today.

Kapalua

This seaside resort north of Kaanapali is famous for its beautiful beaches. Tourism is not as developed here as in neighbouring Kaanapali but a luxury hotel and a golf course complete its exclusivity for tourists.
All in all, the stretch of coast between Lahaina and Kapalua is blessed with great tourist appeal.

A trip through the sugar-cane fields in the Sugar-Cane Train

Kahului   J 4

Kahului, which has almost joined up with Wailuku (see entry), is the largest town on Maui with a population of about 13,000. The airport and the well-developed port are of economic importance. The town's central position proves useful, although it only has a small beach and is generally cooler and windier than other parts of the island. As far as tourists are concerned, Kahului has little to offer. Kahuumanu Shopping Center in the street of that name is worth mentioning, as it includes one of the few restaurants in Hawaii that serves traditional Hawaiian food (Ma Chan. Tel. 877–6475).

General
information

Kahului's history began towards the end of the 18th c. when Kamehameha I left Big Island with his forces and landed here. The town's name means "the winner" and could well refer to the victory which Kamehameha enjoyed against the King of Maui's troops in nearby Lao Valley (see entry).
    In the 19th c. Kahului was chiefly a port, shipping mainly sugar from the surrounding plantations. Kahului's development was arrested in 1900 when much of the town was burnt down in an attempt to rid it of a plague epidemic. During rebuilding the size of the port was increased. The modern airport, located in the 6½ miles/10.5km-wide valley which unites Hallakala (see entry) and the mountains of western Maui, was only completed in the last few years and has made it possible to fly directly from the mainland to Maui.

History

Alexander and Baldwin Sugar Museum

This museum offers a good insight into the sugar cane industry. The museum illustrates its history by means of photographs and original implements, including a sugar refinery, all excellently restored.

Location
3857 Hansen Road,
Puuene, Road 39
Tel. 871–8058

Maui Enchanted Gardens

On the way from Kahului to Makawao (see entry) are the Maui Enchanted Gardens, located in the part of the country called "Upcountry". This recently laid-out garden contains a considerable number and variety of plants and flowers. It comes under the same control as the Nani Mau Gardens in Hilo, Hawaii (see entry). A visit to the gardens can be combined with a visit to the Haleakala Crater (see entry) as they can both be reached via the same route.

Location
Road 37, about
6 miles/10km from
Kahului Airport
Tel. 878–2531

Kapalua

See Kaanapali

Kihei   J4

This village certainly counts as Maui's fastest-developing tourist resort, with a population not far behind that of Kahului (see entry) and Wailuku (see entry). Looked at critically it is a prime example of tourism development gone wrong. Totally uncontrolled building work was carried out on either side of Kihei Road, which runs through the whole village, owing to a lack of central planning. Today, Kihei has far too many buildings such as condominiums and holiday flats – occupied by their owners for only part of each year and rented at other times as time-share projects.
    That apart, Kihei has an almost-continuous 6 miles/10km-long beach, the island's most settled weather and offers beautiful, clear views of Lanai,

Kahoolawe and Molokini. Kihei's hotels are cheaper than elsewhere on Maui, comparable with prices in Kaanapali and Kapalua, but less luxurious.

During the Second World War, Kihei protected itself from a possible Japanese invasion by tank traps and bunkers but no invasion took place. Today pieces of overgrown cement blocks can be seen which bear witness to that period.

Wailea
Makena

South of Kihei the villages of Wailea and Makena are becoming increasingly more developed for tourism with the building of a row of luxury hotels (the Stouffer Wailea Beach Resort, the Maui-Inter-Continental Wailea and the Maui Prince). New golf courses have also been opened here.

★Lahaina   H4

Location and
general
information

Lahaina lies to the west of the island, reached from Kahului Airport via Roads 38 and 30. Although Lahaina's population of 6000 makes it only the fourth largest town on Maui, it remains nevertheless the island's most popular tourist resort. Lahaina offers lively beach and town life and an interesting history, which continues to be celebrated in the town.

History

Lahaina's historical development has been a series of ups and downs. In its 200 years of evolution, Lahaina changed from a small village to Hawaii's seat of government to one of the world's most important whaling ports. The decline of whaling lost Lahaina its identity and it only gained new blood through the onset of tourism. Today, the town's many historically-important buildings are protected and are being renovated and rebuilt.

Before the unification of the Hawaiian islands by Kamehameha I, King Kahekili ruled Maui from Lahaina. Later, after his defeat by Kamehameha, Lahaina became Kamehameha I's seat of government and, until 1840,

Lahaina Harbour

Hawaii's official capital. The two Maui-born queens, Kaahumanu and Keo-puolani, oversaw the conversion of the Hawaiian islands to Christianity from here and allowed the missionaries, who first arrived here in 1823, a free rein in this.

Lahaina's high point as a whaling centre came in 1846 when 429 whaling ships were anchored in its port. For decades, Lahaina maintained its position as the world's most important whaling station and this has left its mark on the town. The large number of sailors who stayed in Lahaina, after spending months on narrow ships, changed the town dwellers' lives considerably. According to one census of Lahaina, taken in 1846, there were 3445 Hawaiians, 112 foreigners, 600 temporarily resident sailors, 155 *adobe* houses (clay houses), 833 grass huts, 59 stone and wooden houses and 528 dogs.

Whaling centre

To prevent a decline in moral standards Governor Hoapili of Maui passed one law after another. Brothels were forbidden, grog could no longer be sold or poured, Hawaiian women (mainly naked) were no longer allowed to swim up to the ships. Unfortunately these measures led more to unrest rather than to an improvement in conditions so that Hoapili felt himself forced to open a prison for the rebellious sailors. Lahaina's stormy whaling times ended in about 1870 and for almost a century the town led a virtually blameless life. Sugar cane and pineapple production became its main source of income.

With the onset of tourism in the 1960s Lahaina gained new life and this has resulted in the town being overrun with tourists almost all year round.

Lahaina

500 m
0,25 mi

Mala Wharf
Front Street
Lahaina-Kaanapali & Pacific Railroad
Mill Street
Kahoma Stream
Honoapiilani Road
Lahaina Luna High School
Jodo Mission
Wainee Street
Train Station
Highway
Pioneer Sugar Mill
Road
Seaman's Hospital
Front Street
Papalaua St.
Whaling Museum
Tong Society House
Lahainaluna
Seaman's Cemetery
Lanakila Church
Lahaina Market Place
Dickenson
Maui Islander
Hale Aloha Church
3 5
4
Canal
Prison
St.
Honoapiilani
Wainee St.
Mill Highway
Street
Harbor
Maluulu o Lele Park
Waiola Church
Shaw
Whaler's Market Place
Front Street
Lahaina Shores Hotel
Pacific Ocean
Auau Channel

1 Baldwin House
   Master's Reading Room
2 Banyan-Baum
   Courthouse
3 Brick Palace
   Carthaginian Museum
   Hauola-Stein
4 Hale Paahao Prison
5 Pioneer Inn

© *Baedeker*

Lahaina today   Front Street, Lahaina's main street, and its neighbouring streets are very
lively, particularly in the evenings when the heat of the day has died down a
little (Lahaina lives up to its name, which roughly translates as "pitiless
sun") and the many shops open. A stroll along Front Street – about
1 mile/1.5km – is always an experience and well worth taking half a day
over. A longer stay should be planned to visit the town's many places of
interest which are to be found for the most part in and around Front Street.

Places of interest in Lahaina

Baldwin House Museum

Tel. 661–3262   The house was built from lava and crushed coral in 1835 and was lived
in from 1837 to 1871 by Dwight Baldwin, the missionary, and the nine
members of his family. It was also used as a doctor's surgery for, in
addition to his work as a missionary, Baldwin was Hawaii's first doctor and
dentist. The furnishings mostly come from when Baldwin lived in the
house, including the Steinway grand piano. Documents honouring the
doctor's achievements are still exhibited in the surgery.

Banyan tree

Location
Front Street
between Canal and
Hotel Street

This tree, which originates from India, measured only 8ft/2.5m in height
when planted in 1873 by Maui's then sheriff to commemorate the 50th
anniversary of the building of the island's first mission house. Since then,
the majestic tree has grown into Maui's biggest banyan tree – it now has a
dozen trunks, is 52ft/16m high, spans more than 197ft/60m and throws
shadows over a third of Court Square, in which it stands.

In the shade of the Banyan trees

Brick Palace

Here only the ruins of Hawaii's first stone-built house can be seen, which Kamehameha had built in 1802 to receive the captains of ships sailing into the port. The house would have covered an area of 39ft/12m by 19½ft/6m with two rooms on each floor. It stood for 70 years and was used later as a warehouse. Unfortunately, a drawing of the house has not survived.

Location
End of Market Street

"Carthaginian"

The "Carthaginian", a reconstruction of a 19th c. sailing ship, is representative of the small, fast freighters which were used for conducting trade between the islands. The original ship was lost in 1972 on a voyage from Lahaina into dry dock in Honolulu. A replacement was found in Norway, from where the "Carthaginian II", with its Lahianan crew, left for its new destination. The ship contains an exhibition about whales and whaling.

Location
At the port, on the corner of Opelekane Street

Courthouse

A bad storm in 1858 destroyed more than 20 houses in Lahaina, including Hale Piula (the courthouse) which King Kamehameha III had built and also used as a palace. A year later a new courthouse was built using stones from the old one and for a year it served as the centre of justice for Maui County. Today it accommodates the Lahaina Art Society Gallery and the police station.

Location
Near the port on the corner of Hotel Street

Hale Paahao (prison)

The prison was built by Governor Hoapili for rebellious sailors who were chained to the walls. All sailors who had not returned to their ships by dusk had to spend the night there. In 1852 a larger prison was built using the coral blocks of the old one, and this contained separate cells for men and women. Most prisoners ended up there either because they had left their ships or were drunk or had worked on Sundays. Prison sentences of more than one year had to be served in Oahu. Today the prison is leased for all types of events.

Location
Corner of Wainee and Prison Street

Hale Pai (printing works)

On the site of the Lahainaluna seminary, above Lahaina, the missionaries developed the first printing works west of the Rocky Mountains, which printed Bibles, dictionaries and school books. From 1834, the first newspaper in the Hawaiian language, the "Lama Hawaii", was printed here.

The printing works was restored by the Lahaina Restoration Foundation between 1980 and 1982 and now houses a museum devoted to the beginning of printing in Hawaii.

Location
Lahainaluna Road
Tel. 667–7040

Hauola Rock

Rocks play an important part in Hawaiian mythology. It is not easy to imagine that the rocks projecting from the sea emit powers. The Hauola Rock, which resembles a chair, had the power to heal persons who sat on it and allowed the sea to wash over their body. As well as holy rocks the *kahunas* (priests) used herbs, diets and massage to restore health to their patients. The Hauola Rock was also used as a birthing chair with the umbilical cords of new-born babies being buried beneath it.

Location
In front of the ruins of Brick Palace

Hawaii Experience

This film, portraying Hawaii's development, history and present-day life, is shown on a 59ft/18m domed screen and can now be seen in Lahiana. The audience can catch a glimpse of tropical gardens and lava-spewing

Location
824 Front Street
Tel. 661–8314

volcanoes, watch whales, see (and hear) roaring waterfalls and experience
a bird's-eye view of the mighty cliffs along the coast. The title of the film is
"Hawaii, Islands of the Gods".

Jodo Mission

Location
On the coast, near
Front and Kenui
Street (the building
is closed)

This Buddhist mission is built on the site of an old village in front of a
majestic coconut grove. It is one of Lahaina's best-known and visited
attractions because of the enormous statue of Buddha – one of the largest
outside Japan – which sits in the mission's small garden. The statue was
erected in 1968 in memory of the first Japanese sugar plantation workers,
who came to Hawaii in 1868. The pagoda which accompanies it is Lahaina's
largest Buddhist temple.

Hongwanji Temple

Another temple, the Hongwanji Temple, dating from 1927, can be found on
Wainee Street, between Prison and Shaw Street.

Lahaina-Kaanapali and Pacific Railroad

Location
Street 30
Paplaua Street
Tel. 661–0089

The commonly-named "Sugar Cane Train" is an authentic replica of the old
train which carried sugar cane along the approximately 4 miles/6km stretch
between Kanaapali and Lahaina at the turn of the century. Today, tourists
are transported along this route by steam locomotive on a return journey of
about 50 minutes, which takes them through sugar cane fields while the
driver entertains them with old songs and stories about the history of sugar
plantations.

Lahaina Whaling Museum

Location
865 Front Street

Lahaina's history as a whaling port is brought to life in this private
museum. Objects from that era are on display here including some unique
and unusual harpoons and harpoon cannons, which were used to shoot the
whales.

Lahainaluna High School

Location
Lahainaluna Road

The one seminary ever founded in Lahainaluna (*lahainaluna* means
"above Lahaina") by missionaries for the education of priests is now the
only high school in the west of Maui. After it was founded in 1831 teaching
was carried out for 40 years in Hawaiian, after which English was adopted
and greater emphasis was placed on maintaining Hawaiian traditions. Part
of the school houses borders and has taken girls since 1980. The campus,
where a row of modern houses now stands, is worth visiting.

Masters' Reading Room

Location
Corner of Front and
Dickinson Street
Tel. 661–3262

The current home of the Lahaina Restoration Foundation was originally
built as a reading room for ships' captains, who often spent a long time in
Lahaina's port. Most captains and officers had their families on board ship
with them and they could withdraw to the shady house and rest. The
ground floor was used by the mission and contained a small chapel. The
reading room was on the first floor.

Pioneer Inn

Location
Corner of Hotel and
Wharf Street
Tel. 661–3636

This hotel, built by a Canadian in 1901, was for a long time the only place to
stay on Maui and is today the oldest hotel in Hawaii (along with the Moana
Hotel in Waikiki which was built in the same year). It remains in the ownership of the founders, George Freeland's family. A thorough renovation and
an extension of the hotel was undertaken in 1964. In the dining room

whaling times are brought to life through the decor – a variety of objects, old photographs and whaling equipment. The bar near the hotel entrance is a favourite meeting place and is always lively. The rooms in the Pioneer Inn are simple and cheap.

Waiola Church and Waiola Cemetery (originally Waine'e)

This church, mentioned several times by James Michener in his novel "Hawaii", has experienced mixed fortunes. The original construction was built between 1828 and 1832 and was the island's first stone church, with room for 300 worshippers. A storm in 1858 damaged it badly, tearing the roof off and causing the bell tower to collapse. It was rebuilt but was burnt down in 1894 by a crowd who considered this an appropriate way of protesting against the abolition of the Hawaiian monarchy. After it had been rebuilt for a second time another fire destroyed the nave in 1947. Rebuilt yet again, the church was then badly damaged by a whirlwind. The present, not particularly impressive, church was erected in 1953.

Location
Wainee Street, near Shaw Street

The neighbouring graveyard dates from 1823 and was Hawaii's first Christian cemetery. The graves of countless important people from the beginnings of the Hawaiian monarchy can be found here, including King Kauanualii of Kauai (1780–1824); Queen Keopuolani, one of the wives of Kamehameha I (1778–1823); Governor Hoapili of Maui (1776–1840), who married one after the other of the two widows of Kamehameha, Keopuolani and Kaahumanu; Miriam Auhea Kekauluohi, one of the five wives of Kamehameha I, later the wife of Kamehameha II and mother of the later King Lunalilo (1794–1845); Princess Nahienaena, daughter of Kamehameha I and sister of Kings Kamehameha II and III (1815–36).

Wo Hing Temple

Only repaired in 1984 by the Lahaina Restoration Foundation, this building is now a museum. It traces the history of the Chinese in Maui and, in particular, their influence on Lahaina. Particularly interesting are the films shown here. The temple was built by Chinese plantation workers as a home and a meeting place for less well-off Chinese workers.

Location
5 Front Street
Tel. 661–5553

Makawao   J 4

Makawao lies south-east of Kahului and is reached via Road 37.

Makawao (meaning "beginning of the forest") is a settlement of Portuguese immigrants mainly involved in rearing cattle. Over the years the place has become well-known in Hawaii on account of the rodeos that are held here throughout the year. The most popular of these takes place on July 4th, American Independence Day. Makawao has about 1100 inhabitants and it has a distinctive flavour of the Wild West, like that of Wailea/Kamuela (see entry) in the north-east of Big Island. The retention of Makawao's character as a Wild West town has been a source of concern for some years. Both Mexican and steak restaurants are located in the two main streets, Baldwin and Makawao Avenue. A peculiarity is Kitada's food stall, said to sell the best *saimin*, a filling noodle soup, which originated in Japan.

The land around Makawao is not typically Hawaiian but is nevertheless attractive with horses and cattle grazing in meadows and on the slopes.

Molokini   H/J 4

This horseshoe-shaped islet lies to the south of Maui's west coast off the village of Makena. Molokini stands 148ft/45m above sea-level and consists of the remains of a crater, the larger part of which has sunk beneath the sea.

Molokini: remains of a sunken crater

Maui Tropical Plantation

The rich fishing to be had in its sheltered bay has caused the island, lying between Maui and Kahoolawe, to be declared a protected marine area. As its clear blue waters are always calm, Molokini is particularly suitable for beginners to snorkelling. Boats sail every morning from Maalea and Lahaina to Molokini. According to Hawaiian legend, Lohiau, the lover of whom the fire goddess Pele dreamed, married a noble Hawaiian woman. In anger, Pele cut their bodies up into pieces. Their torsos became Puu Olai ("earthquake hill"), a hill near Makena, and their heads became Molokini.

Olowalu H 4

This hamlet of just a few houses, located to the south of Lahaine on Road 30, played a part in Hawaii's history. In 1790 the Massacre of Olowalu ("many hills") took place among the native Hawaiians led by an American sea captain – an opponent of Kamehameha I.

Olowalu Massacre

Today's attractions are the 200–300-year-old petroglyphs located near here. They can only be reached on foot and are not easy to find. Different activities of the ancient Hawaiians are portrayed – fishing, canoeing and weaving. It is best to ask for directions at a grocer's shop and petrol station by the roadside. The Lahaina Restoration Foundation is trying to make the area more accessible.

Petroglyphs

Tedeschi Vineyards J 4

The vineyard is located on the almost 40sq.miles/120sq.km grounds of Ulupalakua Ranch, about 9 miles/14km before Kula on Road 37 from Kahului. Maui's only wine producer, it was founded in the 1970s and at first only produced pineapple wine, which is still made today. Later, vines were planted which bore grapes for the first time in 1983. Since then a red table wine and champagne have been produced and these are served in many of Maui's restaurants. Wine-tasting is possible here.

Wine producer

Wailuku H 4

Wailuku, located in windy northern Maui, is Maui County's seat of government and its population of 10,500 makes it the island's second largest town. Wailuku has combined with the neighbouring town of Kahului and together they form the largest town centre on the island.

Town

Wailuku is the older of the two towns and has a historic centre, Wailuku Historic District, which is cut off from the rest of the town by the eight-storey Kalana o Maui, the county offices in the High Street. Bailey House and Kaahumanu Church, both dating from the first half of the 19th c., are located here. At early Sunday services hymns are sung in Hawaiian in the church. A brewery has been started up by some Germans, producing Maui Lager. During the first few years, some 15,000 hectolitres were brewed and now production is considerably greater.

Maui Zoological and Botanical Garden (tel. 244–3276) is situated between Wailuku and Kahului and contains an interesting collection of endemic plants.

Bailey House Museum – Hale Hoikeike

Bailey House originates from 1834 and was inhabited between 1837 and 1882 by the missionary Edward Bailey and his family. During this period it

Location
2375-A Main Street

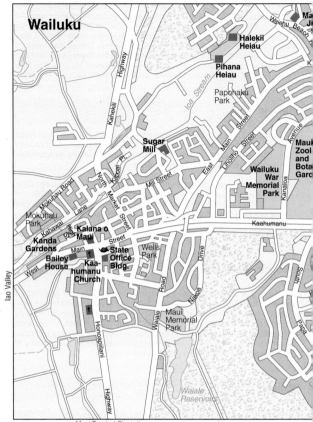

Maui Tropical Plantation

was extended several times. After having stood empty for a long time it was put at the disposal of the Maui Historical Society in 1956. This organisation opened it as a museum the following year. Bailey, who came to Hawaii from Boston, was not only a priest and a missionary but also a teacher, musician, writer, botanist and, above all, an artist. Many of his oil paintings are on show in the museum and capture Maui's appearance in bygone days. The gallery, which also exhibits copperplate etchings, served as the dining room of the Wailuku Female Seminary, a girls' boarding school where Bailey and his wife taught. Also on view here are pieces of handwork from old Hawaii, some made of stones and shells, as well as beautiful examples of *tapa* textiles, carved wooden everyday objects and famous Hawaiian featherwork. In the upper rooms, which were once the Bailey family's bedrooms, stands the furniture that the missionaries brought with them including beds carved from local koa wood as well as wardrobes, toys and china from that period.

Many unusual plants grow in the garden, as well as the different types of sugar cane grown in Hawaii, some of which were introduced to the islands

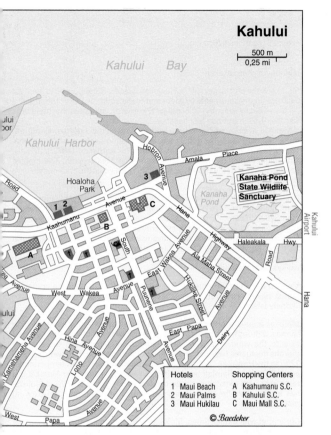

Kahului

500 m
0,25 mi

Kahului Bay

Kahului Harbor

Hoaloha Park

Amala   Place

Hobron Avenue

Kanaha Pond
State Wildlife
Sanctuary

Kanaha Pond

Kahului Airport

Kaahumanu   Avenue

Hana   Highway

Haleakala   Hwy

Haleakala Road

Hana

West   Wakea   Avenue

South   Avenue

East Wakea Avenue

Ala Maha Street

Hukilike Street

Puunene   Avenue

East   Papa   Avenue

Dairy

Hina   Avenue

Kamehameha Avenue

Lono   Avenue

Avenue

West   Papa

Hotels	Shopping Centers
1 Maui Beach	A Kaahumanu S.C.
2 Maui Palms	B Kahului S.C.
3 Maui Hukilau	C Maui Mall S.C.

© Baedeker

by the early Polynesian immigrants. A canoe carved from a single tree trunk and different stone objects are also on view in the garden. It is worth paying a visit to the well-stocked museum shop which sells much literature about the history of Maui and the Hawaiian islands.

Maui Tropical Plantation

The lovely garden, filled with Hawaiian flowers and plants, is located south of Wailuku in Waikapu Valley. Everything about the Hawaiian islands' cultivated plants can be learned here.

Location
On Road 30
Waikapu
Tel. 244–7643

A narrow-gauge railway runs throughout the plantation on which sugar cane, pineapples, coffee, macadamia nuts, guavas and exotic fruits are grown. Demonstrations are regularly given by experts on how to crack coconuts and how to cut open pineapples.

Molokai Island

Area: 261sq.miles/676sq.km
County: Maui
Population: 6900
Main town: Kaunakakai

Location and
evolution

Molokai is the fifth largest of the Hawaiian islands. Neighboured to the west
by Oahu, to the south-east by Maui and to the south by Lanai, the island is
37 miles/60km long by 10½ miles/17km wide. Its coastline measures
88 miles/142km but has few beaches.

Molokai developed from three volcanoes which divide the island into
three distinct areas. The oldest volcano is found in the west (Puu Nana,
1352ft/412m) while the east was formed by Kamakou (4972ft/1515m).
Kalaupapa Peninsula evolved later from a smaller volcano. The highest
point in this part of the island is only 403ft/123m while the crater itself has a
depth of 400ft/122m.

Geographical
features

Despite its small size, Molokai has a variety of geographical features. The
north coast (Pali Coast) has spectacular cliffs reaching to a height of more
than 3282ft/1000m. To the east, three valleys dissect the coastline. The
south coast, by contrast, is flat and characterised by offshore coral reefs.
The fish-ponds established here have used the offshore reefs as a natural
barrier. The western landscape is more undulating but without large
valleys while the east is more typical of Hawaiian landscape with green
valleys and steep hills.

Name

Molokai has the nickname of "Friendly Island". Today, in the course of
tourist development, its image has been reduced to "Lepra Island" or
"Lonely Island".

Climate and
vegetation

Molokai enjoys a climate not very different from the other Hawaiian
islands, although it is perhaps a little cooler because of its extreme expo-
sure to the wind. The average maximum temperature in the summer
months fluctuates between 26°C and 28°C, the minimum between 17°C and
22°C. In the Hawaiian "winter" the maximum and minimum temperatures
are 1–2°C lower. Rainfall levels differ across the island. East Molokai is a
rainy area with extensive, dense tropical rain forests while West Molokai
has a very dry climate and is used as pasture land and for growing
pineapples.

Population

Compared with earlier times, Molokai's population is small. Of its current
6900 inhabitants, 1300 live in the main town of Kaunakakai. Hawaiians and
part-Hawaiians account for almost half of the population – a high proportion compared with the other Hawaiian islands.

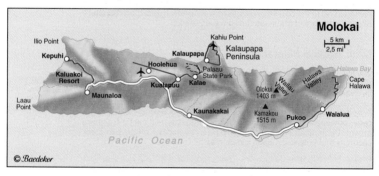

Pineapple growing and cattle rearing were for a long time the main sources of income for the islanders. More than a third of the island is farmed by two cattle ranches, the large Molokai Ranch with approaching 77sq.miles/200sq.km mainly in the west, and the smaller Puuo Hoku Ranch with 22sq.miles/58sq.km in the east.	Farming

Farming on Molokai was never very profitable. On land leased from the Molokai Ranch, Libby and Del Monte began cultivating pineapples in the 1920s and this provided the main source of income for the islanders for half a century. In about 1975 lack of profit forced Dole (which had bought Libby) to stop growing pineapples and in 1982 Del Monte did likewise. This has caused a sharp rise in unemployment on the island.

Until now tourism has developed very slowly on Molokai. The first large tourist complex was built on land along the west coast, bought from Molokai Ranch. The Sheraton Corporation built a hotel complex with bungalows there although the complex has since been sold to another corporation. Today's Kaluakoi Resort Hotel, with its fine golf course and hotel built directly on the beach, is the main tourist attraction. In the surrounding area, some villas have been built for use as holiday homes but their impact on tourism development has been small. This has helped Molokai to protect its original character up to now.

Tourism

Rising unemployment caused by the downfall of farming is supposed to have been countered by the development of tourism. It has not yet been decided how tourism should be encouraged, as development of an infrastructure will, of necessity, follow. Only the future will show which group will win the day – supporters of rapid development or advocates or more controlled growth.

Hawaiian mythology has a unique explanation for Molokai's evolution which is found in the song "*Molokai nui a Hina*" ("Molokai, Hina's Child"). The island is not only Hina's child but also that of Wakea, the creator of all the other Hawaiian islands. Together with Papa, his first wife, he created Hawaii, Maui and Kahoolawe. Another legend says that Maui, the demigod, fished the islands from the sea with a fish hook!

Mythology

Papa then went to Tahiti, whereupon Wakea coupled with Kaula and produced Lanai. Hina became his third wife and bore him Molokai. Wakea's infidelity caused Papa, on her return, to couple with Lua, a young god, and together they produced Oahu. Finally, Wakea and Papa were reconciled and created Kauai, Nihau, Kaula and Nihoa.

James Cook, the British sea captain, sighted Molokai on his first expedition in November 1778 but did not attempt to land because he felt the island appeared to be deserted. Another British seafarer, George Dixon, became the first to land on Molokai eight years later. Molokai was not heard of again until 1832 when the first missionaries went there. Between these periods Kamehameha I had fetched his first wife, Keopuolani, from here and had conquered the island with his troops five years later. Pakuhiwa Battlefield, on which every last one of Molokai's soldiers died, is found on the south coast, about 4 miles/6.5km from Kaunakakai.

History

★Halawa Valley   H 3

Visitors who stay for longer than one day on Molokai should be prepared to accept the difficulties of a journey to Halawa Valley. The beauty of this unique landscape more than makes up for it.	Route

The valley lies to the east of Molokai, no great distance from the west or from Kaunakakei, but the difficult and winding stretch at the end of Road 450 makes the journey time to the valley longer than might be expected. Allow at least four hours for a return journey and longer if stops along the route are envisaged.

A vantage point along the route offers a good view of Halawa Valley and Halawa Bay. Molokai's first inhabitants probably settled in Halawa Valley

Halawa Bay
Halawa Valley

Halawa Bay at the end of Halawa Valley

(*Halawa* means "curve" in Hawaiian). Taro was extensively grown here on layered terraces until a particularly strong *tsunamis* (spring tide) in 1946 flooded the whole valley and deposited so much salt that plants would no longer flourish here.

There are many traces of this earlier settlement, including the remains of two temples – Mana Heiau and Papa Heiau – on the valley slopes.

Halawa's beach is in a poor condition and particular care should be taken when swimming, especially in high waves.

Camping is allowed here, provided prior permission has been granted. Do not drink water from Halawa River, which has its source here.

Moaula Falls   A poor 2½ miles/4km-long path leads from here to Moaula Waterfall (246ft/75m). It is possible to bathe in the pool at the bottom of the waterfall.

After heavy rain, which occurs quite frequently in this part of the island, the path becomes impassable. Care must be taken to cross Halawa River at the correct point as the waterfall can only be reached from the right bank.

This is one of the loneliest places in the whole of Hawaii and this, in a certain way, is its very attraction.

Iliiliopae Heiau   H 3

This temples lies in the eastern segment of the south coast near the village of Mapuleho, not far from Road 450. It stands on private land and can only be visited with permission.

Of the many temple sites to be found in Hawaii, Iliiliopae Heiau is one of the largest (328ft/100m long, 118ft/36m wide) and is probably Molokai's oldest.

According to legend, the stones used to build the temple were transported from Wailu Valley to the opposite coast, passed from hand to hand by the Menehunes, legendary dwarfs. *Ili'ili* is the word for "stones" but where *opae* comes from remains questionable. It is said to be a tributary of the Wailu but it is also possible that the Menehune people insisted on being rewarded for their work with shrimps (*opae*).

Wizards are also said to have lived here and they had to decide upon human sacrifices, which were certainly the main sacrificial gifts in Iliiliopae Heiau.

To gain permission for a visit, the hotel on Molokai should be consulted. The staff will know the correct telephone number to ring.

★Kalaupapa H3

A good view of Kalaupapa Peninsula can be enjoyed from Kalaupapa Lookout, which lies at the northern end of Road 470. The naturally isolated position of this part of the island becomes immediately apparent from here. The history of the peninsula as a leper colony is described on information boards. The peninsula officially ceased to be a leper colony after 1969 and today it is a national park in which a few lepers still reside voluntarily. Modest tourism provides the colony with an income.

Kalaupapa Lookout

It takes effort and expense to visit Kalaupapa, which is separated from the rest of Molokai by 1970ft/600m-high steep cliffs, with only a single winding mule path, the Kalaupapa Trail, leading down to the peninsula. One way of visiting it is to undertake a 1–1½ hour walk (it begins near former mule stables; at one time some rather exhausting mule rides were offered, but high insurance premiums have made these uneconomic). It is much more comfortable to travel by light aircraft. Both Ait Molokai and Aloha Island Air fly to Kalaupapa each morning and evening (for details, tel. 553–3636 (Air Molokai) or 567–6113 (Aloha Island Air).

Excursions

Kalaupapa Peninsula

There are also relatively expensive flights from Honolulu (Reeves Air, tel. 553–3803). Hawaiian Air (tel. 553–5321, or from Oahu 537–5100) occasionally offers such flights. Polynesian Air flies regularly from Molokai Airport (tel. 567–6697) to Kalaupapa).

Visiting

To avoid disturbing the inhabitants of Kalaupapa visitors must reserve places in advance for a guided tour (tel. 567–6613 and 567–6320), and must be at least 16 years old.

Guided tours are offered by Father Damien Tours (tel. 567–6171; P.O. Box 1, Kalaupapa, IH 96757).

Those who travel to Kalaupapa by air can arrange to have places on a tour reserved by them through the airline concerned.

The tour visits two 19th c. churches, an historically important museum, memorials, parks, the former leper houses, cemeteries created on land where forests once stood, and the black lava coast.

Leper colony

The leper colony is, of course, not so much a tourist attraction as a memorial to cultural history and to superstition. From 1865, under King Kamahameha V, lepers and those whom the doctors of the time thought might fall prey to the disease were isolated from the rest of Hawaii. In this way it was hoped that the spread of the disease would be prevented. It is not known how leprosy reached the Hawaiian islands; possibly it came in with Chinese plantation workers. It first appeared in the 1830s and then spread rapidly, as the Hawaiians, with less immunity against infectious diseases, were extremely susceptible to it.

Only after 1946, when sulphanomide was used to stem the spread of the disease, and shortly after to remove the fear of infection, were new cases drastically reduced.

Today, about 100 patients still live in Kalaupapa, with the right to remain there for the rest of their lives. They are now allowed to move around freely and can leave the small colony at any time. However, there are no children here, as the law states that all new-born babies must leave for fear of infection and cannot return before they are 17 years of age.

To grasp the extent of leprosy in Hawaii, visit the cemetery – about 8000 victims are buried there.

Author's impression

One of the first tourists to visit Kalaupapa was the Scottish author Robert Louis Stevenson who wrote in 1889: "In the chronicles of mankind there exists, perhaps, no more melancholy place . . . (its inhabitants) are strangers assembled together due to illness, disfigured, deathly ill, banished."

Pater Damien

In the same year as Stevenson visited Kalaupapa, Joseph Damien de Veuster (see Famous People), a Catholic priest from Belgium, died. He was ordained in Honolulu and agreed to move to Kalaupapa in 1873 to become the greatest *kokua* (helper) of the unfortunate sufferers there who were cut off from the outside world. For years, he was the only one who stood by them. He built houses and churches, tended to their wounds and when food was scarce he climbed the mule path (built in 1886) to fetch supplies. Until then, Kalaupapa could only be reached by ship. For Damien, the lepers were God's children – he did not agree with those who felt that the disease was a punishment for some ill-defined sins. He certainly had no idea that Hansens Disease (as it was now called after the Norwegian doctor who pinpointed its cause) would also affect him. He died in 1889 after 16 years of work in Kalaupapa. A bronze statue was erected in his memory in Honolulu. His grave lies near St Philomena church at Kalawao, the first leper colony. His mortal remains have since been transferred to Belgium.

Leprosy

A law passed in 1865 decreed that those infected with leprosy had to be isolated on Kalaupapa and were thus forced to lead miserable lives. The way in which lepers (often together with their healthy families) were forcibly bundled off to Kalaupapa and were abandoned on the island as

The beach at Kaluakoi resort

outcasts is one of the darker sides of Hawaiian history. There were even henchmen who were rewarded with head money for every leper (including often people with harmless rashes) they seized.

Kaluakoi Resort   G 3

The best beaches and most luxurious hotels are located in the west of Molokai. Swim at Kepuhi and Papohaku beaches – although the constant west wind causes such high waves and the current is so strong that care must be taken at all times. This is particularly the case in the afternoons and when there are no lifeguards present.

The 10sq.miles/27sq.km resort originally belonged to the Molokai Ranch. A Sheraton Hotel built here has since been sold and is now called the Kaluakoi Hotel and Golf Club. It has its own 18-hole golf course, the only one on the island.

This resort is particularly suited to those who enjoy solitude and impressive scenery but who do not want to go completely without luxury and physical comfort.

Tours to Molokai Ranch Wildlife Park (see entry) begin here.

Kaunakakai   G 3

Its 1200 inhabitants make Kaunakakai the largest town on Molokai. Despite the well-known song "The Cock-eyed Mayor of Kaunakakai," the town has not yet got its own mayor. Kaunakakai is an example of ribbon development with one wide main thoroughfare, Ala Malama Street, forming its centre and only single-storey houses built either side.

Harbour	Kaunakakai's harbour enjoyed particular importance as a centre of trade. The decline in pineapple growing lost it this importance and today it is only a small fishing port.

Nearby are located the remains of King Kamehameha I's summer residence. He was born on Molokai and lived here as Prince Lot before he succeeded to the throne. |
Airport	Molokai Airport is located not far from Kaunakakai in Hoolehua, an area of detached houses.
Waikolu Lookout	A road leads off from the right of Road 460 and passes behind Umipaa. Best tackled with a four-wheel drive vehicle (and then only in dry weather), it leads to Waikolu Lookout. The view down into the deep and inpenetrable Waikolu Valley is unique. Just before the lookout, a large hollow is passed.
Sandalwood Hole	This "Sandalwood Hole" was used to measure the right amount of wood with which to load ships. The hole was filled with sandalwood and its contents could then be transported on to ships. At the beginning of the 19th c. the fragrant sandalwood was a valuable export to China. Shameless deforestation quickly led to the decline of this trade and today sandalwood trees can only be found occasionally on the Hawaiian islands.

Kapuaiwa Grove (coconut grove)

This coconut grove is located on the lagoon, west of Kaunakakai (see entry). It is one of the largest palm groves in Hawaii and originally consisted of 1000 trees planted there by order of King Kamehameha V.

Signs are positioned on the edge of the grove warning of the danger of falling coconuts. Kapuaiwa roughly means "mysterious taboo."

On the opposite side of the road are six churches and a Bible school, built mainly of wood, where services are held on Sundays.

Royal Fish Ponds   G/H 3

Along Molokai's south coast, remains of fish ponds can occasionally be seen. At least 58 ponds, a particularly large number, are said to have been constructed here. Today, only a few remain along Road 450 near Pukoo. Many of the ponds became filled in with washed-up earth or destroyed by flood tides.

The walls of these fish ponds were built of lava stone and constructed in such a way that small fish could enter through a type of sluice gate (called a *makaha*). Once fully grown they could no longer pass through the opening in the wall and were easily caught.

The ponds were certainly built in the 15th c. and indicate how well fish farming had developed by then. Fishing was carried out by the "ordinary mortals" exclusively for the *ali'i* (the upper classes) and was a particularly popular upper-class sport in old Hawaii. Keawanui and Ualapue are two of the largest fish ponds and they have been placed under protection.

Maunaloa   G 3

This small village occupies an elevated position about 1 mile/1.5km from the western end of Road 460. The fate of this former plantation settlement is perhaps symbolic of Molokai's varied development. Founded in the 1920s by the Dole Company for its pineapple plantation workers, Maunaloa died 50 years later when pineapple growing was abandoned owing to field irrigation problems. For a decade it became a ghost town. Only then did a few artists settle here and they have brought the place to life again as a centre of craftwork. Although new buildings have been erected, some houses remain today as examples of Maunaloa's past as a typical planta- tion settlement.

Meyer Sugar Mill   G 3

This protected mill stands in the centre of Molokai at Kala'e.

Location
Road 470
Tel. 567–6436

Rudolf W. Meyer, previously a manager of the large Molokai Ranch, built a sugar refinery in 1878 and this has now been restored to its original form. It offers a good insight into the production of sugar, Hawaii's most important export. On view are the sugar cane presses, the copper vats, the vapor- isation pans and a steam machine, all of which are still in working condition.

Molokai Ranch Wildlife Park   G 3

Located near Kaluakoi Resort (see entry) this is an outdoor park, about 1½sq.miles/4sq.km in size, where mostly African animals from Tanzania and Kenya live. A one-and-a-half hour tour offers close-up views of the wildlife. The journey across the rough land is bumpy but extremely in- teresting. The park was stocked in 1978 with giraffes, zebra, Berber sheep, elk antelopes, cranes and different types of red deer. These have brought a piece of Africa to Hawaii for visitors to enjoy.

Game reserve
Tel. 552–2555

The guided tour departs from Kaluakoi Hotel and Golf Hotel and seats should be reserved here.

Antelopes in the Molokai Ranch Wildlife Park

Molokai Ranch

Molokai Ranch, to which the wildlife park belongs, is the largest private ranch on Molokai. Large areas of western Molokai are pastureland, used by the ranch for grazing cattle (its main commodity).

The Great Mahele of 1848, which governed the allocation of land, caused the founding of the Molokai Ranch and at that time it became the property of King Kamehameha V. Later it passed into the possession of the Bishop Trust. Charles Bishop (see Famous People), a banker, bought half the ranch and the other half was inherited by his wife, Bernice P. Bishop, a sister of Kamehameha V. Since then the ranch has changed ownership several times and belongs today to the Cooke family.

Phallic Rock – Kaule o Nanahoa   G 3

This unusual rock formation is located near the lookout (see Kalaupapa) at the end of Road 470. A signpost stands at the beginning of the path, only a few minutes' walk from Phallic Rock. According to Hawaiian legend, the history of the evolution of Phallic Rock is this. Nanahoa, god of manly fertility, who lived near the rock, stared at a beautiful young girl one day who was admiring her reflection in a pond. Nanahoa's wife, Kawahuna, came upon him and became so jealous that she started to pull the girl's hair. Nanahoa also got worked up and began to hit his wife. She tumbled down a hill and turned to stone. The same fate befell Nanahoa – he turned into stone shaped like a phallus and can be seen in this form today.

Over the years the stone became a symbol of fertility – childless women would spend a night praying at the stone to be cured of their infertility. Sometimes they would sit in one of the pools in front of the rock to catch rainwater in the hope that *mana*, the spirit of fertility, would come to them.

Phallic rock

St Joseph's Church

Palaau State Park

Road 460 ends at a car park, with camping and picnic facilities, at the edge of Palaau State Park. Particularly lovely tropical trees can be found here including ironbark, cypress and pine. A good view of this unique vegetation can be gained both along the path to Kalakaua Lookout and the path to Phallic Rock.

St Joseph's Church   H 3

The church is located in the village of Kamalo on Road 450, 10½ miles/17km east of Kaunakakai. It is one of the churches which Pater Damien (see Kalaupapa) had built during his 16 years on Molokai. St Joseph's Church dates from 1876 and was restored in 1971 although services are no longer held in it.

Kamalo

Nearby is Our Lady of Sorrows Church, about two years older than St Joseph's Church and the oldest Catholic church on Molokai. A life-size statue of Damien, sculpted by John Kadowaki (an inhabitant of Molokai), stands in front of the church.

Our Lady of Sorrows Church

Pilots Smith and Emory Bronte were forced to land here. In 1927 they attempted the first civil trans-Pacific flight, starting from California, and crash-landed here.

Smith and Emory Bronte

Wailau Trail   H 3

The trail begins near Iliiliopae Heiau (see entry) and is the only route that connects south and north Molokai. It leads into Wailau Valley, one of the three valleys beginning in the eastern part of the Pali Coast. The inhabitants of the valley left 200 years ago. The trail is strenuous, needs suitable clothing and footwear, and takes a whole day.

The walk passes first of all through the densely-overgrown land and then leads down into Wailua Valley, following Wailua River to the coast. This area is very isolated – only a few fishermen will be encountered along the river. To follow the Wailua Trail, which is in the care of the Sierra Club in San Francisco, special permission is needed and this can be obtained by telephone (Tel. 558–81 130).

As it is impossible to stay overnight on the northern side of Molokai, walkers must be picked up by boat. Glenn Davis (Tel. 558–8195), who lives in Halawa Valley, is responsible for this. He should be telephoned the day before the planned walk along Wailua Valley in order to arrange a collection time. It should be pointed out once again that this trail is very strenuous and suitable only for strong walkers.

Niihau Island

Area: 70sq.miles/181sq.km
County: Kauai
Population: 210
Main village: Puuwai

Island's special position

Niihau Island has belonged for more than 100 years to the Robinson family. Since then the island has been isolated from the rest of the world and is a prohibited area. The inhabitants of Niihau are at liberty to leave the island but still only certain people are allowed to visit (representatives of the health, tax and school authorities, occasionally a doctor and personal guests). Today the island's inhabitants regard their chosen isolation as the only means of leading a natural Hawaiian lifestyle.

Location and evolution

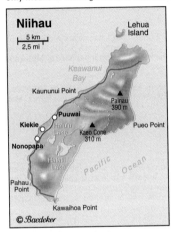

Niihau is the most westerly of the main eight Hawaiian islands. The 70sq.miles/ 181sq.km-large, 17 miles/ 28km-long and about 6 miles/ 10km-wide island is separated from Kauai only by the narrow, approximately 17 miles/ 28km-wide Kalakahi Channel.

Niihau is the oldest of the inhabited Hawaiian islands. The large volcano which originally formed the island was thought to have been between 14769ft/4500m and 19692ft/ 6000m high. Through millions of years progressive erosion has reduced it to its current size.

Geographical features

The mountainous part of the island occupies about one third of its surface. The highest point is Paniau at 1280ft/390m. The remaining surface is flat and relatively bare. Niihau is noted for its two freshwater lakes. Despite the low rainfall Halulu Lake is the largest lake in the Hawaiian islands. Although Halalii Lake is much larger it does not contain water the whole year.

Name

The meaning of the word *Niihau* is not known. The nickname "Forbidden Island" is clear – visitors are not welcome.

Climate and vegetation

Although Niihau is only 44 miles/70km as the crow flies from the rainiest place in the world, Waialeale, Niihau is one of the driest islands in the entire Pacific, with an annual rainfall measurement of only between 4¼in./110mm and 11in./280mm. The reason for the lack of rain is the location of the island. It lies exactly in the rainshadow of the much larger and higher island, Kauai.

Wide expanses of the island are covered by dry grassland – only the most hardy kiawe trees thrive here.

Population

Niihau still has 210 inhabitants. They are pure Hawaiians and lead their lives according to the customs and rituals of the old Hawaiians. Many young inhabitants leave the island, however, which causes the population to decline constantly. It is reported that, in addition to the Hawaiians, about ten Japanese and a German carpenter with a Hawaiian wife live on Niihau.

Daily life on Niihau

The traditional features of modern life are not to be found on Niihau. There is no restaurant, neither alcohol nor cigarettes and tobacco can be bought, policemen and a prison are not needed. There is an elementary school in Puuwai which, together with the main house, are the only two buildings supplied with electricity. There are no telephones, no radios or televisions and only a few cars. Until several years ago, carrier pigeons were the only means of communication with the outside world. The children, who are taught in English and Hawaiian, have to continue their education in Kauai, where the nearest high school is located. Then they only spend the holidays at home on Niihau.

One event, still talked about today, reluctantly brought Niihau into contact with the outside world. In the Second World War Niihau was the only place in the United States which experienced fighting. On Sunday, December 7th 1941, the day of the attack on Pearl Harbor, a Japanese pilot made an emergency landing on Niihau. Not owning a radio, the inhabitants naturally knew nothing of the events in Honolulu. As he regained consciousness, he began to threaten the panicking inhabitants with his machine gun. Two of the Japanese living on the island sided with him. Some inhabitants had already fled by boat to Kauai but when troops arrived from there, the situation was explained to the islanders. One of the them, Ben Kanahele, who had been injured by the Japanese pilot, got into such a rage that he threw him against a rock and killed him. One of the two other Japanese committed suicide with the pilot's gun. Since then the peace on Niihau has not been interrupted.

Contact with the outside world

Through cattle rearing the Robinson family are the main employers on the island. The inhabitants also carry out some bee keeping, fishing and turkey breeding. Particularly fine mats used to be woven but the sheep that have been brought to the island have eaten the sedge grass needed for this craft.

Farming

Particularly valuable are the shell necklaces (see Facts and Figures, Flower Garlands) produced on Niihau. From the multi-coloured shells (hardly bigger than pearls), which can only be found on Niihau Beach, *leis*, consisting of several strands, are made. According to the length of the necklace and the type of shells, up to 10,000 US dollars are paid for these *leis* – as much as the whole of Niihau cost 125 years ago!
    As soon as the tide recedes, the women look for shells on the beach. The *kahelelani* (way to heaven), as the small shells are called, appear in many colours. Red and pink ones are the most unusual. To produce a *lei* takes, according to its length, between 20 and 200 hours of work. They are on sale in many Hawaiian shops although supplies are limited.

Shell necklaces

In 1912, five *heiaus* were excavated on Niihau but little of the island's early history is known. As it has been closed off from the outside world since 1915, no further research has been carried out.
    In 1778, Captain Cook's ships berthed in Niihau and the sailors were received enthusiastically. According to a census of 1831, more than 1700 people lived on Niihau but the population quickly declined as, after several years of drought, many inhabitants moved to neighbouring Kauai. In 1884, King Kamehameha IV sold the island for 10,000 US dollars to Elizabeth Sinclair, the rich widow of a New Zealand cattle breeder. The descendants of one of her daughters, the Robinson family, who also own large areas of land on Kauai, continue to raise cattle and sheep here on the island.
    In 1959, Niihau's inhabitants distanced themselves from the rest of Hawaii. They were the only ones who spoke out as a majority against Hawaii becoming one of the United States of America.

History

Since 1987 it has been possible to fly over the island in a helicopter from Kauai. In addition to this, since 1989, the island can be visited for a short time although contact is not allowed to be made with the inhabitants. In any case, most of the islanders live for the most part on the side of the island (in Puuwai, Kiekie and Nonopapa) opposite the landing point used by visitors. Flights over the island and short visits can be arranged through Niihau Helicopters (Tel. 338–1234 or 335–3500).

Excursions

Oahu Island

Area: 607sq.miles/1574sq.km
County: Oahu. Population: 841,600
Main town: Honolulu

Location and
evolution

Oahu is the third largest island in the Hawaiian archipelago and for almost
150 years has been the political, economic and cultural centre of the
Hawaiian islands. Covering an area of 607sq.miles/1574sq.km, its coastline
measures 137 miles/220km. Oahu evolved from two volcanoes which still
exist today in the mountain ranges, Koolau Range and Waianae Range. The
older of the two, Waianae Range, evolved between about 3.4 and 2.7
million years ago. Strong erosion has had such an effect that the volcanic
craters can no longer be recognised clearly. Oahu is noted for its tuffs
which evolved during the last phase of the volcanic creation of the island
(Diamond Head, Punchbowl, Chinaman's Hat, Rabbit Island).

Geographical
features

The island is divided into four geographical areas – the Koolau Range,
Waianae Range, Schofield Plateau and the flat land around the coast.
Schofield Plateau is formed from lava from Koolau volcano, as is the flat
coastal land. The present mountain ranges and valleys are examples of an
eroded landscape. Particularly impressive is Nuuanu Pali, north of
Honolulu.

Name

The origin of the word Oahu is unclear – it is translated as "meeting place"
by linguists and this is supposed to refer to the meeting of Hawaiian kings
on Oahu. The somewhat down-to-earth nickname "Main Island" reflects the
higher position of Oahu among the Hawaiian islands.

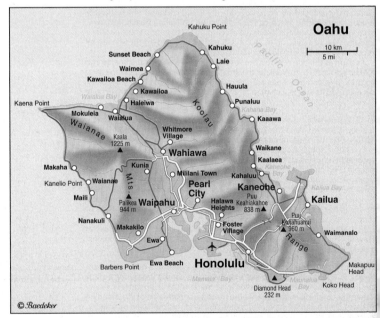

Oahu: flower garlands mark the end of a festival ▶

Climate and vegetation	Oahu's climate resembles that of the other islands. As its mountains are not particularly high, the climate on the side of the island (the west coast) standing in their rainshadow is not nearly so dry as on Hawaii, for example. The island is divided into a windy, damp area (the east coast) and a dry, leeward-facing area (the west coast).
Population	More than 800,000 people, four-fifths of the Hawaiian islands' total population, live on Oahu. The inhabitants of this most densely populated island vary widely. The majority of people live in Honolulu and its neighbouring towns with the rest of the island being thinly populated.
Honolulu capital city	Honolulu is the capital of both the State of Hawaii and the County of Oahu. Since the state reform of government in 1969, whereby the mayor of the principal county town is also the mayor of the whole county, Honolulu is no longer self-governing. The mayor of Oahu County is at the same time responsible for Honolulu so that the importance of the main city, in which more than half of the county's population lives, is not taken into account with regard to government.
Farming	Along with tourism, farming still has a regional importance for Oahu. The main crops are sugar cane and pineapples, which are grown mostly inland on the fertile ground of Schofield Plateau. Ewa District, to the south of the island, is the traditional area for growing sugar cane.
Military	Oahu is of particular importance as a strategic base because of its central position. Large sections of the island (about a quarter of its surface) are military no-go areas where public access is prohibited. The military contributes an important amount to Oahu's economy.
Tourism	Most tourists still arrive on Oahu at Honolulu Airport. About 80% of Hawaii's visitors stay on Oahu itself and spend their holiday almost exclusively on the world-famous beach at Waikiki. This has created an imbalance on the island because Waikiki (Honolulu's beach and tourist quarter) has become devoted solely to tourism and suffers the problems that such mass development can bring. Further development for tourism in the south-west of the island has brought opposition from the native population. As a result, places of interest for tourists are concentrated, for the most part, in and around Honolulu.
Structure of the island	Kailua and Kaneohe, dormitory towns of Honolulu, are located on Oahu's windward side. Further north is the Valley of the Temples (including Byodo-In Temple) as well as Waiahole (primarily a farming area), Punaluu (a large fishing village) and, above all, Laie, the location of the Polynesian Cultural Center and the large Mormon Temple. The northern tip of the island has become famous principally as a surfers' paradise – at the western end of the only road (suitable only for four-wheel drive vehicles) is Kaena Point, where powerful waves break on the shore. The north-west of the island is the least developed and still fairly closed off to tourists. There are almost no hotels and few restaurants here. Places such as Makaha, Waianae and Maili are inhabited purely by natives and surfers who find the best possible conditions for their sport here throughout the year.

Byodo-In Buddhist Temple   F 3

Location
Valley of the Temples
47–200 Kahekili Highway
Tel. 239–88 11

Of the 100 or more large and small Buddhist temples in Hawaii, Byodo-In Temple (Equality Temple) is without doubt the one most worth visiting. It is a copy of the famous temple bearing the same name in the Japanese town of Uji and was opened on June 7th 1968, the 100th anniversary of the arrival of the first Japanese workers in Hawaii. Even the heavy brass bell in front of the entrance is an exact reproduction. Its deep tone creates an atmosphere of peace and contemplation.

Byodo-In Buddhist Temple

As is customary, shoes must be removed before entering the temple. The wooden statue of Buddha inside (almost 10ft/3m tall and covered with gold and lacquer) was carved by the contemporary Japanese sculptor Naszo Inui and is the largest wooden statue of Buddha created in the past 900 years.

Enjoy a stroll around the temple's garden, complete with tea and meditation house, many plants, birds and a carp pond filled with thousands of fish (for Japanese people, the carp is a symbol of order and endurance).

Buses
8/55 (Kaneohe)

Chinaman's Hat   F 3

This conical rock, formed from volcanic tuff stone on Mokolii Island, is noted for its unique shape, which resembles a Chinese hat. A fine view of this rock, pointing out of the sea, can be gained from Kualoa County Regional Park, north of Kaneohe. It is only possible to cover the 1477ft/450m distance to the island by foot at low tide. Suitable shoes are needed because of the jagged coral.

Mokolii means "small dragon" – according to Hawaiian legend the rock is the creature's tail, while its body is beneath the water.

Location
Opposite Kualoa
County Regional
Park
Route 83

Buses
8/55

Haiku Gardens   F 3

These gardens are located on the edge of Kaneohe and have only been opened recently. The entrance leads past a restaurant.

The land was sold as a royal possession in the middle of the 19th c. to an Englishman called Baskerville. He created several water-lily ponds, planted flowers and various trees and had some houses built. Haiku Gardens offer such a picturesque setting that they are often used for weddings.

Location
46–316 Haiku Road
Kaneohe

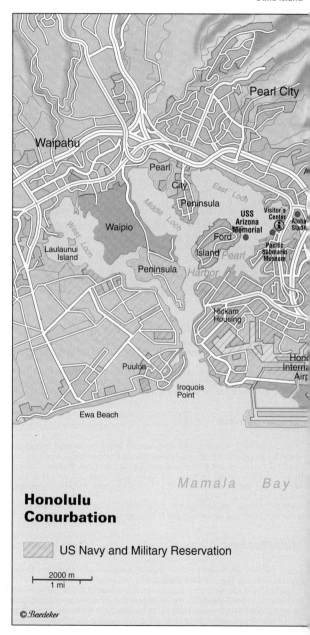

Pearl City

Waipahu

Pearl
City
Peninsula

East Loch

Middle Loch

USS
Arizona
Memorial

Visitor's
Center
ⓘ

Aloha
Stadium

West Loch

Waipio

Ford
Island

Pacific
Submarine
Museum

Laulaunui
Island

Peninsula

Pearl
Harbor

Hickam
Housing

Puuloa

Iroquois
Point

Honolulu
Interna...
Airp...

Ewa Beach

Mamala   Bay

Honolulu
Conurbation

US Navy and Military Reservation

2000 m
1 mi

© Baedeker

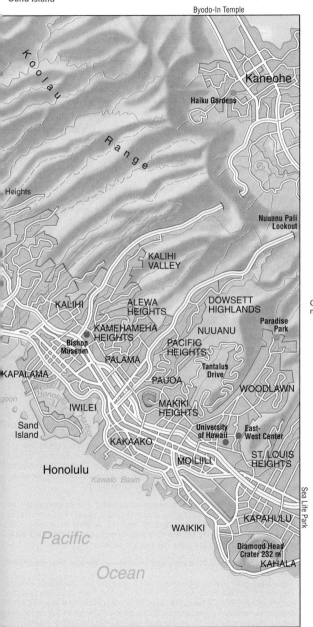

Byodo-In Temple

Koolau

Range

Kaneohe

Haiku Gardens

Heights

Nuuanu Pali
Lookout

KALIHI
VALLEY

KALIHI

ALEWA
HEIGHTS

DOWSETT
HIGHLANDS

General
map

KAMEHAMEHA
HEIGHTS

NUUANU

Paradise
Park

Bishop
Museum

PACIFIC
HEIGHTS

PALAMA

KAPALAMA

PAUOA

Tantalus
Drive

WOODLAWN

Honolulu Harbor

IWILEI

MAKIKI
HEIGHTS

Sand
Island

University
of Hawaii

East-
West Center

KAKAAKO

MOILILI

ST. LOUIS
HEIGHTS

Honolulu

Kewalo Basin

Sea Life Park

KAPAHULU

WAIKIKI

Pacific

Diamond Head
Crater 232 m

KAHALA

Ocean

As Haiku Valley is located near the Valley of the Temples, combine a visit to Haiku Gardens with one to Byodo-In Temple.

Hanauma Bay Beach Park

See Practical Information, Beaches

Honolulu   F 3

Advice

To help understand the layout of Honolulu the following general information is divided into the three neighbouring areas – Pearl Harbor, Downtown and Waikiki. Within these areas the places of interest are arranged alphabetically.

History

The name Honolulu means "protected bay". The city's development first began around the port of Honolulu, Hawaii's safest because of an offshore reef.

In 1792 the British seafarer William Brown was the first to land here and he named the port "Fair Haven", almost a synonym of "Honolulu". Unfortunately it was precisely in this "fair haven" that Brown met his death as a result of an attack orchestrated by King Kalanikupule of Oahu. After Kamehameha I conquered Oahu Honolulu began its rise to become the most important city in the Hawaiian islands. Kamehameha I used the port as a place of transfer and an important stop for Pacific steam ships. Kamehameha III finally declared Honolulu capital city of the Hawaiian Kingdom in 1850.

Pearl Harbor, today so important, was first developed in 1911. Its construction signalled a new phase in Oahu's development as a strategic military position.

Waikiki's tourist development only became possible at the end of the 19th c. when the Ala Wai Canal was built to drain this previously marshy area. From then on, Waikiki's growth into a focal point for tourism began, reaching its zenith in the 1970s.

Honolulu's modern development into a city of tourism was enhanced by the building of the airport, which is situated on a man-made platform in the lagoon between Pearl Harbor and the main part of Honolulu.

Topography

Honolulu today is an extensive, but narrow, city whose topography is determined by the sea and the mountains. Koolau Range, stretching about 31 miles/50km from the south-east to the north-west, is not particularly high but difficult of access. This has hindered the city from spreading out into the mountainous area. Development has been dictated by the cramped terrain and has caused satellite towns (Pearl City and, on the other side of the Koolau Mountains, Kanehoe) to grow up around Honolulu, relieving the city of some of its population pressures.

Highways
Downtown

The dense population necessitated a correspondingly well-developed road network. The most important arterial roads to the north are Pali and Likelike Highways, to the west motorways H1 and H2. A third motorway (H3), between Honolulu and Kaneohe to the east coast, has been approved in principle but construction work has not yet begun.

The Honolulu area

The city of Honolulu falls roughly into three areas – Waikiki, Downtown and Pearl Harbor.

Waikiki, the main attraction, is a peninsula covering almost ½sq.mile/1.1sq.km bordered to the south by the Pacific Ocean and the man-made Ala Wai Canal in the other three directions. In this small area, one of the most densely-populated in the whole of the United States, more hotels, restaurants and shops can be found than in the rest of Hawaii.

View of Honolulu from Kamehameha School

Downtown, the centre and historical part of Honolulu, is not so easily defined. It is bordered to the south by the sea, to the east by Ward Avenue, to the north by Vineyard Boulevard and to the west by College Walk Mall. Most of the places of interest mentioned from now on are to be found here.

In area Pearl Harbor occupies by far the largest part of the city, stretching for kilometres to the west. As well as naval bases, military bases and Honolulu Airport are located here.

Two valleys adjoin the north and the north-west of Downtown. Manoa Valley, which houses the University of Hawaii and the East-West Center, and Nuuanu Valley. Punchbowl Crater and the National Cemetery of the Pacific are to be found here.

Places of interest in Downtown

Aliiolani Hale (Palace of Justice)

Aliiolani Hale bears one of Kamehameha V's forenames which can be translated as "house of the ruler chosen by Heaven".

This magnificent building, more imposing than the Iolani Palace opposite (see entry), was built on the orders of King Kamehameha V as a palace but was only completed after his death and never put to its intended use. Instead, the Hawaiian parliament convened there. It was from here that the call for a Hawaiian republic came, sealing the downfall of the monarchy. Later, the building became the seat of Hawaii's highest court.

The building is located in the centre of historic Honolulu and is a good choice as a starting point for a tour through Downtown Honolulu, which can include a visit to the Mission Houses Museum (see entry), Kawalahao Church (see entry), Iolani Palace (see entry), Iolani Barracks (see entry),

Location
Corner of King Street
and Miliani Street

Bus
2

Town tour

161

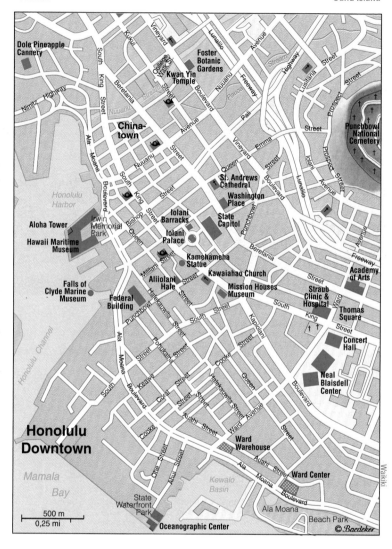

Honolulu Downtown

Washington Place House, the Queen Liliuokalani Memorial and the Hawaii State Capitol.

Statue of Kamehameha I

Standing in front of the Palace of Justice is a statue of Kamehameha I, the founder of the Hawaiian monarchy. Resembling more a figure symbolic of power and strength than a true likeness of the king, it is not the original statue but a second cast. The reason for this is a story in itself.

Downtown Honolulu

Statue of Kamehameha

At the request of King David Kalakaua, the parliament had made 10,000 US dollars available for the statue, which was to be created by the Boston sculptor Thomas R. Gould. A handsome Hawaiian, Robert Hoapili Baker, sat as the model dressed in a cape and helmet and striking the classic pose of a Roman commander. The bronze figure was cast in Paris and was supposed to be brought to Honolulu on board the three-master "G. F. Handel" of Bremen. However, passing the Falkland Islands, the ship ran into a storm, was wrecked and sank, complete with its crew and the statue of Kamehameha. The insurance company willingly paid up the sum of 12,000 US dollars and this was used to order a new statue. By this time, however, Gould had died. His son used the old cast but decorated it differently so that the new statue bore little resemblance to the original. This was placed in front of the Palace of Justice in 1883 and is now one of Honolulu's most photographed attractions. On Kamehameha Day (June 11th), a garland of flowers more than 16ft/5m long is draped around its neck and outstretched arms.

In the meantime, the original statue was recovered and taken to Stanley, capital of the Falkland Islands, where it stood unnoticed in front of a house. An American captain called Jervis discovered the statue accidentally, recognised Kamehameha, bought it for the sum of 500 US dollars and brought it to Honolulu. As the square in front of the Palace of Justice was already occupied by the copy, it was decided to erect the original near to Kamehameha's birthplace, Kapaau (see entry), on Hawaii's north coast. It stands there now, fairly unnoticed, in front of an unprepossessing office block belonging to the Kohala district of the island.

Aloha Tower

When built in 1921, this nine-storey tower was Honolulu's tallest building and it symbolised the city for decades. Even today a good view in all directions can be enjoyed from the top floor.

Location
Pier 9

Before the age of jet planes, large steamships with considerable numbers of visitors docked here. The visitors were greeted as friends by the natives and given flower garlands. Today all has become quiet around the protected tower – only the movement of freighters is overseen from here. The only passenger ships are the "Constitution" and the "Independence", which begin and end their relatively expensive, weekly round-trips to the other islands from piers 9 and 10.

The Aloha Tower Shopping Center, with numerous shops and restaurants, has now been built in the tower. There are also special shuttle services from here to Waikiki and back.

★★Bishop Museum

Location
1525 Bernice Street
Tel. 847–3511

Buses
2 (to Kapalama
Street)

The Bishop Museum (full name Bernice Pauahi Bishop Museum) is not only Hawaii's largest museum but also one of the four most important folklore museums in the United States of America. The other three are the Smithsonian Institution, the Museum of Natural History in New York and the Field Museum of Natural History in Chicago. The museum was founded by Charles Reed Bishop, Hawaii's first banker, in memory of his wife Bernice Pauahi Bishop, great-granddaughter of Kamehameha I and Hawaii's richest woman (see Famous People). Part of her fortune was used to found the Kamehameha School, situated above the museum.

The Bishop Museum held its centenary celebrations in December 1989 but this date actually commemorates the beginning of the building – the museum was only opened to the general public in 1892. It was extended two years later and not long after that the planetarium, the only one in Hawaii, was built.

Contents

The original contents came from the Bishop family's private collection, which included many unique artefacts. The collection has since been extended and consists today of 100,000 Hawaiian and South Pacific

**Plan of
Museum**

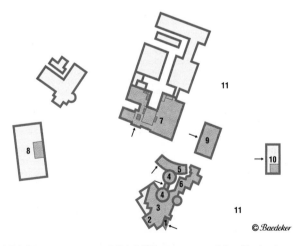

11

11

© Baedeker

1 Main Entrance	7 Main Exhibition	8 Hawaii Immigrant
2 "Pacifica" Shop	Hawaiian Hall	Heritage Preservation
3 Jabulka Pavilion	Hawaiian Vestibule	Centre
4 Planetarium	Hall of Hawaiian National	9 Atherton Halau
5 Hall of Discovery	History, Polynesian Hall	10 Members' Office
6 Lanai Restaurant	Kahili Room	11 Car Park

exhibits, a collection of twelve million insects, six million shells, 250,000 plants, 200,000 invertebrate marine creatures, 100,000 fish, 20,000 birds and 15,000 mammals.

Only a small number of these can be exhibited at any one time.

The somewhat unprepossessing outer building, through which the museum is entered, is a more recent extension. It leads on the right-hand side to the planetarium and on the left-hand side to a well-stocked museum shop where books, records (featuring Hawaiian music) and Hawaiian craftwork are sold.

Main entrance

Before entering the main building, visitors pass an impressive stone sculpture on the lawn, which originates from the Easter Islands.

The main building was designed by the well-known American architect, Henry H. Richardson.

Main building

The most impressive part of the Bishop Museum is, without doubt, the Hawaiian Hall. The Hall is so poorly lit that taking photographs without a flash – which is forbidden without permission – is useless. In the Hawaiian Hall, extensive material relating to Hawaii's history is exhibited. Hanging from the ceiling of this tall room, framed with galleries, is the first exhibit – a 49ft/15m-long sperm whale – which weighed 20 tons when alive.

On the ground floor are the Hawaiian crown jewels, the throne and other furnishings from Iolani Palace (see entry), an early Hawaiian house; carved wooden idols from pre-1819; particularly fine examples of the materials made from tree bark (*tapas*), produced exclusively in the Pacific region by Hawaiians; cloaks made from feathers, as well as photographs illustrating Hawaiian life. Also on the ground floor is an extensive collection of containers carved from the very hard wood of the koa tree. On the first floor there are Hawaiian exhibits dating from the 19th c. and on the second floor exhibits illustrating the cultures of those who immigrated to Hawaii (Japanese, Chinese, Filipinos, Samoans and Portuguese).

Hawaiian Hall

Another important exhibition hall is the Hall of Hawaiian Natural History in which more can be learned about the evolution of Hawaii's volcanoes, the development of plant life on the islands and the effects of human settlement on the land.

In the Polynesian Hall visitors can discover more about the lives of the South Pacific people, their social system, their religion and their daily life. Masks, ceremonial clothes, weapons, musical instruments and pictures of the Polynesian Islands, from Micronesia to Melanesia, complete the portrayal of past times on the island world of the South Pacific.

Kahili Room and Hawaiian Vestibule are galleries in which special exhibitions are mounted, almost always of unusual objects. In Atherton Halau (Hula School) hula dancing can be seen daily at 1pm, performed mainly by children taught at one of the many hula schools.

In the library 90,000 books about the history of Hawaii and the people of the South Pacific are available. The film section shows the history of Hawaii and the people of the South Pacific by means of old photographs and films. Showings at the planetarium in the afternoons and evenings. In clear weather, it is possible to view the starry Hawaiian night sky through a telescope at the evening showing.

Further exhibition halls

Chinatown

Chinatown is the exotic quarter of Honolulu but smaller than the equivalent quarters in San Francisco or New York. Its origins can be traced back to the Chinese contract workers who came to Hawaii in the 1860s and it has been able to protect its Far Eastern appeal until now.

Many Chinese landworkers soon began to give up their work on the sugar plantations in order to open shops and restaurants in Honolulu for

Location
Downtown
Honolulu
between Nuuanu,
N. Beretania and
S. King Street

Chinatown: Wo Fat Chinese restaurant

Bus
19

their countrymen. Two fires in 1886 and 1900 made new building necessary. The last fire was the result of arson. It grew out of control and destroyed large parts of Chinatown. It was hoped that by burning down certain areas of Chinatown, the increasingly widespread plague epidemics would be wiped out. Chinatown enjoyed its greatest expansion and importance in the 1930s. Today it should be called "Asiatown" since, in addition to the Chinese, there are also Vietnamese, Filipinos, Thais and Koreans living here.

Chinatown is currently classed as one of the areas of the city in need of renovation. This would lead to future revaluations of the area's properties. Of greatest interest to tourists are the many shops selling all manner of oriental foodstuffs in Hotel and Smith Street as well as the *lei* shops located on the edge of Chinatown in Mauna Kea Street. Here, the finest flower garlands can be bought considerably more cheaply than in other parts of the city (particularly Waikiki).

Guided tour

No difficulties are foreseen in exploring Chinatown alone during the day even if parts of Hotel Street are used for prostitution. The Chinese Chamber of Commerce, 42 North King Street (Tel. 533–3181), offers a two-three hour guided walk through the area every Tuesday, starting at 9.15am.

Wo Fat
(Tel. 533–6393)

The name of the Chinese restaurant Wo Fat, Hawaii's oldest restaurant still trading, can be translated as "harmony and welfare." In 1866, only a year after its opening, the original restaurant fell victim to the Chinatown fire. It reopened in two different houses until 1906 when it took up residence in its current position at the corner of Mauna Kea and Hotel Street. In 1938 the building was given its present Chinese appearance – as a pink pagoda. After the lifting of prohibition in 1933 Wo Fat was the first restaurant to apply for a drinks licence in Hawaii, receiving Licence No. 1.

Dole Pineapple Cannery

Even at a distance it is possible to recognise the building housing the largest pineapple cannery in the world by the Dole-Pineapple, a water tank shaped like a pineapple. Unfortunately there are no longer any tours of the factory. Instead there are showings of a film about the work of James Dole and pineapple production. Viewers can see how pineapples are peeled and husked as well as the modern machines which prepare almost 100 pieces of fruit a minute. There is also the opportunity to sample a variety of pineapple products.

Location
650 Iwilei Road
Tel. 531–8855

Buses
19 or Pineapple
Transit Bus (12)

The Dole Pineapple Pavilion is located outside Honolulu 2½ miles/4km from the town centre, on Highway 99 to Haleiwa, at Wahiawa and can be reached by taking Bus 52. It also provides information about pineapple growing, offers tours of pineapple fields and sells fresh pineapples cheaply.

Dole Pineapple
Pavilion

Below the Dole Pineapple Pavilion, where Roads 80 and 99 cross, the "competition" has been established. The very informative Del Monte Variety Garden is located here, planted with all the different types of pineapple trees available and offering commentaries on the history of the fruit and its importance to Hawaii.

Del Monte Variety
Garden

★Foster Botanic Gardens

The origins of the Botanic Gardens, now situated in the centre of Honolulu, can be traced back to 1855, when Queen Kalama sold a five acre/two-hectare piece of land to the German doctor William Hillebrand, who had also made a name for himself as a botanist. He planted a group of trees here, which are still in existence today. When Hillebrand returned to Germany in 1867 he sold the gardens to Thomas Foster and his wife who presented them to the city as a gift in 1930.

Location
180 N. Vineyard
Boulevard
Tel. 533–3406

Bus
4

Guided tours

As time has passed the gardens have quadrupled in size.

Particularly worth viewing are the trees planted by Hillebrand – an enormous kauri tree from Australia, a kapok tree from Indonesia and a baobab tree from Central Africa. There is also a fine example of a banyan tree, found frequently throughout Hawaii. The one planted here is of Chinese origin, other banyan trees originate from India and Malaysia.

The Botanic Gardens also have an extraordinary collection of orchids, ranging from the tiny pleurothallis to the giant grammatophyllum, which all grow wild here – in the earth, on rocks and trees. More useful plants such as coffee, cocoa and cinnamon bushes can be admired here, as well as vanilla, pepper and clove plants.

On the occasion of the centenary of the arrival of the first Japanese immigrants in Hawaii in 1868, the Botanic Gardens were presented with a 13th c. bronze statue of Buddha by the town of Kamakura.

Buddha statue

Hawaii Maritime Museum

The Hawaii Maritime Museum was first opened in the summer of 1989, evolving from the former Hawaii Maritime Center.

On entering the one-storey building, the visitor's attention is immediately drawn to the large outrigger under construction there. It is a copy of one of the boats used by the Polynesian people when they settled on Hawaii centuries ago.

Here in the museum, the world of the sea comes alive. Countless exhibits illustrate surfing, maritime weather, the sinking of ships, traditional local fishing techniques and the coastal changes of the Hawaiian islands. A boat in which children can play is located on the roof of the building.

The real attractions are to be found docked at the museum's pier – ships more than a century old, the four-master "Falls of Clyde" and the seaworthy outrigger "Hokule'a".

Location
Pier 7
Ala Moana
Boulevard
Tel. 523–6151

Bus
19

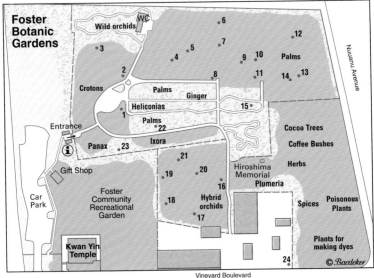

Foster Botanic Gardens

© Baedeker

Vineyard Boulevard

1 Bo Tree	9 Kapok Tree	17 Chauimoogra Tree
2 Pagoda Tree	10 Tropical Almond Tree	18 Yokewood Tree
3 Guana Tree	11 Ring Spruce	19 Hongkong Orchid Tree
4 Plum-nut Tree	12 Double Coconut Palm	20 Rainbow-shower Tree
5 False Fig Tree	13 Loulu Palm	21 Doum Palm
6 Kauri Tree	14 Wax Palm	22 Quipo Palm
7 Pod Tree	15 Cannonball Tree	23 Pandanus Tree
8 Travellers' Tree	16 Baobao Tree	24 Gupang Tree

"Falls of Clyde"   Built in Glasgow in 1878, this sailing ship, the only one of its kind still in existence, served the Matson Steam Ship Company from 1898 until 1920, first as a passenger ship and later as a freighter. After being laid-up the "Falls of Clyde" was taken in tow to Alaska and used as a floating fuel supplier for the fishing boats there. When the Hawaiians heard that the ship was going to be broken up, money was immediately collected to enable the four-master to be returned to Honolulu. The ship was restored and has been open to visitors since 1986.

"Hokule'a"   The "Hokule'a" (Star of Joy) is a realistic copy of a canoe used by the Polynesians to travel between islands. The vessel became well known through spectacular Pacific voyages undertaken in 1976 and 1980. These almost 6214 miles/10,000km-long return voyages between Honolulu and Tahiti were led by Mau Piailug, an inhabitant of the Caroline Islands. The crew relied on the same navigational aids as the islanders centuries before – the position of the stars and studying the waves.

Although modern materials such as plywood and glass-fibre have been used, the shape of the almost 66ft/20m-long vessel has been built based on old pictures and rock drawings. The voyages revealed how difficult it must have been for more than a dozen men to live on a canoe measuring less than 10ft/3m at its widest point.

Hawaii State Capitol

The Capitol Building of the youngest American state is architecturally unusual – modern, full of symbolism and open. The plan for the building was drawn up by the Californian firm of architects Carl Warnecke & Associates and cost 25 million US dollars. The official opening took place after Hawaii's ten-year affiliation to the United States of America as a separate state. The architecture of the building is said to express the element of water (the ocean) and Hawaii's volcanic evolution. The almost 66ft/20m-high fluted columns, which surround the building, are reminiscent of the royal palms found all over the islands. The open inner courtyard of the atrium is tiled with a blue mosaic floor coloured in sea tones. Combined with the ponds found in the grounds surrounding the outside of the building, they symbolise the ocean surrounding the islands. The volcanic rock which has been used and the open "crater-shaped" roof above the inner courtyard are evocative of the volcanic evolution of the Hawaiian islands.

The conference halls of the two chambers are visible from the inner courtyard through the windows. The lower house, the house of representatives, is decorated in blue and green while the upper house, the senate, makes use of the earth colours – red and brown.

Go up by lift to the fifth floor from where a fine view of Honolulu can be gained.

During the course of a one-hour guided tour, best booked in advance by telephone, the governor's study can be viewed.

Above the entrances to the two opposite sides of the building – the *mauka* side of the Capitol (facing the sea) and the *makei* side (facing the mountains) – hang enormous casts of the Hawaiian coats of arms, each weighing five tons.

On the *mauka* side stands a statue of the priest Joseph Damien (see Famous People), sculpted by the Venezuelan artist Marisol.

Location
Beretania Street
Richards Street
Tel. 548–7851

Guided tours

Bus
2

Hawaii State Capitol

A copy of it can be found next to the statue of King Kamehameha I in the Statuary Hall in the US Capitol in Washington, where each of the 50 states is represented by two famous figures.

Statue of Queen Liliuokalani

On the *makei* side stands a statue of the last Hawaiian monarch, Queen Liliuokalani, who spent the years after her abdication not far from here in Washington Place (see entry), today the residence of the governor.

★Honolulu Academy of Arts

Location
900 S. Beretania Street, opposite Thomas Square
Tel. 538–1006

Guided tours

Bus
2

The Honolulu Academy of Arts owes its existence (like the Bishop Museum) to a private individual, Mrs Charles M. Cooke, a family member of the "Big Five", the "sugar barons" of Hawaii. She not only financed the building of the Academy, but also donated her family's private collection to the museum to start it off.

The building, whose exterior appears somewhat sober, is built in a Spanish style, adapted to its Hawaiian setting, with an overhanging roof. The four small inner courtyards are grouped around a large central court-yard. The museum was originally opened in 1928 and is worth visiting for its varied collections and, above all, its exhibits of Hawaiian art.

Exhibits

In the 28 galleries on the ground floor permanent exhibits are on diplay while, on the small first floor, special exhibitions are mounted. It is interesting to note that the very extensive collection of oriental art is situated in the western part of the museum, with the occidental art located in the eastern part.

The European-American art, found on the right-hand side of the entrance, includes stone and bronze sculptures, as well as antique ceramics and work from the 20th c.

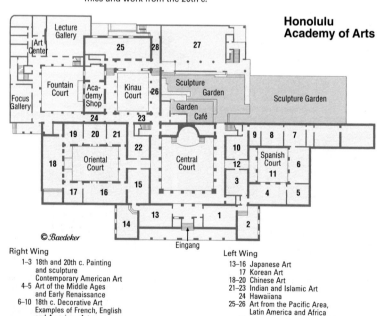

Honolulu Academy of Arts

© Baedeker

Eingang

Right Wing
1–3 18th and 20th c. Painting and sculpture Contemporary American Art
4–5 Art of the Middle Ages and Early Renaissance
6–10 18th c. Decorative Art Examples of French, English and American Art
11–12 Art in Antiquity

Left Wing
13–16 Japanese Art
17 Korean Art
18–20 Chinese Art
21–23 Indian and Islamic Art
24 Hawaiiana
25–26 Art from the Pacific Area, Latin America and Africa
27 Contemporary Hawaiian Art
28 Art of the American Indians

Galleries 1 to 3 are particularly worth visiting as they contain pictures and sculptures from the 19th and 20th c., including works by Delacroix, Whistler, Homer, Gauguin, van Gogh, Pissaro, Picasso and Rivera, to name but the most famous, as well as American artists up to and including the major producers of Pop Art.

Located to the left of the entrance is eastern art, offering a comprehensive view of the development of Japanese and Chinese art forms.

Hall 24 is of particular importance as exhibits of old Hawaiian culture are on view here – they complement well the collection in the Bishop Museum (see entry). Here, particularly well-preserved examples of the *tapa* textiles (produced from tree bark) can be seen. Their design is still copied today, although the secret of the materials' manufacture has been lost. Paintings and drawings from earlier times, feather cloaks and much more are also displayed here.

A sculpture garden, a gift shop (selling reproductions, original artwork, craftwork and literature) and a restaurant complete the museum complex.

★Iolani Palace

The only royal palace in the United States of America, little is known of its evolution. King David Kalakaua ordered its construction in 1879 and after three years it was completed together with its gardens – the banyan tree here was apparently planted by Queen Kapiolani. Costs ran to 350,000 US dollars, which the Hawaiians put down to the extravagant whims of their ruler. It was the first building in Honolulu to be supplied with electricity, and both the king's and the queen's rooms had direct telephone lines to the royal boathouse.

The palace, which only served its intended purpose for eleven years until the fall of the monarchy, has recently been fully renovated and now reflects, at least from the exterior, the splendour of the previous century.

Location
King Street
Richards Street
Tel. 523–1471
(Reservations)
538–1471
(Information)

Bus
2

Iolani Palace

Attention should be paid to the Corinthian columns as well as the windows imported from San Francisco, the fences and the entrance doors, on which the royal arms are resplendently mounted. Little remains of the original interior furnishings – some of them are to be found in the Bishop Museum (see entry), the rest have been lost. However, internal architectural features such as the woodwork of the ceilings and walls and the lighting have been restored to their original state. To the right of the entrance is the throne room, to the left the reception room and the large dining room used for state banquets. The royal bedrooms and the guestrooms are located on the upper floor.

Seat of Parliament	From 1895 until the completion of the Hawaii State Capitol (see entry) in 1969, this was the seat of the Hawaiian Parliament. Of the two chambers, the House of Representatives sat in the former throne room while the senate sat in the large dining room – this being of as little symbolic relevance as the fact that the governor carried out his duties in the former royal bedroom.
Coronation Stand	In front of the palace, King Kalakaua had the Coronation Stand erected. It has since been moved into the garden to the left of the main entrance. The king, following the example of Napoleon I, had himself and his queen crowned here – with crowns made specially for the occasion. On every Friday at noon, the Royal Hawaiian Band – which still bears this name – gives a free concert and this always proves very popular.
Iolani Barracks	Also located in the palace grounds are the Royal Barracks where the king's bodyguards lived. Originally built in 1871 close to the site of the present Hawaii State Capitol, the barracks only moved to their current position when the Capitol was built. The building resembles medieval battlements with embrasures, which appear somewhat odd in these surroundings.
Hawaii State Archives	To the right of Iolani Palace are the Hawaii State Archives, built in 1953 and containing an extensive collection of state documents, reports and many old photographs – a real treasure trove for all those interested in the history of Hawaii.
Library of Hawaii	Immediately next door is the Library of Hawaii with a lovely shady courtyard used by many of the government officials working nearby as a place to spend their lunch hour.
Honolulu Hale City Hall	Opposite the State Archives, on the other side of Punchbowl Street, is City Hall (Honolulu Hale). This dates from 1928 and was built in the early Renaissance style. It is used today for cultural events and exhibitions.

Kawaiahao Church

Location 957 Punchbowl Street Tel. 538–6267 **Bus** 2	No other church has played such a decisive part in the history of Hawaii as Kawaiahao Church, located between Aliiolani Hale (see entry) and Mission Houses Museum (see entry). It is certainly not Hawaii's oldest church but definitely the most historically significant. It was built between 1836 and 1842 from 140,000 blocks of coral taken from the coral reefs off the coast. The plans for the church were drawn up by the priest Hiram Bingham (see Famous People).
Spring	To the left of the entrance to the church is the spring from which the church got its name. It bubbles today just as it did in the days of the chief's wife Hao. The water from this spring was not allowed to be used by the *ali'i*, the upper classes of the country. This included the chief's wife Hao, to whom the church owes its name (Kawaiahao – Water of Hao).
Place of history	Originally several straw huts which stood here were used as a church by those first converted to Christianity by the missionaries. It was not until

Kawaiahao Church

1836 that the present church began to be built. On July 31st 1842, the "Great Stone Church" was officially opened. Between 3000 and 4000 believers stood in the grounds (many more than there was room for in the church), including King Kamehameha III. He announced on this occasion what was to become Hawaii's state motto – *Ua mau ka ea o ka aina* – meaning, roughly, "The life of the state will always be shaped by honesty".

The marriage of King Kamehameha IV and Queen Emma took place here. Hawaii's first elected king, Lunalilo, was sworn in here and is buried in the adjoining cemetery. As the first monarch not belonging to the Kamehameha clan, he did not want to be interred in the Royal Mausoleum (see entry) in Nuuanu Valley.

Inside the church the seats can still be seen where the members of the royal household sat. Four *kahili* (feather poles), symbolising the status of the kings, stand nearby. On the walls of the gallery hang portraits of the Hawaiian *ali'i*, 21 pictures in all, beginning with one of Kamehameha I.

Sunday services are held either at 8am or 10.30am in the Hawaiian language with Hawaiian hymns. Kawaiahao Church is the only church on Oahu (and one of the few on the Hawaiian islands) which continues this practice. — Services

Behind the church is the missionaries' churchyard where most of Oahu's missionaries and their families are buried. — Churchyard

Adjoining the missionaries' churchyard is the Adobe Schoolhouse, built seven years before the church in 1835 from adobe (hardened lime). The Oahu Charity School was first accommodated here, then a kindergarten, the Hawaiian Bible Society and the Kawaiahao Sunday School. Today, the 157-year-old building is used as a day nursery. — Adobe Schoolhouse

Kewalo Basin

Location
Ala Moana
Boulevard
Ward Avenue near
Fisherman's Wharf

Bus
19

Kewalo Basin, also known as Fisherman's Wharf, is a small picturesque port, where a number of excursion, sailing and motor boats are also moored.

It is possible to hire a boat here to go fishing out in the open sea. If doing this, do not dwell on the fact that in early Hawaiian times people who had been made outcasts and had been banished were drowned here. Fishing boats can be hired here with a captain and a crew for a whole day (7am–3.30pm) or for a half-day. Costs vary between 250 and 375 US dollars for a group of six people. Many companies charge per person at a price of about 75 US dollars for a full day. Bait, rods and other equipment are supplied.

What can be fished in the waters of Honolulu? Blue or striped marlin, the former being one of the biggest fish there is. In Honolulu, a story is often told of the heaviest of these fish ever to be caught which, when hauled aboard, weighed more than 1764lb/800kg – generally they weigh no more than between 309lb/140kg and 397lb/180kg. The best time to catch marlin is from the end of June to the end of September. There are also ahi and aku (both types of tuna fish, the latter recognisable by its yellow fins), and swordfish and sailfish (recognisable by the fins on its back) and, above all, mahimahi, still to be found on menus.

It is expected, incidentally, that fish caught on Sundays are left for the captain, together with a tip. Some of the charter companies, with whom trips should be booked a day ahead, are Coreene-C's Charter (Tel. 536–7472), Happy Time Charters (Tel. 329–9630), Island Charters (Tel. 536–1555) and Sportfishing Hawaii (Tel. 536–6577).

Boat trips can be taken from Kewalo Basin to Pearl Harbor (see entry).

★ Mission Houses Museum

Location
S. King Street near
Kawaiahao Church
Tel. 531–0481

Bus
2

Today the three houses dating from the beginning of the times of the missionaries, are protected as a national historic landmark and have been opened to the public as a museum. They are the oldest buildings standing which were created in a western style and comprise the Mission House (1821), the Chamberlain House (1831), built by Levi Chamberlain for himself and his family of eight when they came to Honolulu from Vermont in 1823, and the printing works (1841). It was here that books in the Hawaiian language, used by missionaries as a written language, were first printed.

Missionaries on
Oahu

On the one hand missionaries contributed to Hawaiian culture by creating an alphabet essential to the preservation of Hawaiian, hitherto purely a spoken language; on the other hand they helped erase Hawaiian culture by their spreading of Christianity. Kamehameha II, who in 1819 had participated in the destruction of the traditional *kapus*, viewed the missionaries with mistrust, curtailed their stay to one year and allocated them a barren place somewhere between Waikiki and present-day Downtown Honolulu in which to live. They could only construct a few grass huts there, which afforded them little shelter and the dry earth made farming on a large scale impossible.

Building of the
Mission Houses

Shortly before Christmas 1820 parts of a wooden house arrived on board a freighter from Boston. The missionaries could not erect it, however, as they needed permission from the king to stay where they were for more than a year. Just before the end of the year the king came to make an inspection. He visited a class belonging to the school held in one of the grass huts, ate a sumptuous meal, allowed himself to be persuaded by the missionaries ideas – their desire to fight alcoholism, gambling, incest and other "shameful" practices – and granted them permission to stay for longer.

As a result of this, work began immediately on the first house, which can now be visited. Of course, few of the original furnishings have survived

Mission Houses Museum

Steps leading to the National Memorial Cemetery of the Pacific

although two large desks from the 1830s (sent to Honolulu from Boston) and a rocking chair (designed by the missionaries' leader, Father Hiram Bingham – see Famous People – for the king and his queen, Kaahumanu), still exist. Two hurricane lamps from New England, almost 250 years old, can also be seen.

The printing press, now located in the printing house, is certainly not the original. It is certain, however, that it is a true copy of the original press, on which the first Hawaiian words were printed.

A second printing press from that time is to be found at Lahaina (Maui), on the campus of Lahainaluna Seminary.

Visits

Tours of the houses take place daily during opening times.

On Saturdays, a programme entitled "Honolulu 1831" is presented on the lawn, during which visitors have the opportunity to meet Hawaiians. A Mission Houses Fancy Fair takes place annually, though at different times of the year, selling mainly craftwork made by native artists.

Neal Blaisdell Center

Location
Kapiolani Avenue
Ward Street

Bus
2

This relatively modern building, the interior and exterior of which are not particularly attractive, was originally called Honolulu International Center. It now bears the name of a long-standing (1955–69) mayor of Honolulu. The building comprises a multi-purpose hall offering a variety of entertainments – such as a circus, a boxing match or a rock concert.

In the concert hall that forms part of the complex both the Honolulu Symphony Orchestra and the Hawaii Opera Theatre perform.

★Nuuanu Pali Lookout

Location
Koolau Mountains
above Honolulu on
the Pali Highway
(No. 61)

Buses
None

The finest vantage point on Oahu is undoubtedly the Nuuanu Pali Lookout (*nuuanu* means cool hills, *pali* means cliffs). This is one of the few vantage points which cannnot be reached by local buses. By car, the journey takes about fifteen minutes from Waikiki, following Pali Highway to the Pali Lookout exit.

Already popular in the 19th c. with visitors, the lookout is reached by following a road originally built for carriages. Built in 1898 by 200 very poorly-paid workers, it is said to have cost a mere 37,500 US dollars!

Arriving at Nuuanu Lookout, visitors find themselves at the top of an approximately 985ft/300m cliff, from which an uninterrupted view of the Kaneohe Plain and the mountains can be enjoyed. However, even if there is fine weather in Honolulu, Pali Lookout can be in cloud or experiencing rain. These periods of bad weather do not usually last long, so it is worth while being patient. The constant strong winds here cause a considerable drop in temperature from that in Honolulu. It is strongly advisable to take a jacket on this outing. The view, however, more than makes up for all the rigours of the weather.

Scene of battle

Nuuanu Pali played an important part in Hawaii's history, although the historical details are disputed. In 1795, as part of his campaign to unite the islands, Kamehameha I had pushed the King of Oahu's troops back to the cliffs – there was no way out. According to one account, Oahu's defenders were massacred. According to another, most of them threw themselves off the cliffs in order not to fall into the hands of Kamehameha's troops. This action was similar to the time 1600 years earlier when the Jews in Massada threw themselves off the West Bank of the Dead Sea to escape imprisonment by the Romans. Even the number of dead is disputed, varying between four hundred and several thousand. In later years, remains of the fallen were found in the area at the foot of the cliffs.

Nuuanu Valley

By taking a small detour through the densely-forested Nuuanu Valley, there is a chance to visit a series of other places of interest – Queen Emma's

Summer Palace (see entry), the Punchbowl National Cemetery (see entry) and the Royal Mausoleum (see entry).

Its beautiful scenery and its pleasant and cool climate combine to make Nuuanu Valley a popular place to live. Honolulu's finest villas are to be found here.

Punchbowl National Cemetery

Punchbowl Crater is one of the tuffs created during the last phase of eruptions on Oahu. Located above Honolulu, the 46-hectare cemetery is called *Puowaina* (Hill of Sacrifices) by Hawaiians because human sacrifices were brought here for the Hawaiian gods. During the time of the Hawaiian monarchy, Punchbowl was a fortress and it was then used as an observation post for Honolulu harbour during the Second World War. After the war, Hawaii's territorial government offered the land to the United States for use as a military cemetery and this was inaugurated in 1949.

Location
2177 Puowaina Drive
foothills of the Koolau Mountains

In 1966, a memorial building, reached by a long flight of steps, was opened to the public. It incorporates a chapel, the Court of the Missing and a series of wall mosaics portraying the course of the decisive Pacific battles during both the Second World War and the Korean War. The area for gravestones, many of them decorated with flowers, extends on both sides of the flight of steps.

Buses
2 (as far as Beretania and Alapai Street, then in the direction of Pacific Heights as far as Puowaina and Hookui Street, then fifteen minutes on foot)

In the National Cemetery of the Pacific the remains of nearly 30,000 American soldiers are buried, including 22 honoured with the highest war decoration – the Congress Medal. Often visited is the grave of war correspondent Ernie Pyle, whose reports on the theatre of war brought him posthumous fame.

The names of 22,000 victims missing in war are engraved on a marble wall in the Court of the Missing.

A good view can be enjoyed from the cemetery – over Waikiki and Diamond Head from one side and of Pearl Harbor from the other.

View

Queen Emma's Summer Palace

Standing in front of this simple white-painted house, built in a typically 19th c. New England style, it is hard to believe that it is a palace. Queen Emma named the building after a Hawaiian demi-god called *hanai-a-ka-malama*, which roughly means "adopted child of the light" or possibly also "of the moon".

Location
913 Pali Highway
Tel. 595–3167

Bus
4

Queen Emma (see Famous People), the adopted daughter of a British doctor in Honolulu, did not have the house built. It was constructed in 1847 by the businessman and later sugar plantation owner Henry Augustus Peirce and sold a few years later to John Young II, the son of a British confidante of King Kamehameha I and uncle of the later queen. After his death, Emma inherited the house in 1857, a year after her marriage to King Kamehameha IV.

She furnished it as a summer palace where the royal couple could enjoy the coolness of the valley and maintain a court.

The single-storey house has two bedrooms (Emma had its only guest-room built at the back of the house in order to accommodate Prince Alfred, one of Queen Victoria's sons, who ultimately did not come to Hawaii). Emma and her husband often visited European courts and spent a long time in England. They were strongly influenced by the English lifestyle. They introduced, for example, the Anglican high church to Hawaii and had St Andrew's Cathedral (see entry) built.

After Emma's death the house threatened to fall into decay until it was finally saved by the Daughters of Hawaii, a women's society. This organisation has run it as a museum since 1915.

177

Queen Emma's summer palace

Furnishings

The English influence becomes obvious in the palace furnishings, particularly the Victorian style. In the entrance stand *kahili* (feather poles), which are supposed to symbolise the owner's high rank and *lauhala* mats, woven in a way no longer used in Hawaii. Portraits of the Hawaiian kings and queens hang on the walls and there are many Hawaiian artefacts on show.

The canoe-shaped koa-wood cradle, built for Prince Albert (the royal couple's only son) is of historical interest. He was, incidentally, the godson of Queen Victoria but died when he was only four. In the same room are exhibited a shirt, a pair of trousers and shoes that belonged to the young prince as well as a lock of his hair.

Enjoy a stroll around the garden, well stocked with many Hawaiian flowers and plants.

Guided tours generally take place at 2pm.

Royal Mausoleum

Location
2661 Nuuanu Ave
Nuuanu Valley
Tel. 536–7602

Bus
4

Were this neo-Gothic building not surrounded by palms, ginger, plumeria and other Hawaiian plants and flowers, it could be taken to be in England. Built in 1865 during the reign of Kamehameha V, the mausoleum contains the remains of six of the eight kings who ruled Hawaii in the 19th c., as well as those of many of their families. Kamehameha I is not interred here – his body was buried, according to Hawaiian custom, in an unknown part of the Island of Hawaii. To provoke the Kamehameha family, to whom he did not belong, Lunalilo, Hawaii's first elected king, chose his own burial plot in the grounds of Kawaiahao Church (see entry).

Chinese Buddhist Temple

Around the corner from the mausoleum stands a Chinese Buddhist Temple (42 Kawanana Place), which is particularly richly decorated with gold lacquer.

St Andrew's Cathedral

The idea to build this originally Anglican cathedral dates back to the time when King Kamehameha IV and his wife visited London. An Anglican priest arrived on Hawaii soon after their return and received the queen into the Anglican Church (this religious denomination had not previously existed on Hawaii). Meanwhile her husband introduced the Book of Common Prayer. It was his brother Kamehameha V, however, who laid the foundation stone for the cathedral in 1867. Construction took longer than a decade and the cathedral was not officially opened until 1902.

A few years later, when the United States of America asserted their influence on Hawaii, St Andrew's was changed from an Anglican into an Episcopalian cathedral. This is the American form of the Anglican high church and has few members in Hawaii today.

Some of the building materials for this neo-Gothic cathedral came from England, although it is supposed to resemble more the Gothic cathedrals of northern France rather than those on the other side of the English Channel. About 30 years ago the cathedral was given an inappropriate new portal whose modern style does not suit the rest of the building.

Not far away, at the end of Fort Street Mall, stands one of Hawaii's few Catholic churches. The Cathedral of Our Lady of Peace was built from blocks of coral in 1843.

Location
Queen Emma
Beretania Street

Bus
2

Cathedral of Our
Lady of Peace

Tantalus Drive

This is one of the most worthwhile car journeys that can be made in the city of Honolulu and can be interrupted at regular intervals for walks. Tantalus Drive begins immediately behind Punchbowl National Cemetery (see entry) and leads first of all through the elegant suburb of Makuku Heights. It then begins the very winding climb to the top of Tantalus Mountain (about 2133ft/650m). Thanks to heavy rainfall the summit is covered by dense rain forest including ginger, eucalyptus and bamboo trees.

Of course the whole route can be covered on foot by following the paths marked along Round Top Drive, passing banana and guava trees.

At some points along the route a fine view can be had of Honolulu and its many surrounding valleys, particularly the 1149ft/350m-high Puu Ualakaa Hill ("hill of the rolling sweet potatoes", which Kamehameha I had planted here). The summit is reached via the park bearing the same name.

Location
Northern Honolulu

Ward Center and Warehouse

This shopping centre, located near to Ala Moana Shopping Center and divided into two linked complexes, has about 75 shops and restaurants.

The Warehouse is the older of the two buildings and has been built to look as though it dates from an earlier time by the use of wooden beams and joists instead of steel.

The shops have enjoyed increasing popularity as they sell mainly goods of very high quality. Those seeking souvenirs will find an extensive selection here. No fewer than ten shops sell art and craftwork. In both buildings there is a bookshop and in the Ward Center there are several shops selling men's and women's fashions.

The shopping centre is calmer than Ala Moana Shopping Center and the shops are both smaller and more specialised.

Location
1050 Ala Moana
Boulevard
Tel 531–6411

Bus
19

Washington Place

Washington Place, located in the administrative quarter on Beretania Street, is neither a square nor (as is common in America) a street, but a building. It was the home of the sea captain John Dominis and his son John

Location
Beretania Street

Bus 2	Owen Dominis (see Famous People). Dominis was governor of Oahu for many years and in 1862 married the sister of the later king, Lydia Kamakaehe, whom David Kalakaua chose as his successor. Shortly after her accession to the throne in 1891, her husband died. Queen Liliuokalani, as she named herself, had been deposed by 1893 with the end of the monarchy. After her abdication and up until her death in 1919 she lived at Washington Place. Today the building is the official residence of the governor of Hawaii.
War Memorial	Very close by is a memorial dedicated to the Hawaiian victims of the Second World War. It is a metal sculpture, incorporating copper, with an eternal flame.

★★Waikiki

Dream resort	Waikiki enjoys endless associations as the world's most famous ideal beach resort – blessed with South Sea magic – as a world of opposites, as Miami with a hint of Japan, as pure pleasure. It is difficult to characterise this small, flat area of Honolulu where more than 80% of visitors to Hawaii spend their holidays.
Location	Waikiki ("bubbling water") is the 2 mile/3.2km-long and about 2626ft/800m-wide heart of Honolulu, if not of the whole of the Hawaiian islands. It is bordered to the west by Ala Moana Park, to the north by Ala Wai Canal and to the east by Diamond Head. Gathered in this small area is the largest choice of hotels. They are to be found either on the beach, on Kalakaua Avenue (which runs parallel to the beach), with views over the sea, only a stone's throw away in Kuhio Avenue (parallel to Kalakaua Avenue) or in the side streets. Accommodation consists mainly of tower blocks which have been developed rapidly over the last 30 years.
Former marshland	What is today known as Waikiki was originally marshland and was only completely eradicated at the beginning of the 1920s with the completion of the Ala Wai Canal. The beach, however, was certainly a favourite bathing place for Hawaiians long before Hawaii was declared a kingdom at the beginning of the 19th c. – even if it took making Honolulu into the capital city in order to develop the beach. The kings who succeeded Kamehameha I had bathing houses built on Waikiki Beach and received foreign guests here.
Tourist development	Only after 1898 when the territory of Hawaii became part of the United States of America, was the first hotel built on the beach. The oldest hotel, the totally-white Moana Hotel (1901), now belongs to the Sheraton chain and has hotel skyscrapers on either side. Only at the end of the 1920s was a second hotel built, the pink-painted Royal Hawaiian, recently renovated but overshadowed by a hotel tower block, and the Royal Hawaiian Shopping Center (see entry). These two quite small hotels were sufficient for those visitors arriving by ocean liner, including the super-rich from the east coast and stars from Hollywood. The great turning point came in the 1960s when Hawaii became accessible from the mainland in only a few hours thanks to the age of the jet plane.
Beginnings of mass tourism	Countless hotels were built in rapid succession, each one bigger than the last. The "Manhattanisation" of Waikiki made quick progress. Mass tourism altered the face of Waikiki and some of the sparkle and attraction, which had made the resort so famous, was lost. Only in the last few years have hoteliers – about one quarter of the hotels are owned by Japanese – concerned themselves with the tradition of

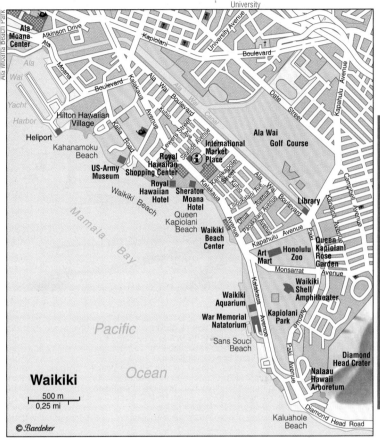

Waikiki and invested millions of US dollars in the restoration and renovation of existing hotels (work which is still being carried out) as well as building new hotels. Elegant shops opened their doors on Kalakaua Avenue and found themselves surrounded by cheap souvenir shops – a mixture still typical of Waikiki today. Waikiki is, however, not just a beach. It is also a city whose large number of tourists make it one of the world's most densely populated.

Waikiki has not simply one beach but a series of beaches, almost all ideal for swimming and all types of watersports. The beaches begin in the west with Kahanamoku Beach (named after the famous Olympic swimmer – see Famous People), immediately in front of the Hilton Hawaiian Village, and extend to Sans Souci Beach at Diamond Head in the east. As they so smoothly overlap one another, tourists find them indistinguishable. Kahanamoku Beach is separated from Gray's Beach (originally called Kawekewehe Beach, meaning "opening" as a narrow channel is located here, now called Gray's Channel). This is followed by the Royal Hawaiian Beach (from

Beach life

181

On the beach of Waikiki

the hotel of the same name to the Moana Hotel) – without doubt the most famous and crowded part of Waikiki. Next comes Kuhio Beach Park (the western part has a stone wall – Kapahulu Wall – built in front of it and is the only part of the beach unsuitable for swimming), followed by Kapiolani Beach Park and Sans Souci Beach.

Further beaches, located outside the true Waikiki, comprise the small Kaluahole Beach, Diamond Head Beach Park, Kuilei Cliffs Beach Park (made somewhat dangerous because of high waves), Kaalawai, Kahala Beach (where the Kahala Hilton Hotel is located) and Wailupe Beach Park on the western side of the artificial peninsula of the same name. For further information about Oahu's beaches see Practical Information section, Beaches.

Places of interest in Waikiki

Ala Moana Shopping Center

Location
Ala Moana
Boulevard

Bus
8

Hawaii's oldest and largest shopping centre lies between Ala Moana Boulevard, Pikoi Street, Kapiolani Boulevard and Atkinson Boulevard. It is only five minutes by bus from Waikiki and can easily be reached from there on foot. More than 100 shops, several department stores, many restaurants, two banks and a post office (the only one in Honolulu which stays open on Saturdays until 4.30pm) are to be found under one roof. There is hardly anything that cannot be bought here, making it an essential place to visit. No fewer than four department stores are in this shopping centre – Sears, Liberty House, Penney's and Shirokaya (a Japanese concern only selling Japanese goods). There is also an enormous Woolworths, the Honolulu Book Shop (the largest in the state with an unbeatable range of literature about Hawaii) and Long's Drugs – almost a small department store in itself (and the cheapest supplier of photographic equipment, particularly films, which are less expensive in Hawaii than on the mainland). In the Makai Market Food Court on the ground floor there are food shops and about a dozen snack bars.

The expensive fittings in the shops – such as marble floors – have caused the shopping centre to gain the reputation during recent years as a "shopping temple". Rich customers, often Japanese tourists with filled shopping bags, are everywhere to be seen here.

There is no problem parking in the huge car park. Be sure to buy a plan of the shopping centre in order to avoid unnecessary walking.

Very close by is the Ala Moana Beach Park (Ala Moana means "road by the water"). The beach park is not as busy as the beaches in Waikiki and tourists can enjoy sharing the beach with local families.

Ala Moana Beach Park

★Diamond Head

This approximately 812ft/225m-high extinct volcano at the eastern end of Waikiki is the symbol of Honolulu and, at the same time, one of the finest lookouts from which the beach and the city can be viewed from close at hand.

Mark Twain, who visited Hawaii more than 100 years ago and was known as someone who exaggerated at times, said that Diamond Head was one of the most impressive works of nature that he had ever seen.

The Hawaiians had called the extinct volcano *Leahi*, which could mean "place of fire". It gained its current name when sailors, on an expedition led by British seafarer George Vancouver, landed here and thought they had found diamonds on its slopes. Unfortunately, they were disappointed – the supposed diamonds were worthless pieces of limestone. Named "Pele's Tears", (Pele was the goddess of fire), they have in the meantime been taken as souvenirs by visitors.

Location
To the east of Waikiki

Bus
Beach bus, then ¾ mile/1.1km on foot

Diamond Head: the landmark of Waikiki

Hawaiian temple

On the western slopes, approximately where the Hawaiian School for Girls is now located, there used to be a *heiau* – a Hawaiian temple – in the days of King Kamehameha I. The king had human sacrifices brought here to appease Ku, the insatiable god of war.

Climbing the crater

It is interesting to climb Diamond Head, not only for a close-up view of the crater of the extinct volcano but also to gain a fine view from the edge of the crater.

The path to the summit poses no great difficulties. As two tunnels have to be negotiated it is advisable to take a torch. At the beginning of the path warnings are given about its length and its potential hazards – apart from the tunnels, 99 steps have to be climbed and, just before the top, a short ladder has to be negotiated. Despite these hurdles the visitor is rewarded with a fine view at the top.

Climbers will pass gun emplacements from the Second World War. These are relics of the time when Diamond Head was a high-security American military base.

★East-West Center

Location
1777 East-West Road
University of Hawaii Campus
Tel. 944–7111

Bus
4

The East-West Center, located on the campus of the University of Hawaii (see entry), was set up in 1960 by the American Congress with the aim of promoting better relations and understanding between the people of Asia and of the Pacific and of the United States of America through common education and research. The centre initially concerned itself with cultural exchanges but over the years has turned to more practical issues such as technology, economy and population problems. Since 1961 more than 30,000 men and women, two-thirds of them from Asian countries and the Pacific, have taken part in courses run by the East-West Center. Every year more than 200 research grants are awarded. In addition, 400 students who

Wall painting by Affandi

study at the University of Hawaii for their degree or thesis, take part in projects and events organised by the centre. Its work is financed by the United States of America, Asian countries, endowments and donations.

Belonging to the East-West Center is the Imin Conference Center, with rooms for between ten and 300 people. It was designed by the famous architect I. M. Pei. In the stairwells can be seen the well-known wall paintings by two artists – the Hawaiian Jean Charot and the Indonesian Affandi – which they created during their time at the East-West Center. In Charlot's work hands surround flames – a symbol of human endeavour and creativity. Affandi's fresco portrays the wisdom of the orient – in the palm of God's hand are three wise Asians, Ghandi, a Buddhist monk and the Indonesian legendary figure Semar.

Imin Conference
Center

In the John A. Burns Hall (named after the second Governor of the State of Hawaii) the centre's art collection is on display. It consists mainly of gifts from the Asian and Hawaiian artists who have worked in the centre.

John A. Burns
Hall

A Japanese garden with a tea house, a Thai pavilion made of teak (a present from King Bhumipol Adulyadej) and a grove of plumerias are worth visiting.

Japanese garden

Honolulu Zoo

Even if Honolulu Zoo is not one of America's most famous, it is nevertheless worth visiting. For those visitors interested in Hawaiian fauna, specimens of Hawaii's rare birds and those threatened with extinction are a particular attraction.
    It is also possible to see the *nene* (the Hawaiian goose), Hawaii's national bird, which is difficult to find in the wild.
    A peculiarity is the hairy bat, one of two types of mammal found in Hawaii when the first settlers arrived almost 1500 years ago. The monk seal, another example of an endemic mammal, can also be found in the zoo. For the Hawaiians, three snakes merit particular attention – they are the only snakes to be found on the Hawaiian islands.
    There are also the usual zoo inhabitants – elephants, giraffes, monkeys, lions, tigers, a hippo and a brown bear.

Location
151 Kapahula
Avenue
Kapiolani Park
Tel. 923–7723

Every Tuesday, Saturday and Sunday (from 9am until 1pm), an art market takes place outside the zoo at which mostly Hawaiian artists sell their work.

Art Mart

Kahala

Kahala enjoys a favourable climate and is noted for its particularly dry weather in contrast to the mountain slopes above Honolulu where, nevertheless, many groups of villas are located. Kahala is Honolulu's most exclusive address. It is the most delightful part of Honolulu with the most expensive houses in the city. The Kahala Hilton is situated here (probably the quietest and certainly the most elegant hotel on Oahu) as is the Kahala Shopping Center (which is not very large but is certainly upmarket).
    There is also Waialae Country Club with the finest golf course on Hawaii. This is, however, only open to club members. Growing against the fence that runs along Kealaolu Avenue, and which is intended to protect the golf course from the outside world, is what is probably Hawaii's longest hibiscus hedge.

Location
A suburb of
Honolulu,
north-east of
Diamond Head

Buses
7 or beach bus

Many of Kahala's houses (including Waialae Country Club) have been bought up in the last few years by the Japanese. This has led to an enormous increase in house prices and speculation everywhere in Hawaii but, above all, in Kahala.

Japanese
investment

According to newspaper reports one of Kahala's largest houses was sold for 21 million US dollars to a Japanese man. Another bought ten houses for almost ten million US dollars and sold them a few days later in Tokyo at great profit without the buyers having looked closely at his motives. An estate agent in Honolulu reported that the price of houses in Kahala had doubled within a year. He named an average price of 1.2 million US dollars for houses sold in 1988.

Kahala Hilton

The 20-year-old Kahala Hilton is used by more prominent figures than any other hotel in Honolulu. Queen Elizabeth II, King Juan Carlos and Queen Sofia of Spain, Ronald Reagan and his wife (during the time of his presidency), Frank Sinatra, Michael Jackson, Prince Charles and Princess Diana have all stayed here. This, however, is only a small selection of the famous names in the visitors' book.

Kalakaua Avenue

Location
Parallel to
Waikiki Beach

Waikiki's main street, named after King David Kalakaua, stretches for 1 mile/1.6km from Beretania Avenue (Beretania is the Hawaiian word for Britain) in Downtown Honolulu to the end of Kapiolani Park.

Along Kalakaua Avenue – the heart of Waikiki – which runs parallel to the beach, are countless hotels, restaurants and shops. If visitors are looking for a change from the beach, they need never be bored in this always-lively street. Very close by are the Waikiki Shopping Center (on the corner of Seaside Avenue), the International Market Place (between Seaside Street and Kanekapolei Street) and the Royal Hawaiian Shopping Center (see entry), which stretches from Lewers Street as far as Seaside Avenue. Many shops can also be found in the hotels, particularly the upper floors of the Hyatt Regency (2424 Kalakaua Avenue).

In the last few years redevelopment has taken place in and around Kalakaua Avenue and the area has been planted with more than 100 trees.

Carvings on sale in Kalakaua Avenue

This old market place remains a meeting point, a shopping area and a lively part of Honolulu. On busy Waikiki Square there is a chance to sample the city's hustle and bustle.

International Market Place

These four stones stand quite inconspicuously at the Waikiki Beach Center near the Sheraton Moana Hotel, their position giving little indication of their supposed magical qualities. Four powerful priests (*kahunas*), who came to Oahu from Tahiti in the 16th c., are said to have transferred their spiritual strength (their *mana*) to these stones before they left the island. Here the visitor finds himself at a point between two different worlds – the magical world of the early Polynesians and the modern world of beach life and luxury hotels.

Wizard Stones of Waikiki

Kapiolani Park

This 28-hectare park, which King Kalakaua gave to the city and which now bears the name of his wife, divides Waikiki from the small residential area on the south-west side of Diamond Head (see entry).

Location
Eastern Waikiki

Kapiolani Park is Honolulu's oldest public park and also the best loved. It contains a series of attractions – Waikiki Zoo (see entry); Waikiki Aquarium (see entry); and the Kodak Hula Show in the Waikiki Shell Amphitheater (free admission), in which summer concerts also take place, given by the Honolulu Symphony Orchestra.

Every Sunday, the Royal Hawaiian Band entertains in a music pavilion.

All in all Kapiolani Park is a pleasant recreational area with a large selection of leisure activities. Even tennis courts and picnic areas are available.

Jogging is certainly one of the favourite activities that take place in Kapiolani Park. At all times of the day, in all corners of the park, visitors will encounter panting and sweating runners. Every year in December this passion for running is stirred up again when native and international runners arrive at Kapiolani Bandstand, the finshing point of the 26 miles/42.2km-long Honolulu Marathon.

Honolulu Marathon

On the corner of Paki Street and Monsarrat Avenue lies the beautiful Queen Kapiolani Rose Garden, which has been open since 1972 and has many different types of roses. One particular variety is noteworthy – the lokelani, a rare Hawaiian rose.

Queen Kapiolani Rose Garden

Kodak Hula Show

The Kodak Hula Show offers a quick and instructive (but free) introduction to the Hawaii national dance, the hula (see Facts and Figures, Music and Dance) – there is even an opportunity to join in. The Kodak Hula Show is, even if inevitable changes have to be made during the course of the year, the longest-running show not only in Hawaii but in the whole of the United States of America. It began in 1937 and since then has been presented three or four times a week, apart from a few interruptions due to war.

Location
Kapiolani Park
Monsarrat Avenue
Tel. 833-1661

Reachable on foot

Accompanied by traditional Hawaiian music, the Hawaiian women dance some of the traditional hula dances, wearing Hawaiian skirts. Tahitian dances are also performed and, during an interval in the hour-long show, the audience is taught the basic steps and movements of the hula dance. To reach a professional level, several years of training are necessary, as offered by the many hula schools (*halaus*).

To be assured of a good seat, it is advisable to arrive at least 30 minutes before the performance at the venue near the music pavilion. Remember also to take some sort of headwear for protection against the sun.

The Kodak Hula Show

Paradise Park

Location
3737 Manoa Road
Manoa Valley
Tel. 988–2141

Buses
5 (from Ala Moana
Center)
Free bus service
offered by Waikiki
Park

Paradise Park is reached by driving along Manoa Valley above Waikiki. This scenic and attractive valley is a popular residential area for those who want to escape the hustle and bustle of the city.

Heavy rain has caused a dense tropical rain forest to grow here with more than 100 tropical plants and almost as many species of exotic birds. A safari offers the opportunity of observing this lush vegetation and, more importantly, of taking numerous photographs (for this place, perhaps more than any other on the islands, really captures the wonders of Hawaiian nature). A show entitled "Dancing Waters" is presented three times a day and hardly less well-known is the show called "Quacking Ducks".

Lyon Arboretum

Visitors can look around the Lyon Arboretum (only a few minutes' walk away), a garden of trees maintained by the University of Honolulu.

Manoa Falls

Those who would like a walk can follow the 1½ miles/2.5km Manoa Falls Trail. This runs behind the park to the waterfall – bathing is possible.

Royal Hawaiian Shopping Center

Location
2201 Kalakaua
Avenue
Tel. 922–0588

Reachable on foot

This shopping centre, located in central Waikiki, is the newest and most modern on offer in Honolulu. It is situated on the south (seaward) side of Kalakaua Avenue with its main entrance in Lewers Street.

It contains about 25 clothes shops together with a dozen boutiques, more than 20 souvenir shops, approximately fifteen jewellers' and ten restaurants. There is also a currency exchange, a shop which will pack parcels (GBC Packaging), a post office (on the second floor), an excellent book shop (Waldenbooks) and an information stall manned by the Polynesian Cultural Center (see entry).

University of Hawaii

The approximately 37-acre/15-hectare campus of the University of Hawaii is located in Manoa Valley, north of Waikiki, and can be reached easily and quickly by bus or car. Those interested in American university life should first visit the Student Center, decorated with a wall painting depicting life in Hawaii before the arrival of the *haole*, the white men. An information desk here gives details of all aspects of university and student life.

Located on the second floor of the Student Center is a gallery (free admission), which mounts a series of exhibitions, showing mainly the work of Hawaiian artists.

The university book shop is of interest (open: Monday–Friday 8.15am–4.15pm, Saturday 8.15–11.45am). It offers the complete selection of books published by the University of Hawaii Press, in particular Hawaiian and South Sea classic literature.

This relatively young university has developed quickly. Today 25,000 students are registered here, some of whom live on the campus. The current university arose from the College of Agriculture and Mechanic Arts (founded in 1907), originally located at Thomas Square in Honolulu. It transferred to Manoa Valley in 1911 and immediately changed its name to the College of Hawaii. It gained its present name in 1920. The University of Hawaii has another campus at Hilo on the Island of Hawaii and also incorporates seven Community Colleges, offering two-year apprenticeships.

Over the past few years the high cost of living in Hawaii coupled with the lack of housing in Honolulu has caused the university authorities difficulties in attracting teachers, and several professors have moved to the mainland. To prove more attractive the university has plans to build homes for its staff on the campus.

Location
Manoa Valley
Tel. 948–8855

Bus
4

US Army Museum

Among the exhibits in this small military museum are weapons from the time of the Hawaiian wars in the 18th c. to the Second World War and the Vietnam War. Also on display are American soldiers' uniforms from the last 200 years as well as enemy uniforms. Most interest is doubtless aroused by the old Hawaiian weapons studded with skarks' teeth – used in battles between former Hawaiian tribes.

The museum is located in a 1909 building originally built to defend Honolulu and Pearl Harbor.

Location
Fort DeRussy
Tel. 438–2821

Reachable on foot

Waikiki Aquarium

Opened in 1954 the aquarium houses about 300 types of Hawaiian and other Polynesian fish and sea creatures in four self-contained galleries, each illustrating a different theme. "Hawaiians by the Sea" uses pictures and drawings to show how the early Hawaiians built fish ponds, extracted salt, made nets and claimed part of their daily food from the sea. In "South Sea Marine Life", fish, turtles, eels, starfish, shellfish and coral can be seen (notice the butterfish on account of its unpronouncable name – *lauwiliwili-nukunukoioi*). "Micronesia Reef Builders" offers a view into the world of living coral around which trained seals perform their tricks.

Location
2777 Kalakaua Avenue
Tel. 923–9741

Bus
2

Pearl Harbor

Pearl Harbor gained its name through the oysters which were alleged to be found here. They are possibly as legendary as the "diamonds" at Diamond Head (see entry).

Name

Pearl Harbor, which gained tragic fame as a result of the Japanese air attack on it on December 7th 1941, was not America's first military base in Hawaii.

Strategic military USA base

Hawaii's strategic importance is based on the fact that, owing to their central Pacific location, the Hawaiian islands are an ideal place from which the whole Pacific region can be controlled.

Today, Hawaii is still the most highly-militarised state in the United States of America – enormous areas, in particular in the west of Oahu Island, are under the jurisdiction of US forces and are closed off to civilians. It was only under pressure that King Kalakaua handed over Pearl Harbor to the USA as a base in 1887. Pearl Harbor, known for its narrow entrance leading to an unusually-deep bay, had already been examined by the Americans in 1872 for military use. The harbour, where dredging began in 1908, was finally inaugurated on December 11th 1911 – almost 30 years to the day before the Japanese attack. Today, the whole area in and around the harbour is still used for military purposes.

Attack on Pearl Harbor

Despite its great strategic importance, Pearl Harbor was hardly known to the world as a military harbour. This changed suddenly on December 7th 1941 at 7.59am when the first of many bombs dropped on to it. Within the space of two hours, the Japanese had sunk or badly damaged battleships and cruisers (including the two large ships USS "Arizona" and USS "Utah") and had destroyed 188 aircraft. Human losses were high – 2325 sailors and members of the Marine Corps as well as 57 civilians died. On the USS "Arizona" alone, 1177 officers and sailors were killed.

Declaration of war

On that day, President Roosevelt declared war on Japan and three days later, on December 11th 1941, Germany and Italy declared war on the United States of America – the Second World War had begun.

★★USS Arizona Memorial

Location
Near Ford Island
Tel. 422–0561

Buses
20 (from Waikiki),
50,
51, 55 (Ala Moana Center)
Express bus
(Tel. 926–4747)

The USS Arizona Memorial is Hawaii's most-visited attraction, with more than 1½ million visitors a year. In memory of the dead who drowned aboard the sinking USS "Arizona", a memorial was opened in 1962 which accommodates up to 3000 visitors daily thanks to the Visitor Center, completed in 1980.

The memorial was erected above the sunken battleship, parts of which still project above the water. The gleaming-white floating building, about 197ft/60m long, contains a large semi open-air room in which visitors gather. At the end of the memorial there is a shrine on which the names of the 1177 victims, including the commander and his deputy, are engraved on a wall of Vermont marble.

Visitor Center

The memorial is reached via the Visitor Center where free entry tickets are handed out. A purpose-built cinema shows a 20-minute film about Pearl Harbor and the Japanese attack (the first showing begins at 8am, the last at 3pm). A naval cutter then ferries visitors to and from the real memorial at regular intervals.

Boat trips around the harbour

From Kewalo Basin (see entry), boat trips can be made to Pearl Harbor and back although this is regarded as an expensive alternative way of viewing the USS Arizona Memorial as the boat sails past it. The advantage of such a trip, however, is that much of the harbour which is only visible from the water can be seen. Trips are offered by several companies including Paradise Cruise (Tel. 536–3641) and Pearl Harbor Cruise (Tel. 924–4969).

Pacific Submarine Museum

Location
Pearl Harbor near
Visitor Center
USS "Arizona"
Tel. 423–1341

A visit to the USS Arizona Memorial (see entry) can be combined with one to the Pacific Submarine Museum and the American submarine "Bowfin", moored nearby.

Displayed in the Pacific Submarine Museum are mainly parts of American submarines, as well as those of German and Japanese origin which

The United States Arizona Memorial

fell into American hands during the Second World War. They are exhibited in such a way that visitors can not only touch them but also move them.

Bus
10

Located in Bowfin Park, the USS "Bowfin" – a submarine built during the Second World War – was restored by a private organisation, the Pacific Fleet Submarine Memorial Association. This association also maintains the park as a memorial to the 52 US submarines sunk during the war and their 3505 dead sailors and officers. The "Bowfin" sunk a total of 44 Japanese ships.

USS "Bowfin"

Wander around the ship at will, climb the command tower and gain an all-round view of Pearl Harbor through a periscope. Many photographs and other memorabilia illustrate life aboard a submarine both on friendly patrols and in wartime situations.

Kahala

See Honolulu, Waikiki.

★Mormon Temple   F 2

The Mormon community has a membership of more than 30,000 and this makes it the largest non-Catholic Christian community in Hawaii. Mormons first came to Hawaii in 1850 and had already founded their first community there by the following year. The missionaries were called away again, however, because of internal disputes. Only in the next decade, when the missionaries returned and were able to buy about 5930 acres/2400 hectares

Location
Laie
Coastal road 83
Tel. 293–5055

The temple can
only
be viewed from
the
outside

Bus
55

of land in Laie, did the gradual rise of the "Church of Jesus Christ of Latter Day Saints" (the official name of this faith) begin. They built on the land and also planted many flowers. When in 1874 King David Kalakaua (see Famous People) visited the by now well-developed village community, he is supposed to have said that wherever Mormons were, he had found "health and thrifty loyal subjects".

The building of the temple began in 1916 and three years later it could be officially opened. Building costs amounted to 250,000 US dollars. The completely-white building, which stands out from the *pali* (mountain-sides), can only be entered by Mormons but its location alone makes it an attraction. On the right-hand side of the temple grounds is a visitor centre where a film about the history of the Mormons can be seen and printed information about the community and its ongoing missionary work is available.

Brigham Young
University

In Laie there is also part of the Brigham Young University of Salt Lake City, whose students in Hawaii originate from the many South Pacific islands and earn their fees through their work in the Polynesian Cultural Center (see entry), run by Mormons. About 400 students are singers or dancers who take part in performances given in the Polynesian Cultural Center. The young students are chosen by missionaries working there to study in Laie.

Nuuanu Pali Lookout

See Honolulu, Downtown.

Paradise Park

See Honolulu, Waikiki

★★Polynesian Cultural Center   F2

Location
55–370
Kamehameha
Highway, Laie
Tel. 293–3333
(in Waikiki, tel.
923–1861)

Bus
55 (from Ala
Moana)

After Pearl Harbor the Polynesian Cultural Center (built in 1963) is Hawaii's second largest attraction. Despite high admission charges and its consid-erable distance from Honolulu (33 miles/53km), its various productions are attended by more than one million people a year. The Polynesian Cultural Center was founded almost three decades ago by Laie's Mormon commu-nity in grounds of about 14 hectares. Its purpose is to portray as authen-tically as possible, through music and dance, the culture and daily life of the Polynesian islanders in Hawaii, Tahiti, Marquesas, Tonga, Samoa and Fiji as well as that of the Maoris in New Zealand. The centre is set out in the style of a village with each group of islands represented by several houses in which the respective island inhabitants practise traditional handwork and other daily activities. Two performances, the "Festival Production of the Long Canoes" by day and the evening show called "This is Polynesia", are dance displays in the style of an exotic musical with the most modern lighting and sound effects. See Map pages 194/195.

Actors

As not only the performers in the two shows but also the people at work in the houses come from the islands which they represent, a certain amount of authenticity is guaranteed. The actors are almost all students chosen by the Mormons to study in Laie at the offshoot of the Brigham Young Uni-versity of Salt Lake City. They earn their fees by taking part in the different productions.

Polynesia

Thus, for example, in Tonga Village – Tonga is by the way the only inde-pendent kingdom in the South Seas – women can be seen making

Mormon temple in Laie

materials from tree bark (the Hawaiians call it *tapa* while in Tahiti it is called *ngatau*). Photographs of past kings and current rulers, beautiful floor coverings and much more are also on show. In the neighbouring Tahiti Village, women can be observed making *leis* from shells as well as grass skirts, which really originate from the Gilbert Islands. There is also much keen singing and playing of musical instruments. The Marquesas Islands, on which only about 6000 people live, are represented by one house for the chief and a second for the women and children. In Hawaii Village there is to be found inside a chief's house a bed with a cover made of feathers surrounded by *kahilis*, the feathered poles which are symbols of the *ali'i*. Visitors can also see here how *poi*, the Hawaiian national dish, is made from the roots of the giant taro plant. The four-roomed chief's house in Fiji Village is also worth seeing as all its rooms are covered in mulberry tree *tapas*. The Samoans portray themselves by practical demonstrations – here visitors can learn the expert way of opening a coconut. In Maori House, a more than 39ft/12m-long canoe with room for 40 people can be seen. The Maoris, who no longer call their part of the world New Zealand but Aotearoa, can be watched performing their stick dance, often wearing full war paint.

Admission charges are staggered. The lowest price of 25 US dollars allows access to the "Festival Production of the Long Canoes" (performed several times a day) and the opportunity to stay for as long as desired in the native villages. The price rises to 39 US dollars to include food and admission to the evening show. These are without doubt the highest admission charges for an attraction in Hawaii but it alone offers visitors the opportunity to enjoy seeing the culture and lifestyle of some of the South Sea peoples. — *Admission charges*

A selection of bus companies offers trips to the Polynesian Cultural Center, including Noa Tours (Tel. 599–2561) and Transhawaiian (Tel. 7356–6467). Information is available from a Polynesian Cultural Center office located in — *Organised tours* the Royal Hawaiian Shopping Center (see entry), Waikiki, where admission tickets can also be bought.

Puu O Mahuka Heiau   E2

Location
Above Waimea Beach Park, north-west coast of Oahu

Bus
55 from Ala Moana

The temple can be reached on foot as well as by car from Waimea Beach Park (see Practical Information, Beaches) by turning on to Pupukea Road in Waikiki. After about ¾ mile/1.1km, an unmade-up red sandy road (please heed the street sign) is reached – follow this also for ¾ mile/1.1km.

From the temple there is a lovely view on to Waimea Beach Park and the sea.

Puu O Mahuka Temple is one of the largest of the few remaining *heiaus* on Oahu. Typical of this temple site is its totally rectangular shape, which extends to the size of a football field. The temple was once surrounded by a stone wall. Inside, small stones were piled up and tree trunks were presumably laid on top to create a platform. The buildings erected on top of this no longer exist as perishable materials, such as wood, leaves and grass, were used.

Puu O Mahuka was apparently one of the temples to which human sacrifices were brought. According to legend three sailors from the crew of one of the ships that brought George Vancouver to Hawaii were supposed to have been sacrificed along with others here – because they had angered the natives. Human sacrifice was originally unknown in Hawaii. Polynesians from Tahiti brought this religious custom here for the first time in the 13th c., and it was then practised for more than 500 years until the abolition of the *kapu* system by King Kamehameha II and his mother Kapiolani (see Famous People). Visitors to Puu O Mahuka are often surprised by the fact

Polynesian Cultural Center

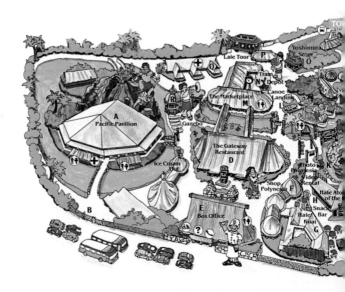

that "sacrifices" are still brought here. On the stone walls can be seen stones, bones or fruit wrapped in ti-leaves or other leaves and bound together with grass – a sign that even 170 years of Christianity has not been able to extinguish completely the old religious customs.

Sacred Falls – Kaliuwaa Falls   F 2

The path along Kaluanui River to the waterfall begins at the Sacred Falls Bazaar (a map of walks is available here). The 2 mile/3km path is not totally easy – stout footwear and waterproof clothing are necessary, and do not attempt to begin the walk after rain showers as the path is then too soft. The difficulty of the walk is more than compensated by the countless wonders of nature to be seen. Pass through a narrow gorge where only a small amount of daylight penetrates. The path is not only narrow but many rocks have to be negotiated and, towards the end, there is a fairly steep climb. The area is called Kaliuwaa Valley ("Canoe Room" or "Canoe Leak"). Located here is the territory of the pig demi-god Kamapua'a ("Pig's Boy"). According to legend, he could lean to the left of the waterfall toward the rocks and so allow his family to flee from an enemy.

The pool beneath this 98ft/30m-high waterfall, although much colder than the water of the Pacific, invites a refreshing dip. Do not stay too long here so as to be back on Kamehameha Highway before nightfall.

Location
West coast of Oahu between Punaluu and
Hauula
Kamehameha Highway

Bus
55 from Ala Moana

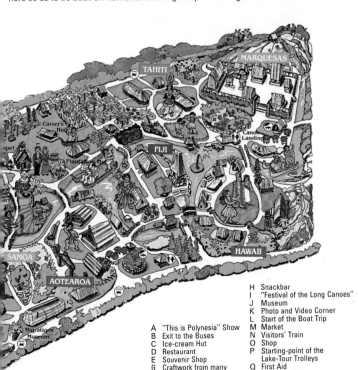

A	"This is Polynesia" Show
B	Exit to the Buses
C	Ice-cream Hut
D	Restaurant
E	Souvenir Shop
G	Craftwork from many countries
H	Snackbar
I	"Festival of the Long Canoes"
J	Museum
K	Photo and Video Corner
L	Start of the Boat Trip
M	Market
N	Visitors' Train
O	Shop
P	Starting-point of the Lake-Tour Trolleys
Q	First Aid
R	Wind-band Concerts

195

Remains of the Puu O Mahuka Heiaus

★Sea Life Park

F3

Location
Near Makapuu
Beach
Park at south-east
tip of Oahu
Tel. 259–7933
or 923–1531

Bus
Shuttle service
from Waikiki
Tel. 923–FISH

On Oahu's eastern tip at the foot of the impressive Makapuu Cliffs can be found the Sea Life Park – a favourite destination for outings. More than 2000 types of fish swim about in an enormous pool which can be viewed through a glass wall.

Displays given by whales, dolphins and sea lions are very popular and their feeding times are a major attraction. Particularly impressive are the tricks performed by whales and dolphins. In the shark section visitors learn about sharks that can be found in the waters of the Pacific and, in particular, whether swimmers might encounter these predators.

In the Pacific Whaling Museum the skeleton of an enormous whale is on display, as well as an extensive collection of objects carved from whales' teeth. A replica of a whaling ship from earlier times is anchored in the lagoon.

From the Sea Life Park there is a fine view of the offshore island known as Rabbit Island or Manana Island. On this small volcanic needle of rock the odd rabbit, reared by a Hawaiian farmer, can still be seen hopping around. Today, the island is a protected bird sanctuary.

Makapuu Cliffs

These more than 985ft/300m-high rocky cliffs provide an ideal launching point for the many hang-gliders who dare to take a leap downward here. Some of the more courageous among them are supposed to have succeeded in gliding across the water to Rabbit Island.

Halona Blow Hole

Near Road 72, between Hanauma Bay and the Sea Life Park and close to Koko Head Crater, visit Halona Blow Hole. Sea water is forced at high

Performing sealions in the Sea Life Park

pressure through holes in the lava stone and shoots noisily into a high fountain, similar to a geyser. This activity follows the pattern of the waves.

Senator Fong's Plantation and Gardens   F 3

Located in Kaneohe, these gardens once belonged to the Hawaiian Senator Fong and have been open to the public in their present state for a short while.

At the first elections for the American Congress in Hawaii in 1959, Hiram Leong Fong was elected as the first US senator of Asian descent. Fong came from a large Chinese family of landworkers and achieved the astonishing rise to the Senate for the Republican Party. When he retired from political life in 1979 after 17 years of public service, he decided to create (on an approximately 150-hectare area of land) a tropical forest open to everyone, together with a plantation and gardens. Among other things, 90 types of edible nuts and fruits grow here.

Location
Kaneohe
47–285 Pulama
Road
Tel. 239–6775

Bus
55 (to Pulama
Road)

Wahiawa Botanic Garden   E 2

In the middle of Oahu, in Wahiawa (the farming centre of the island), there is an attractive botanic garden where a stop can be made on the way to the pineapple fields in the north of the town or on the way back to Honolulu.

Here the trees from tropical areas of Africa, Australia and the South Sea Islands, planted about 40 years ago, are eye-catching. Only some of them are named – the strongly-smelling camphor trees from China and Japan, cinammon trees from Sri Lanka and a particularly fine rubber tree from New Guinea.

Location
13396 California
Avenue
Wahiawa, east of
Road 99

197

Waimea Falls Park E 2

Location
9864 Kamehameha
Highway, Haleiwa
Tel. 638–8511

This former nature park lies on Oahu's northern coast in Waimea Valley. Leave Haleiwa on Road 83 and, after 4 miles/7km, turn off on to a side road which leads directly to Waimea Falls Park.

Buses
85 or 55

With an area of 1730 acres/700 hectares and containing more than 5000 different tropical and sub-tropical plants, this park is the largest botanic garden on the Hawaiian islands. Travel on an electric narrow-gauge railway to view the different gardens and the 49ft/15m-high waterfall – an additional attraction. Those who prefer to walk can wander along the paths of the park for hours. Cultural events also take place here. Guided tours give information about the plant life and the history of Waimea Valley.

Along with the many plants and trees, which are all labelled, many rare birds can be observed in a bird enclosure, including (occasionally) the *nene*, the Hawaiian goose, and the koloa duck. The souvenir shop contains a large selection of books about Hawaii and is worth visiting. There is a restaurant (Proud Peacock) and a snack bar (Country Kitchen). On nights when there is a full moon the park remains open so that people can walk in the moonlight (admission charges are not increased for this).

Waimea Valley

Waimea Valley, located in the Koolau Mountains, was densely populated in early Hawaiian times. Today attempts are being made to allow not only the natural beauty of this valley but also the cultural life of the Hawaiians to revive. The dance troupe called Halau o Waimea performs hula dances here which have no commercial benefit but recall the time when the dance had a ritual function and the songs sung by men and women to accompany it provided a way for them to speak in unison to their gods. At different times, some of the old Hawaiian plays are performed near the waterfall.

Water-lilies in the Waimea Falls Park   *Surfboards on Waikiki Beach* ▶

Practical Information

Accommodation

See Camping, Hotels, Youth Hostels

Air Transport

The best way to get from island to island fairly cheaply and quickly is by air. The main routes are serviced by Hawaiian Airlines and Aloha Airlines, which fly from Honolulu to Hawaii, Maui, Kauai, Molokai (Hawaiian Airlines only) and Lanai, as well as Discovery Airlines.

In addition there are a number of smaller airlines using propeller-driven aircraft and the smaller airports. These include Aloha Island Air, Princeville Airways, Panorama Air and Reeves Air.

Bookings can be made at:
Aloha Airlines; tel. 800–652–1211
Hawaiian Airlines; tel. 800–367–5320 and (Maui) 244–9111

Airlines

In addition to six American airlines (American, Continental, Delta, Northwest Orient, TWA and United), as well as the three largest Hawaiian companies (Aloha, Discovery Airlines and Hawaiian Airlines), a large number of other airlines also fly to and from Honolulu. These are:

Air Micronesia, Air Nauru, Air New Zealand, Air Niugini, British Airways, Canadian Pacific, China Airlines, Japan Airlines, Korean Airlines, Philippine Airlines, Quantas (Australia), Samoa Airlines, Singapore Airlines and South Pacific Island Airways. In addition many charter companies run regular flights to Honolulu, especially during the main tourist season.

As all airlines fly to Honolulu its airport has become a "turntable" for air traffic between the USA and the South Pacific.

Airports

As a direct consequence of the increased air traffic between the islands and the mainland, Hawaii now boasts twelve public and fifteen military and private airports, as well as eight helicopter pads.

Airports

The main airports are:
Honolulu International Airport (Oahu)
Hilo Airport (Hawaii)
Kona Airport (Hawaii)
Lihue Airport (Kauai)
Princeville Airport (Kauai)
Kahului Airport (Maui)
Kapalua Airport (Maui)
Hana Airport (Maui)
Molokai Airport (Molokai)
Lanai Airport (Lanai)

International air traffic

For a number of years Honolulu was the only international airport in the islands. Now, however, as a result of the increase in tourism, airlines fly direct to Kona (Hawaii), Kahului (Maui) and Lihue (Kauai).

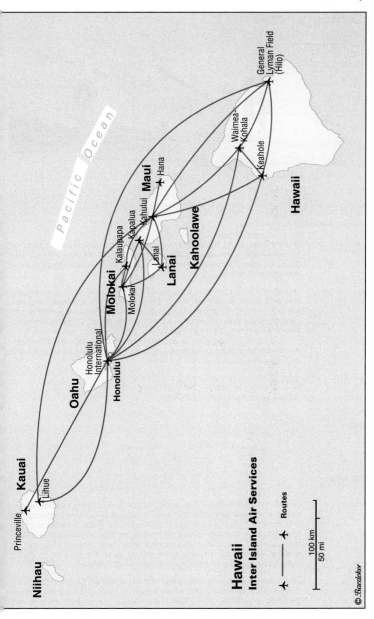

Hawaii
Inter Island Air Services

✈ Routes

100 km
50 mi

© Baedeker

A plane of Hawaiian Airlines

Standard of service
Generally speaking formalities are completed speedily at all airports; at Honolulu delays can occasionally occur when a number of aircraft arrive at the same time. The larger car rental firms have desks at all airports, close to the luggage reclaim.

Honolulu Airport
Honolulu is by far the best equipped of all Hawaiian airports. It is the only one with a bank where money can be exchanged (Perera Deak), and also the only one with a number of shops offering such Hawaiian specialities as pineapple, papayas, Kona coffee, macadamia nuts, etc. for the return flight. Hawaiian Airlines, the largest within the islands, has its own terminal.
   The airport building itself is also interesting, having many works of art, murals and decorated ceilings, sculptures, paintings and tapestries mainly depicting Hawaiian themes.

Information
Honolulu International Airport; tel. 836–6411
Hilo Air Terminal, Hawaii; tel. 969–1545 or 1547
Kona Airport, Hawaii; tel. 329–4868

Banks

See Currency

Beaches

General
Scarcely anywhere else in the world will you find so many beaches within such a small area as here in the Hawaiian islands. In all there are more than 100 "county parks", as they are known, beaches under the control of the four Hawaiian counties, where swimming, surfing, snorkelling, sunbathing, hunting for mussels and various other seaside pleasures can be enjoyed. On at least a third of these county parks it is possible to obtain permission to camp in a tent for the night (see Camping).

Dangerous currents
First a word of warning: only a few of the beaches are guarded. Normally there are just warning signs, which should be strictly obeyed at all times. Beaches vary between quiet bays and stretches where waves are high and there are dangerous currents and undertow. The need to take great care cannot be over-emphasised.

The sun presents another danger. Hawaii is not very far from the Equator, and even during the winter months the sun is considerably more intense than most Europeans are used to. Start with a few minutes and gradually increase the time spent out in the sun, and use an effective sun-cream (factor 15 or more) on the exposed parts of the body. Sunburn can completely ruin a holiday.

Protection from the sun

Hawaii Island

With its total coastal length of 165 miles/266km Hawaii boasts a considerable number of excellent beaches, more than 25 of them being officially listed. The remaining 75 or so can be discovered in the course of exploring the island. All beaches are open to the public, some being accessible only by water. Generally speaking, Hawaii enjoys less protection from off-shore coral reefs than the other islands. and for this reason heavy waves can be expected, especially when the tide is flowing. Strong undercurrents are also common, so care must be taken when swimming and indulging in water sports, as most beaches are unguarded.

Introductory remarks

The following is a selection of beaches beginning in the north of the island and moving in an anti-clockwise direction:

6 miles/9.5km north of Honokaa, at the end of Route 240, a path leads down into the valley and to this beach of black sand; strong currents make it somewhat dangerous for bathers.

NORTH COAST
Waipio Bay

A beach of white sand, ideal for swimming and snorkelling, lies just off Route 270 at Kawaihae. There are facilities for picnics and camping.

WEST COAST
Samuel M. Spencer Park

South of Kawaihae, on Route 19 and in front of the Mauna Kea Beach Hotel, lies this beach of white sand protected by reefs. It is ideal for all kinds of water sports.

Mauna Kea Beach

Also on Route 19, and a little way south of Mauna Kea, this beach of brilliant white sand is also ideal for all water sports.

Hapuna Beach State Park

The beach lies in front of the Mauna Lani Bay Hotel. From Route 19 there is a path to the hotel car park. The sea is calm except in winter, when surfing is possible.

Kalahaipuaa

Some 20 miles/30km north of Keahole-Kona airport, on Queen Kaahumanu Highway, lies this beautiful, semicircular beach lined with coconut palms. It belongs to the Royal Waikoloa Hotel but is also open to non-residents and is ideal for bathing, diving and snorkelling. Immediately behind the beach lie two old fish-ponds. In the hotel precincts are some well-preserved rock drawings dating from c. 1500 B.C.

Anaehoomalu Bay

4 miles/6.5km north of Keahole-Kona airport a small road branches off to a beach of white sand broken up only by a few lava rocks. It is popular with the locals for swimming, fishing and surfing.

Maniniowale Beach

Also known as "Magic Beach" or "Disappearing Sands Beach", this beach lies close to Alii Drive and 5 miles/8km south of Kailua-Kona. It owes its name to the fact that every winter the waves completely flood it and wash away the existing sand, but subsequently deposit a new layer. In the summer months it is ideal for surfing, but swimmers must beware of currents.

White Sands Beach Park

This beautiful beach of white sand lies in a sheltered bay 6 miles/9.5km south of Kailua-Kona on Route 11. It is ideal for bathing and snorkelling.

Kahaluu Beach Park

A white sand beach sheltered by a reef, Napoopoo lies 13 miles/21km south of Kailua-Kona and is a nature reserve with waters rich in fish. It is ideal for bathing and snorkelling.

Napoopoo Beach Park

Beaches

Hookena Beach Park

Lying 25 miles/40km south of Kaiua-Kona, this beach – a mixture of white and black sand – is suitable for swimming and snorkelling. There are also picnic facilities.

SOUTH COAST
Mahana Bay/ Green Sand Beach

The south coast with its beaches of black sand is the result of countless volcanic eruptions over thousands of years. The glowing, hot lava flowed into the sea and then, as a result of the sudden cooling process, exploded into small particles which the tides subsequently broke down still further to form sand. Deposits of volcanic olivine (magnesium iron silicate) have given a section of the beach a greenish tint.

Mahana Bay, known also as Green Sand Beach, stretches more or less northwards from South Point, the southernmost point of the island (accessible only via South Point Road in a four-wheel drive vehicle).

Punaluu Beach Park

A detour off Route 11 leads to this very beautiful "black beach". Bathing, surfing and snorkelling are safe only off the northern section, and even here there are some dangerous undercurrents, so it is wise to be careful.

Kaimu Beach Park

Near Kaimu lies Kaimu Beach, a favourite with photographers. However, as it lies in the path of subterranean lava tunnels it becomes covered in ash and debris whenever Kilauea erupts and its continued existence is in doubt.

Close by can be found Harry K, Brown Park which, unfortunately, has been completely covered in ash following recent eruptions.

EAST COAST

The east coast is rainy and the beaches are black and mainly rocky. Little Reed's Bay Beach Park lies on Hilo Bay. Some 4½ miles/7km north of Hilo lies Honolii Beach Park, popular with surfers. The remaining beaches (Leleiwi, Keahola Park, Onekahakaha, Hilo Bayfront Park and Kolekole) have little to recommend them.

A "black" beach on the coast of Hawaii Island

Kauai Island

With a coastline measuring 90 miles/145km, Kauai possesses many beaches of varying quality and degrees of danger for swimmers and water-sportsmen. Bathers are strongly advised never to swim alone and always to obey the warning signs.

SOUTH COAST
Salt Pond Beach Park

This beach, near Hanapepe (see entry), is one of the best, safest and most popular on the island. Water sports are possible almost all the year round. Coming from Hanapepe, turn right at the "Veterans' Cemetery" sign into Lolokai Road.

Poipu Beach Park

There is a wide beach in the south of the island, almost 2 miles/3km long, where swimming and surfing can be enjoyed throughout the year. Only at the eastern end do rocks make swimming more dangerous. Take Routes 520 or 530 via Koloa and turn left into Poipu Road.

EAST COAST
Kalapaki Beach

Situated near the Westin Kaui Hotel, this beach is particularly suited to bathing and surfing.

Lydgate State Park

A completely safe beach for swimming all the year round. It lies on the west bank of the Kailua River, and is signposted from Route 56.

Wailua Beach

Wailua Beach, on the opposite bank of the river in front of the Coco Palms Resort, is not protected by coral reefs. It should therefore be used only when the sea is calm and when lifeguards are present.

Anahola Beach

Situated in the bay of the same name (signposted from Route 56) this beach is safe for swimmers in summer, thanks to the offshore coral reef. In winter, however, the almost ever present heavy seas make it somewhat dangerous.

NORTH COAST

Most of the beaches on the north coast are quite small; some are suitable for swimming and snorkelling in the winter months as well.

Larsen's Beach

Larsen's Beach, sandy with a few small rocks, is suitable for bathing.

Waiakalua Iki Beach

From North Waiakalua Road a small path leads to the sandy Waiakalua Iki Beach, which is also suitable for swimming.

Kaupea Beach

Kaupea Beach, also known as "Secret Beach", is situated at Kilauea Point (from Route 19 turn off on to the Kahiliwai Road as far as the end of the track across the fields); a small footpath leads straight to the beach of white sand where swimming and surfing can be enjoyed.

Anini Beach Park

This beach, sheltered by a long coral reef, is suited to swimming all the year round. From Route 56 turn Kalihiway Road, then take Anini Road to the beach.

Lumahia Beach

Lumahai Beach, adjoining Hanalei Beach, is certainly one of the finest and most photographed beaches on Kauai. However, it is not sheltered by a coral reef and so suffers the full force of the waves. Because of the currents and the waves swimming is very dangerous, and bathers should enter the water only if they are certain that it is calm, which is not very often. At milestone 33 there is a viewing point where you can park and from where a steep, sometimes very muddy path leads to the beach.

Hanalei Beach

In Hanalei Bay, formerly one of Kauai's three berths for ships and where yachts still lie at anchor, is one of the island's most beautiful beaches. However, swimming is safe only at both ends of the bay. Surfing is popular especially at the eastern end. In the middle of the bay the swell is high even in summer, and in winter it is very stormy there.
From Route 56 the beach is accessible via Aku Road or Weke Road, on either side of the town of Hanalei.

Hanalei Bay on the north coast of Kauai Island

Haena Beach Park   This beach of white sand at the north-eastern tip of Kauai opposite the Maniniholo Caves, just before the end of Route 66, is divided into three parts; going from east to west, these are known as Tunnels, Haena Beach Park itself, and Cannons. In summer all three are equally suitable for bathing.

Lanai Island

Beaches on this island are described under A to Z, Lanai Island

Maui Island

The island of Maui has more than 50 beaches; most of them lie along the west coast between Kapalua and Makena, some in the Hana region and other less attractive ones around Paia, Kahului and Wailuku (see A to Z, Maui Island).

The following is a selection, moving from north to south:

Kapalua (Fleming) Beach   One of Maui's most beautiful and safest beaches for bathers, with good snorkelling.

Napili Bay Beach   A long, horn-shaped beach of white sand, suitable for swimming and snorkelling, but the latter can be dangerous when there is a heavy swell.

Hanakoo and Kaanapali Beaches   These beaches lie north of Lahaina and are excellent for bathing. (A map of the beaches is on display in the hotels.)

Wahikuli State Wayside Park (Lahaina)   One of the most popular beaches on Maui, with picnic tables, showers, toilets and a paved car park. Bathing and snorkelling are good. Watch out for rocks in the water.

As well equipped as Wahikuli Park, with a good view of the islands of Molokai, Lanai and Kahoolawe. Here, too, bathers should watch out for rocks in the water.

Launiopoko State Wayside Park (Lahaina)

The name of this State Park means "forget me not", and was dedicated in 1956 to the soldiers and sailors who died in the Second World War. It is a fine beach for bathing, and there are shady pavilions, picnic areas and showers.

Maipoina Oe Iau Beach Park (Kihei)

Three beaches lying close to one another, with the soft sand reaching far out into the sea. Excellent bathing, snorkelling and surfing.

Kamaole Beach Park I, II, III (Kihei)

This beach lies somewhat hidden behind an apartment site. To reach it, proceed southwards along South Kihei Road which runs parallel to the shore; this road ends in a cul-de-sac. From here steps lead down to the beach. Superb swimming and surfing. A beautifully laid-out park adjoins the beach.

Mokapu Beach Park (Wailea)

This beach, too, adjoins a park, and there is excellent bathing, snorkelling and surfing.

Polo Beach Park (Wailea)

A small but beautiful beach of white sand, superb for swimming.

Palauea Beach (Makena)

A beautiful, wide beach of white sand, good bathing.

Polenalena Beach Park

Not far from Nahuna Point is a 19th c. graveyard. There is no beach here, but Nahuna Point is well-suited for snorkelling and scuba-diving.

Nahuna Point

Almost 220yd/200m in length, this beach of fine, white sand is bordered by two rocky promontories. At the southern end can be seen some interesting multi-coloured coral formations. Bathing is good, but snorkelling only if the winds are not too strong, which is usually in the afternoons.

Maluaka Beach (Makena)

Although it is not officially allowed, Puuolai Beach, a flat beach of white sand, is actually the only nudist beach on Maui. Prospective bathers can drive only to a point about 110yd/100m from the beach and must then walk the rest. Bathing is good, except in winter, although there is often a high swell. Snorkelling is average only.

Puuolai Beach (Little Makena)

Of all the beaches around Hana this is the safest. There are seats in the shade, picnic tables, showers and toilets.

Hana Bay State Park (Hana)

Molokai Island

Molokai is not very well blessed with beaches, especially good ones. Those on the west coast have already been mentioned under Kaluakoi (see A to Z, Molokai). On the south coast lies a chain of beaches of which only a few can be described as very good. One Alii Park, about 4 miles/6km from Kaunakai, with Kakahaia Beach Park and Kumimi Beach adjoining it to the east, together form what is perhaps the best area for bathing on Molokai. The best place for snorkelling is Halawa Bay, while surfing is possible off Moomoni Beach, in the north-west of the island. For water sports in general the larger islands are undoubtedly the best.

General

Oahu Island

The island of Oahu boasts some 115 miles/185km of coastline and many beautiful beaches, some better for bathing, others well suited to surfing or snorkelling. However, the ebb and flow of the tides is unpredictable and a constant danger. For that reason it is essential to obey the warning signs, especially on unguarded beaches.

Part of the beach on the Kaanapali coast of Maui Island

Particular care should be taken during the winter months, from October to February, when the heavy seas wash the sand out into the sea, leaving the beaches – especially on the north and west coasts – narrower. It is not until early spring that the sand is washed back again and the beaches resume their normal appearance. Even then it is essential to watch out for dangerous undercurrents.

Beginning in Honolulu on the south coast, the following beaches are to be found by proceeding in an anti-clockwise direction:

Ala Moana Beach Park

This beach in the centre of the town is very popular with local people and is good for bathing.

Waikiki and Kuhio Beaches

Waikiki Beach and Kuhio Beach are described under Waikiki (see A to Z).

Diamond Head Beach Park

Worth visiting, although the bathing is not very good.

Hanauma Bay Beach Park

This is perhaps the most beautiful – but also the busiest – beach on Oahu. The bay forms a crater partly filled with water. The sea is always calm here, and with hardly any danger of undercurrents it is ideal for snorkelling and scuba-diving. As Hanauma Bay is a protected area and fishing is prohibited, divers can observe numerous multi-coloured fish at play.

Following Route 72 we reach Koko Head Beach Park, also known as Sandy Beach, one of the most dangerous stretches on Oahu. Only experienced divers venture here; numerous undercurrents and rocks make it quite unsuitable for the average swimmer.

Bathers should also exercise extreme caution in Makapuu Beach Park; better still, stay well clear!

Hanauma Bay on Oahu Island, an ideal place for snorkelling

A few miles further north Waimanalo Beach Park, 3 miles/5km long, is the longest beach on Oahu and – in contrast to the two we have just described – quite suitable for swimmers of average ability.

Waimanalo Beach Park

This beach is reserved for members of the US Air Force on weekdays, and thus is open to the public only from noon on Friday to Sunday evening. Good swimming, pleasant for picnics.

Bellows Field Beach Park

This is made up of three beaches: Kailua, Kalama and Oneawa, with a total length of more than 2 miles/3km. White sand and reef-sheltered seas make Kailua one of Oahu's best beaches, favoured more by local people than by tourists. To get to it take the Kamehameha Highway (H1), Pali Highway (61) as far as Kailua, then Kailua Road to the beach.

Kailua Beach Park

Further north along Route 83 lies one of the finest beaches, directly opposite the island known as Chinaman's Hat, with plenty of picnic places and shady trees.
North of Laie you will find the Malekahana State Recreation Area, and offshore the Goat Island bird sanctuary.

Kualoa County Regional Park

The beaches on the north coast lie very near to one another; from north to south, they are Sunset Beach, Ehukai Beach, KeWaena Beach and Waimea Beach.
These beaches, stretching over several miles, are a surfer's paradise, but the breakers can often be too high for bathing; in winter they can be as much as 25ft/8m. Warning signs must always be obeyed. While local surfers seem to prefer Makaha Beach on the west coast, Californians are usually found here on the north coast.
Heavy breakers up to 30ft/9m in height are also often encountered in Waimea Bay Beach County Park, so the less experienced would do well to watch from the beach instead of risking the water themselves. Particular care is necessary in the winter months.

NORTH COAST

Bookshops

On the west coast, from south to north, a string of easily accessible beaches lie along Route 93. These are: Kahe Beach Park, Nanakuli Beach Park, Ulehawa Beach Park, Maili Beach Park, Lualualei Beach Park, Pokai Beach Park, Makaha Beach Park, Keeau Beach Park and Yokohama Bay, at the end of the road.

Apart from the latter, all these beaches are well equipped, although Keeau is better suited for surfing than bathing. As already mentioned, Makaha is above all else a rendezvous for surfers, swimming being somewhat dangerous when the swell is high. Maili lies between the two rivers of Ulehawa and Mailiili which flow down from the mountains and enter the sea at this point. Conditions for bathing are excellent here.

Bookshops

Most bookshops offer a good selection of Hawaiian literature; some of the principal ones are:

Oahu
Honolulu

Upstart Crow and Co., 1050 Ala Moana Boulevard (Ward Warehouse); tel. 533–17614
and 1200 Ala Moana Boulevard (Ward Center); tel. 536–4875
Honolulu Book Shop, Ala Moana Shopping Center; tel. 941–2274
Honolulu Book Shop, downtown Honolulu, 1001 Bishop Street; tel. 537–6224
Waldenbooks, 2201 Kalalaua Avenue (Royal Hawaiian Shopping Center); tel. 926–3200
Bishop Museum, 1525 Bernice Street; tel. 847–3511

Hawaii

Basically Books, 169 Keawe Street, Hilo; tel. 961–0144
Book Gallery, Kaikoo Mall, Hilo; tel. 935–2447

Kauai

Stones Books, Kukui Grove Shopping Center, Lihue; tel. 245–3703
Waldenbooks, Kikui Grove Shopping Center, Lihue; tel. 245–7162

Maui

Upstart Crow and Co., The Wharf, Lahaina; tel. 667–9544
Waldenbooks, Maui Mall, Kahului; tel. 877–0181

Libraries

Most of the larger places have public libraries, the addresses of which can be found in the local telephone directory.

Business Hours

See Opening Times

Camping

General

On the Hawaiian islands there are in all more than 50 parks with chalets offering overnight accommodation, or which provide camping sites. However, caravans are not allowed. There are only a few private camp sites; most sites are in National Parks, State Parks and City and County Parks. The latter offer the least in standards of comfort. The theft risk is very high, especially near large towns and on the west coast of Oahu. Requirements vary: for some a simple free permit is all that is necessary, while others must be reserved at least a week in advance. In addition, campers should obtain from each site details of the length of stay allowed (mostly only 3 to 5 days, 7 to 14 days on Hawaii Island). Some sites are closed on one or two days each week (often Wednesdays and Thursdays). Although some of these regulations may appear somewhat unfriendly, this is offset to a considerable degree by the fact that the charges per night are often very

low; at some sites it is only one US dollar. In all cases it is advisable to write
to the department concerned in good time for information and bookings.

Department of Parks and Recreation   **Hawaii**
25 Aupuni St., Hilo, HI 96720; tel. 961–8311

Division of State Prks
75 Aupuni St., Hilo, HI 96720; tel. 961–7200

Hawaii Volcanoes National Park, HI 96718; tel. 967–7311
Recommended sites: Keokeo County Beach Park (in the north of Hawaii),
Samuel Spencer County Beach Park (west of Kawaihae), Punaluu County
Camping (near Punaluu), Namakani Camping (in the Volcanoes National
Park).

Parks and Recreation   **Kauai**
4193 Hardy St., Lihue, HI 96766; tel. 245–8821

Division of State Parks
3060 Eiwa St., Lihue, HI 96766; tel. 241–3444
Recommended sites: Haena Beach Park Camping (near Haena), Niumalu
Beach Park Camping (near Lihue, at Nawiliwili Harbour), Anini Beach Park
Camping (west of Kilauea, near Princeville), Polihale State Park Camping
(west of Kekaha).

Koele Company   **Lanai**
P.O. Box L, Lanai City, HI 96763; tel. 565–6661

Lanai Company
P.O. Box L, Lanai City, HI 96763; tel. 565–8232
Recommended sites: Hulopoe Beach Camping (in the south of the island)

Department of Parks and Recreation   **Maui**
War Memorial Gym, 1580 Koahumanu Ave., Wailuku, HI 96793; tel.
243–7389

Division of Parks
54 High St., Wailuku, HI 96793; tel. 243–5354

Haleakala National Park
P.O. Box 369, Makawao, HI 96768; tel. 572–7749
Recommended sites: Seven Pools (on the coast in the Haleakala National
Park, south of Hanai), Waianapanapa State Park Camping (near Hana),
Pecusa Camping (south of Lahaina)

Department of Parks and Recreation   **Molokai**
Kaunakakai, HI 96748; tel. 553–5141

Division of Parks
P.O. Box 153, Kaunakakai, HI 96748; tel. 567–6083

City and County Parks of Molokai
P.O. Box 526, Kaunakakai, HI 96748; tel. 533–3221
Recommended sites: One Ali Camping (east of Kaunakakai, near Kewala),
Papohaku State Park Camping (west coast of Molokai)

Department of Parks and Recreation   **Oahu**
650 S. King St., Honolulu, HI 96813; tel. 523–4525

Division of Parks
1151 Punchbowl Street, Honolulu, HI 96813; tel. 587–0300
Recommended sites: Kaiaka State Park Camping (north of Haleiwa), Waimanalo State Park Camping (Kailua, south of Waimanalo), Sand Island

State Park Camping (on Sand Island, between Honolulu Airport and Hono-lulu Downtown). All State Park and County Park camp sites on Oahu are closed on Wednesdays and Thursdays.

Car rental

General

For anyone wishing to explore the islands independently a hire car is often essential. Oahu is the only island with an excellent public transport system, but even there – to save time – it is best to rent a car for excursions of any length. On the other islands it is absolutely imperative, especially on Hawaii because of its size and the relatively long distances to be covered. In Honolulu and on the other islands all the major rental firms, as well as a number of local ones, have desks at the various airports. It is best to book a car in advance, especially during the high season and at week-ends. Tariffs vary considerably, so it is advisable to compare charges. Often car rental charges are at their cheapest when included in a Fly & Drive holiday package.

Rental conditions

Two things are needed in order to hire a car: an internationally valid driving licence, which should be obtained before leaving home, and a credit card (American Express, Mastercard, Visa, Diners' Club). Otherwise a cash guarantee deposit of several hundred US dollars will have to be made. Drivers must be at least 21 years of age – some firms insist on 25 – and some impose an upper age limit of 70. To the relatively low tariffs – especially if the car is rented for a week – must be added the premium for personal accident and third party liability insurance, unless the use of a credit card gives cover automatically.

Generally the hirer must agree not to use the vehicle on unmade-up roads. The majority of the main roads and most side roads are made-up, and so are the mountain roads on all the islands.

International
car rental firms

The following have offices on all the islands:
Dollar Rent-A-Car; tel. 800–342–7398/944–1544

The following have offices on all the islands except Lanai:
Budget Rent-A-Car; tel. 537–3600

The following have offices on all the islands except Molokai and Lanai:
Alamo Rent-A-Car; tel. 800–327–9633
Avis Rent-A-Car; tel. 800–831–8000
Hertz; tel. 800–654–3011
National Interrent; tel. 800–CAR–RENT or 800–227–3876

The following have offices only in Hilo, Hawaii:
Harper Car & Truck Rentals; tel. 969–1478

Cars and minibuses suitable for disabled persons on Maui, Oahu and Hawaii (Kona, Hilo) can be rented from:
Over the Rainbow; tel. 800–303–5521

Chemists

Drugstores and
pharmacies

American drugstores, occasionally called pharmacies, are quite different from European chemists; for most of them dispensing prescriptions is only a very small part of their business. Many are like small supermarkets also selling food and drink, and a few include a snack bar as well.

Most drug stores are listed in the "yellow pages" of the telephone directories which are available in almost every hotel and motel room.

The largest and most efficient drugstore chain, with branches on the other islands too, is Long's in the Ala Moana Shopping Center in Honolulu; tel.

941–4433. It is open Mon.–Fri. 9.30am–9pm, Sat. 10am–5.30pm and Sun. 10am–5pm.

In Waikiki two drugstores are worthy of mention: Outrigger Pharmacy, 2335 Kalalaua Avenue; tel. 923–2529, and Kuhio Pharmacy, 2330 Kuhio Avenue; tel. 923–4466.

There are branches in Maui in the Lahaina Cannery Shopping Center; tel. 667–4384, and also in Kauai in the Kukui Grove Shopping Center; tel. 245–7771, on the island of Hawaii in the Lanihau Center in Kona; tel. 329–1380, in the Prince Kuhio, Plaza in Hilo; tel. 959–5881, and at 555 Kilauea Avenue, also in Hilo; tel. 935–3358.

On Molokai Drugs can be found in Kaunakakai on Molokai; tel. 553–9913.

No drugstores provide a special night-time service outside normal opening hours. In the event of an emergency help should be sought from the nearest hospital. They are open 24 hours a day and have a dispensary. **Emergencies**

Clothing

Light summer clothes are usually sufficient, although the weather can become somewhat cooler in the winter months of November to January. Casual leisurewear is normal, as well as Aloha shirts for men and muumuus (white Hawaiian dresses) for the ladies. Sandals are the best footwear. Do not forget to take a raincoat, as each island has its wetter parts.

Only a few restaurants expect their male guests to wear a jacket and tie; this is generally speaking the exception. When a table is reserved – and this is usually necessary – it is best to check on the position regarding dress.

If mountaineering and walking are envisaged, good stout climbing boots or shoes are essential. Warm clothing should also be taken as temperatures in the higher mountainous regions are considerably lower than on the coast (see Facts and Figures, Climate), as well as light rainwear and protection from the sun, especially for the head.

Credit Cards

See Currency

Currency

The unit of currency is the US dollar (US $). There are notes with values of 1, 2, 5, 10, 20, 50 and 100 US dollars (in internal banking business there are also larger notes), and coins of 1 (penny), 5 (nickel), 10 (dime) and 25 (quarter) cents; occasionally 50 c (half dollar) and 1 dollar coins can be found.

The exchange rate of the US dollar fluctuates against most foreign currencies; current rates can be obtained from banks and tourist offices and are published in national newspapers. Visitors from Europe are recommended to change their money into US dollars before they leave Britain, and above all to make sure they have sufficient change (notes of $1 to $10 and coins) available. There is a bank (Perera Deak) at Honolulu Airport where foreign currency can be exchanged for US dollars, and there is usually no problem in doing so at banks in Honolulu, but the exchange rate is usually poorer than in the UK. Shops and restaurants generally do not accept foreign currency; the larger hotels will do so but will charge a high commission. **Exchange rates**

There are no restrictions on the import and export of foreign currency, but if bringing in more than 5000 US dollars a customs declaration must be completed in the aircraft. **Currency regulations**

Customs regulations

Travellers' cheques

For security reasons travellers' cheques should be obtained prior to departure, made out in US dollars by a European branch of American Express or Barclays. These can be exchanged at any bank, and in most hotels and restaurants, on production of a passport. For these travellers' cheques a commission of 1% is charged when they are purchased. If travellers' cheques are lost or stolen they can be replaced by the nearest branch of the issuing firm providing the control coupon is produced.

Credit cards

Visitors are recommended to take credit cards – American Express, Mastercard, Visa, Diner's Club and Carte Blanche are generally accepted. They are useful for paying bills of all kinds – for airline tickets, in hotels and motels, petrol stations and most shops. When a car is rented credit cards are accepted both in payment and (where required) as a security deposit, whereas cash is not liked.

Banks

In Hawaii banks are generally well organised, being primarily branches of regional banks such as the Bank of Hawaii and the First Hawaiian Bank. At least one branch of a bank will be found in every large shopping centre in Honolulu and on the other islands.

As Hawaii is primarily geared to tourism there is normally no problem in changing sterling into dollars if the need arises.

Most banks are open from 8.30am–3pm or 3.30pm, 6pm on Fridays. Most close on Saturdays, and all on Sundays and public holidays.

Banks in Honolulu

The following is a selection:
Bank of Hawaii, 2220 Kalakaua Avenue; tel. 923–2011
Central Pacific Bank, 2400 Kalakaua Avenue; tel. 923–3176
Deak Perera Hawaii Inc., 2335 Kalakaua Avenue; tel. 537–4928
First Hawaiian Bank, 2181 Kalakaua Avenue; tel. 923–0745
Hawaii National Bank, 2280 Kalakaua Avenue; tel. 923–3802
Deak Perera, branch at the airport; tel. 836–3603.

Customs regulations

Entry into the USA and to Hawaii

Articles for personal use (clothing, toilet articles, jewellery, photographic and film apparatus, binoculars, portable typewriters, portable radios and tape recorders, video and television apparatus, sports equipment and even a car for one year) can be imported without payment of duty. In addition adults can bring in one quart (about one litre) of alcoholic drink, 300 cigarettes or 50 cigars or three pounds (about 1350g) of tobacco. In addition every person can import presents up to a value of 100 US dollars including, for adults, up to one gallon (3.78 litres) of alcoholic drink and 100 cigars. There are special and complex regulations for the importation of live animals, meat, fruit and plants; information can be obtained from customs offices. For Hawaii there are special regulations regarding the importation of agricultural products; further information can be obtained from the Hawaii Visitors Bureau (see Information).

Electricity

Current in Hawaii, as on the American mainland, is supplied at 110 volts, 60 cycles AC. European visitors will require an adaptor for apparatus designed to run off 220 volts, and this is best purchased from a hardware or electrical store prior to departure, although adaptors are also available in local hardware stores.

Emergencies

Emergency dial 911

First aid, police and fire brigade can be called on 911 on the islands of Oahu, Maui, Kauai, Molokai and Lanai.

For police, fire brigade and ambulance on Hawaii, call 961–6022

See Medical Assistance   Hospitals

See Motoring   Breakdown

Events

Most events are held out of doors. Details of the exact dates and times can   General
be obtained from the local press or advertising brochures. In most cases
further details of a particular event can usually be obtained from the
telephone numbers listed below. With very few exceptions, all events are
free of charge. To avoid any confusion, the term "Big Island" has been used
to indicate Hawaii Island itself.
   The Hawaii Visitors Bureau (see Information) will also provide a Calendar
of Events, with details of dates and places.

January

Hawaiian Open Golf Tournament, Waialae Country Club Golf Course,   Early
   Honolulu, Oahu; tel. 526–1232

Narcissus Festival in Chinatown, Honolulu   Middle to late
Chinese New Year Festival with colourful lion- and dragon-dances, fire-
   works and flower shows; tel. 533–3181
Cherry Blossom Festival in Honolulu, usually lasting until early March

February

Punahou School Carnival, Honolulu; tel. 944–5711 and 944–5753   Early

Surfing competitions, etc. on Oahu, Makaka Beach; tel. 593–9292; on Maui,   Middle
   Honolulu Bay and Hookipa Beach Park; tel. 572–4883

March

Mauna Kea Ski Meet, slalom races on Mauna Kea, Big Island; tel. 943–6643   Early
Marathon from Wailuku to Lahaina, Maui; tel. 242–6042
Cemiesee Windsurfing Championship, Hookipa Beach Park, Maui; tel.
   572–4883

Cherry Blossom Queen Pageant, grand Japanese festival held in Honolulu,   Middle
   Oahu; tel. 949–2255
Kamehameha Schools Song Concert, in the International Center, Hono-
   lulu; tel. 842–8338 and 842–8495

Prince Kuhio Festival, Kauai; held at the week-end following the State   Late
   Festival on March 26th; tel. 245–3971
Kona Stampede, Big Island; tel. 885–7949
Start of the polo season (which lasts until September), Hawaii International
   Polo Club Games, Oahu; tel. 637–POLO; Honolulu Polo Club Games,
   Waimanalo, Oaho; tel. 396–7656

April

Wesak (Buddha) Day, held on the first Sunday following April 8th   Early
   (Buddha's birthday). Dawn Service with dancing in Ala Moana Park and a
   choral concert in Kapiolani Park in Honolulu; tel. 538–3805

Events

Middle	Whale Day in Kihei, on Maui; tel. 879–8860
	Hawaiian Festival of Music, Waikiki Shell, Honolulu; tel. 637–6566
Late	Hula Pakahi & Lei Festival, Maui Inter-Continental Resort, Wailea, Maui; tel. 879–1922

May

May 1st	"Lei Day", May Day Festival. Celebrated on all the islands, with garlands of flowers, wreaths of walnut leaves and feather adornments. The White Queen, accompanied by her seven maids-in-waiting, is crowned in Kapiolani Park, Honolulu; tel. 521–9815
Early	Captain Cook Festival, with Hawaiian games, angling competitions and musical events on Big Island, Kailua Kona
Middle	Bankoh Kayak Challenge, kayak races from Molokai to Oahu; tel. 521–2345
	Fiesta Filippina, a Philippine folk-festival lasting several days, with the crowning of Miss Philippina in Honolulu
Late	Bankoh Ho'Omana'O Challenge, sailing regatta from Maui to Honolulu; tel. 537–8660
	Keahou-Kona Triathlon, Keauhou Bay, Kailu-Kona on Big Island; tel. 329–2692
	Memorial Day Festival. On the last Monday in May wreaths are placed on thousands of graves in the Punchbowl National Cemetery in Honolulu

June

June 10th	King Kamehameha Day on all the islands, with street parties (hoolaulea) in Waikiki and Kona, parades in Kailua-Kona, Lahaina and Kahului; for information tel. Honolulu 586–0333
Late	Hawaii State Farm Fair in Honolulu; tel. 848–2074

July

July 4th	Parker Ranch Rodeo, Waimea, Big Island; tel. 885–7655
	Makawao Rodeo, Hawaii's biggest rodeo, Makawao, Maui; tel. 572–9928
	Naalehu Rodeo, Naalehu, Big Island; tel. 928–8326
	MacFarlane Canoe Regatta and Surf Race, Waikiki, Honolulu; tel. 921–1400
Early	Na Wahine O Hawaii, performances of music and dancing in Ala Moana Park, Honolulu; tel. 239–4336
	Na Hula O Ka'Ohikukapulani, a hula festival held in Lihue, Kauai; tel. 335–576 and 335–6466
	Big Island Marathon, Hilo, Big Island; tel. 961–6651
	Transpacific Yacht Regatta, Los Angeles–Honolulu. This world-famous yacht race starts on July 4th and the first boats arrive in Honolulu after about 9 days
	Festival of the Pacific, Hilo, Big Island; tel. 961–6123
	Prince Lot Hula Festival, Moanalua Gardens, Honolulu; tel. 839–5334
	Ukulele Festival with music and dancing in Kapiolani Park, Honolulu; tel. 737–3739
Late	International Jazz Festival, Waikiki Shell, Baisdell Center; tel. 941–9974
	Kilauea Volcano Marathon and Rim Runs, in Hawaii Volcanoes National Park, Big Island; tel. 967–8222

August

Early	Hanalei Stampede, Po'oka Stables, Princeville, Kauai; tel. 826–6777
	Hula Festival, Kapiolani Park, Honolulu

Kapalua Music Festival, Kapalua Bay Hotel, Kapalua; tel. 669–5656

Macadamia Nut Harvest Festival, Honokea, Big Island; tel. 755–7276   Middle to Late
Admission Day Celebrations (celebrated on all the islands on August 17th)
Hawaii Intercultural Dance Festival, Big Island; tel. 965–7828
Hula Festival in Kapiolani Park, Honolulu; tel. 266–7654

September

Polynesian Festival (dancing competitions), Kaneohe, Oahu; tel. 247–6188   Early
Parker Ranch Round-up Rodeo, Waimea, Big Island; tel. 885–7447
Kapalua Open Tennis Tournament, Kapalua, Maui; tel. 669–0244
Queen Liliuokalani World Championship Long Distance Canoe Races for
    men and women, in Kailua-Kona, Big Island; tel. 323–2565
Okinawan Festival, dancing, handicrafts and other cultutal events held in
    Kapiolani Park, Honolulu; tel. 676–5400
Chinese Moon Festival Day, held in honour of the Chinese Emperor Minh
    Huang. Details from Chinese Chamber of Commerce; tel. 533–3181
Hawaiian Ocean Festival: The Diamond Head Wahine Windsurfing Classic,
    Waikiki, Oahu; tel. 521–4322

Hawaii County Fair, Hilo Civic Auditorium, Hilo, Big Island; tel. 935–5022   Middle
Aloha Week (street festivals on all the islands lasting until early October);
    for information tel. Honolulu 944–8857

October

Maui County Fair, Kahului, Maui; tel. 877–3432   Early
Mukahiki Festival, Waimea Falls Park, Oahu; tel. 638–8511
Ironman Triathlon in Kailua-Kona, Big Island, with international
    competitors

Orchid Show in Honolulu; tel. 395–3689   Middle

November

Lincoln Mercury Kapalua International Golf Tournament, Kapalua, Maui;   Early
    tel. 669–0244
Kona Coffee Festival, a folk-festival in Kailua-Kona, Big Island; tel.
    326–7820

King Kalakaua Keiki Hula Festival, Kailua-Kona, Big Island   Middle
Veterans Day Parade from Fort DeRussy to Kapiolani Park, Honolulu

International Surfing Championships, lasting until December, on Sunset   Late
    Beach and Makaha Beach on Oahu

December

International Film Festival on Oahu and neighbouring islands   Early
Festival of Christmas Trees in Honolulu; tel. 547–4780

Honolulu Marathon; tel. 734–7200   Middle
Buddha Day, in all Buddhist temples on the islands; tel. 245–6262

Food and Drink

In addition to the many restaurants (see entry), there are numerous snack   Snacks
bars like those on the US mainland, where hamburgers, hot dogs, pizzas
and sandwiches can be bought.

Food and Drink

International cuisine

The various ethnic groups residing on the Hawaiian islands have each brought with them their national specialities. As well as Chinese, Japanese cuisine has become very popular.

Hawaiian cuisine

It is not all that simple to obtain genuine Hawaiian fare. The best way is to attend a *luau* (see below), where there will be such specialities as *poi*, a sort of porridge prepared from the root of the taro plant, which is widely found in the Pacific. Depending on its consistency, the "porridge" is described as one, two or three finger poi; the thicker it is the lower the number. Other typical Hawaiian dishes are *uala* (sweet potatoes), *haupia* (coconut pudding) and, of course, the ubiquitous roast pork.

The word *pupus* has come to include "starters" in the broadest sense in everyday parlance, but these are seldom of Hawaiian origin.

Fruit

The best way to "eat Hawaiian" is with fruit, a wide selection of which is offered on every occasion.

Papaya fruit is available almost all the year round; particularly tasty is what is known as strawberry papaya, with pinkish-red flesh. Visitors should also try mangoes, which ripen between April and October. Coconuts are on sale all the year, and chilled coconut milk is a special delicacy. Hawaiian bananas are small but sweet and tasty. Pineapples are found here in abundance, as well as bread-fruit, guavas and avocados.

Drinks

As well as the delicious fruit juices and fresh coconut milk, mention should also be made of the various cocktails available, even though they are not of true Hawaiian origin. Names such as Mai Tai, Blue Hawaii, Chi Chi, Ono and Halekulani Sunset are but a few of many drinks mixed mainly from fruit juices, white rum and various liqueurs. A genuine Hawaiian drink is "okolehao", a sort of gin distilled from the roots of the ti-palm.

A wide selection of wines and beers is on sale in bars and restaurants, especially in Waikiki.

Luau

Banquets

Going to a luau – the Hawaiian word for festival or party – will give visitors the opportunity to join in a traditional Hawaiian feast. Many hotels and restaurants lay on luaus for tourists. A luau is made up of an evening meal combined with a dancing display, mainly of traditional Hawaiian dances and those from other Polynesian islands. It is divided into three sections:

6pm–7pm: the guests arrive and help themselves to a drink which is included in the price.

7pm–8pm: a buffet meal is taken at the (generally long) table.

8pm–9pm: the dancing display provides entertainment.

Oven-roasted pig
The imu ceremony

The main item on the menu is roast pig, cooked in the traditional way in an imu, an underground oven. The almost ritual preparation procedure, which starts about noon, is something which should not be missed; ask about the exact time the ceremony is to take place.

A fire is kindled on stones, often lava-deposits; as soon as this goes out and the stones are hot enough, the ashes are removed. Now the imu can be filled. Two men lay the prepared pig in the centre of the hole in the ground, and cover it first with ti leaves and then with banana leaves. The pig's abdominal cavity is stuffed with hot lava-stones, and then further leaves are laid over the animal. Thus prepared, the pig is wrapped in a sack and covered with soil. It takes four to six hours for it to be cooked through. At the start of the luau it is dug up, divided up into small pieces and served to the guests. Thanks to this method of preparation – which the Hawaiians call "kalua" – the flesh is juicy and tender.

Other foods

There is a lot more on the menu at a luau, including fruit, salad, fish (usually mahi-mahi and huhu), poi, sweet potatoes and haupia, which is often the only sweet dish. Visitors will find it difficult to try everything!

The Imu Ceremony: Ti leaves are laid on the open-air oven

The cost of attending a luau will vary between US$30 and US$60, including tax and tips. It is always necessary to book in advance.

Organisers

King Kamameha's Hotel, 75–5660 Palani Road, Kailua-Kona; tel. 326–4969
Hilton Waikoloa Village, 425 Waikoloa Beach Drive, Kamuela; tel. 885–1234
Kona Village Resort, Kailua-Kona; tel. 325–5555

Hawaii

Kauai Coconut Beach Resort, Coconut Plantation, Kapaa; tel. 822–3455/800–22–ALOHA

Kauai

Royal Lahaina Resort, 2780 Kekaa Drive, Lahaina; tel. 661–3611
Grand Wailea Resort, 3850 Wailea Alanui Drive, Wailea; tel. 875–1234
Maui Maui Marriott, 100 Nohea Kai Drive. Kaanapali; tel. 661–5828
Maui Lu Resort, 575 So. Kihei Road, Kihei; tel. 879–5881

Maui

Paradise Cove Luau, 92–1089 Alii Drive, Kapolei; tel. 973–5828
Polynesian Cultural Center Luau, 55–370 Kamehameha Highway, Laie tel. 293–3333/367–7060
Hilton Hawaiian Village, 2005 Kalia Road, Honolulu; tel. 949–4321

Oahu

Getting to Hawaii

The only way to get to the Hawaiian islands is by air, as there are no longer any shipping links between the USA and Hawaii. Only cruise ships put into Honolulu harbour.

By air

Flight connections, on the other hand, are very frequent. Being situated in mid-Pacific the Hawaiian islands are directly accessible from several continents; there are flights to Honolulu from Asia (Tokyo, Bangkok, Singapore, Manila), Australia (Sydney, Melbourne), New Zealand (Auckland) and from the islands of the South Pacific.

If travelling from the UK or Europe, the normal way is to go by transatlantic flight from London or other airports to Chicago, San Francisco or Los Angeles, and then fly on from there to Hawaii.

The following American airlines fly to Honolulu: America West, American, Continental, Delta, Northwest Orient, TWA and United Airlines, as well as Hawaiian Airlines from Los Angeles.

Direct flights
to other Hawaiian
islands

From the west coast of the USA there are also direct flights to Kahului (Maui), Kailua-Kona (Hawaii) and Lihue (Kauai). There are also non-stop flights fron Chicago to Kahului.

For flights between the islands see Air Transport.

Special tariffs

Some US airlines, such as Delta Air and United Airlines, for example, offer cheap combined flight tickets (Skypass and tour tickets). Generally speaking fares for flights within America are relatively low, so it is well worthwhile combining a transatlantic flight with a domestic flight. Detailed advice should be obtained before arranging the journey.

Golf

Hawaii Island

On "Big Island" there are a number of excellent golf-courses, with the added bonus of beautiful views of the Pacific Ocean and the high mountains. Some of the courses which belong to the luxury hotels are reserved for hotel guests; in any event the fees are rather high. Telephone for details in advance.

Golf-courses

The following is a selection:

Francis H. I'l Brown North Course and South Course, Mauni Lani Resort. P.O. Box 4959, Kohala Coast; tel. 885–6655

Hapuna Golf Course, 62–100 Kauna'oa Drive, Kamuela; tel. 880–3000

Kona Country Club, 78–7000 Alii Drive, Kailua-Kona; tel. 322–2595

Mauna Kea Beach Hotel Golf Course, 62–100 Mauna Kea Beach Drive, Kamuela; tel. 80–3480

Waikola Resort Golf – Beach Golf Course, 1020 Keana Place, Kamuela; tel. 885–6548

Waikola Resort Golf – King's Golf Course, 600 Waikola Beach Drive, Kamuela; tel. 885–4647

Kauai Island

Even though it boasts fewer golf-courses than its neighbouring islands, the golfer will still be able to enjoy himself on Kauai. Most of the courses are owned by hotels or clubs, so it is always best to telephone first to enquire about the fees and whether non-residents can play there.

Golf-courses

The following is a selection:

Kiele Golf Course and Lagoons Golf Course, Golf and Racquet Club, Kalapi Beach, Lihue; tel. 241–6000 and 800–634–6400

Princeville Golf Club – Prince Course, Princeville Corporation, 53900 Kuhio Highway, Princeville; tel. 826–5000 and 800–826–4400

Kaluakio Golf Course on Molokai Island

Princeville Golf Club – Makai Course, Princeville Corporation, Lei O Papa Road, Princeville; tel. 826–3580 and 800–4400

Maui Island

Maui has some excellent golf-courses, including several which are run by clubs or hotels. Some are not open to the public. One of the best known is Bay Course at Lahaina (in the north-west of Maui), which Arnold Palmer helped to construct. An international tournament is held here every November.

The following is a selection: Golf-courses

The Bay Course, 300 Kapalua Drive, Lahaina; tel. 669–8044
Kaanapali Golf Course – North and South, Kaapalani Beach, Lahaina; tel. 661–3691
The Plantation Course, 300 Kapalua Drive, Lahaina; tel. 669–8044
Silversword Golf Course, 1345 Pilani Highway, Kihei; tel. 874–0777
Wailea Blue Course, 120 Kaukahi St., Wailea; tel. 875–5111
Wailea Emerald and Gold Course, 100 Wailea Golf Club Drive, Wailea; tel. 875–5111

Molokai Island

On Molokai there is only one 18-hole golf-course, at the well-developed Kaluakoi tourist resort.

Kaluakoi Golf Course, P.O. Box 26, Maunaloa; tel. 552–2739 and 800–521–1625

Oahu Island

There are a large number of golf-courses on Oahu, although many belong to clubs or hotels

Golf-courses

The following is a selection:

Del Mar Golf College at The Sheraton Resort and Country Club, 84–626 Makaha Valley Rd., Waianae; tel. 695–5561
Ko Olina Golf Club, 92–1220 Aliinui Drive, Kapolea; tel. 676–5300
The Links at Kuilima, 57–091 Kamehameha Highway, Kahuku; tel. 293–8574
Sheraton Makaha Resort & Country Club – West Golf Course, 84–626 Makaha Valley Road, Waianae; tel. 695–9544
Turtle Bay Country Club, 57–091 Kamehameha Highway, Kahuku; tel. 293–8574/800–HILTONS

Lanai Island

Lanai has two golf-courses in addition to those owned by the larger hotels

Challenge at Manele, P.O. Box L, Lanai City; tel. 565–2222
Experience at Koele, P.O. Box L, Lanai City; tel. 565–4653

Hotels

General

There are numerous places to stay on the Hawaiian islands. In all there are about 70,000 hotel rooms available, and the number is increasing. New hotels are opening up all the time, mainly large establishments on the coast, offering very high standards at prices to match. Cheaper accommodation is also available, of course, ranging from very simple tourist hotels to those less attractively situated some way from the beaches and with nothing much to offer in the way of a view.

Bed and Breakfast

Another means of obtaining overnight accommodation at cheap rates is bed and breakfast with local families. Charges are usually from about US$ 50 per night. For information and to make reservations: Hawaii Bed and Breakfast Hawaii, P.O. Box 449, Kapaa/Hawaii, HI 96746.

Hotels are divided into five groups, and the following is an indication of what the visitor can expect to have to pay for a double room:

Price categories

Group I+	over 225 US $
Group I	125–225 US $
Group II	85–125 US $
Group III	60–85 US $
Group IV	under 60 US $

In most cases up to four people can sleep in one double room without any additional charge. Usually it is also worth enquiring about special terms for longer stays of a week or a month.

In the lists of selected hotels below the following abbreviations are used: C = condominium (see below), r. = number of rooms, SP = swimming pool, T = tennis court(s).

Additional costs

To these prices must be added sales tax, which is charged throughout Hawaii, and hotel tax, totalling about 10%. Nothing extra is charged for children up to about eighteen years of age sleeping in the same room; for additional adults a further five to twenty dollars is charged. Breakfast is seldom included in the price. Many hotels also charge extra for garage space.

There are hardly any motels like those on the American mainland.

Apart from hotels there are also many condominiums on the islands, i.e. mainly small, furnished dwellings comprising several rooms, which are particularly advantageous if more than three or four people are travelling in a party. They have fully-fitted kitchens, but the disadvantage is that users have to stay more than one day, usually two to five.

In the lists which follow condominiums are either listed separately or are marked with the letter "C".

It is advisable to book overnight stays in advance; most hotels have "800" telephone numbers, on which calls to reserve a room are free of charge. Hotel rooms on Hawaii, Kauai, Maui and Molokai can be reserved through a number of agencies in Honolulu; these agencies will arrange bookings for hotels, flights and car rental for an "all-in" price, which is usually cheaper than doing them separately (see Travel Bureaux).

An Accommodation Guide can be obtained from the Hawaiian Visitors' Bureau in Honolulu (see Information).

The following is an alphabetical list of hotels and condominiums on each of the islands. Where applicable, the "800" reservations number is given as well as the normal telephone number. The SDT code for the whole of Hawaii is 808.

Condominiums *(margin note)*

Reserving rooms *(margin note)*

Note *(margin note)*

Hawaii Island

Manago Hotel (64 r.), IV, Capt. Cook, HI 96704; tel. 323–2642
Captain Cook

Volcano House (60 r.), II, HI 96718; tel. 967–7321/800–736–7140, SP, T, golf
Volcanoes National Park

Dolphin Bay Hotel (18 r.), III, HI 96720; tel. 935–1466
Hawaii Naniloa Hotel (325 r.), I, Banyan Drive, HI 96720; tel. 969–3333/ 800–442–5845, SP, golf
Hilo Bay Hotel (140 r.), III, 87 Banyan Drive, HI 96720; tel. 961–5818/ 800–442–5841, SP
Hilo Hawaiian Hotel (283 r.), II, 71 Banyan Drive, HI 96720; tel. 935–9361/ 800–367–5004, SP
Hilo

Aston Royal Sea Cliff Resort (C–154 r.), 75–6040 Alii Drive, HI 96740; tel. 329–8021/800–321–2558, SP, T
Keauhou Beach Hotel (310 r.), II, 78–6740 Alii Drive, HI 96740; tel. 322–3441/800–448–8990, SP, T
Kona Bay Hotel-Uncle Billy's (140 r.), III, 75–5739 Alii Drive, HI 96740; tel. 329–1393/800–442–5841, SP
Kona Surf Resort & Country Club (530 r.), I, 78–128 Ehukai St., HI 96740; tel. 322–3411/800–367–8011, SP, T, golf
Sea Village (C–131 r.), II, 75–6002 Alii Drive, HI 96740; tel. 329–6488/ 800–367–5168, SP, T
Kailua-Kona

Parker Ranch Lodge (21 r.), III, Highway 19, P.O. Box 458, HI 96743; tel. 885–4100
Puako Condominium (40 r.), II, 3 Puako Beach Road, HI 96743; tel. 965–9446, SP
Kamuela/ Waimea

The Royal Waikoloan , A Royal Outrigger (547 r.), I, 69–275 Waikaloa Beach Drive, HI 96743; tel. 885–6789/800–688–7444, SP, T, golf
Shores at Waikoloa (120 r.), I, 5460 Beach Rental, HI 96743; tel. 467–3311/ 800–223–7037, SP, T, golf; minimum booking 3 days
Waikoloa

Hotels

Fountains outside the Westin Kauai Hotel

Kauai Island

Hanalei

Cliffs at Princeville (C–40 r.), I, Edwards Road, HI 96714; tel. 826–6219/
800–367–7052, SP, T, golf

Hanalei Bay Resort (C–40 r.), I, 5380 Honoiki Road, HI 96722;
tel. 826–6585/800–222–5541, SP, T, golf

Hanalei Colony Resort (C–52 r.), I, P.O. Box 20, HI 96714; tel. 826–6253/
800–628–3004, SP

Kapaa

Aston Kauai Beachboy Hotel (243 r.), I, 4-484 Kuhio Highway, HI 96766;
tel. 931–1400/800–321–2558, SP, T

Hotel Coral Reef (24 r.), IV–III, 1516 Kuhio Highway, HI 96746;
tel. 822–4481

Lae Nani (C–84 r.), I, 410 Papaloa Road, HI 96748; tel. 822–4938/
800–367–7052, SP, T

Plantation Hale (C–151 r.), II, 484 Kuhio Highway, HI 96746; tel. 688–744/
800–688–7444, SP

Koloa
(Poipu Beach)

Kiahuna Plantation (C–333 r.), I, 2253 Poipu Road, HI 96756;
tel. 800–367–7052; minimum booking 2 days

Nihi Kai Villas (C–70 r.), II, 1870 Hoone Road, HI 96756; tel. 742–7220/
800–742–1412, SP, T; mimimum booking 3 days

Poipu Kai Resort (C–350 r.), I, 1941 Poipu Road, HI 96756;
tel. 800–688–2254, SP, T

Poipu Shores (C–39 r.), I, 1775 Pe'e Road, Poipu, HI 96756; tel. 742–7700/
800–367–5004, SP

Prince Kuhio Resort (C–13 r.), III, 5160 Lawai Road, HI 96756;
tel. 245–4711, SP

Sheraton Kauai Garden Hotel (226 r.), I, 2440 Hoonani Road, HI 96756;
tel. 800–325–3535, SP, T

Sunset Kahili Condo. Apt. (C–36 r.), II, 1763 Pe'e Road, HI 96756;
tel. 742–7434/800–827–6478, SP; minimum booking 3 days

Banyan Harbor Resort (C–148 r.), II, 3411 Wilcox Road, HI 96766; tel. 245–7333/800–422–6926, SP, T   **Lihue**

Coco Palms Resort (390 r.), I, 4–241 Kuhio Highway, HI 96746; tel. 822–4921, SP, T; with wedding chapel!

Garden Island Inn (21 r.), IV, 3445 Wilcox Road, HI 96766; tel. 245–7227

Kaha Lani (C–65 r.), I, 4460 Nehe Road, HI 96766; tel. 822–9331/ 800–321–2558, SP, T

Hanalei Bay Resort (C–134 r.), II, 5380 Honoiki, HI 96722; tel. 826–7444, SP, T, golf   **Princeville**

Pali Ke Kua (C–98 r.), 5300 Ha Haku Road; tel. 800–688–2254, SP

Princeville Condominiums (C), II, HI 96722; tel. 826–6585/800–222–5541, SP, T, golf

Puu Poa (C–56 r.), I, 5454 Ka Haku Road, HI 96722; tel. 826–6585/ 800–222–5541, SP, T, golf

Kauai Resort Hotel (228 r.), II, 3–5920 Kuhio Highway, HI 96746; tel. 591–2235/800–272–5275, SP, T   **Wailua**

Lanai Island

Lanai Bed and Breakfast (3 r.), III, 312 Mahana Place, HI 96763; tel. 565–6378/800–476–0557

The Lodge at Koele (102 r.), I+, P.O. Box L, HI 96763; tel. 565–3800/ 800–321–4666, SP, T, golf, croquet lawn and bowling green, library, horse stables; minimum booking 5 days

The Manele Bay Hotel (250 r.), I+, P.O. Box, HI 96763; tel. 565–7700/ 800–321–4666, SP, T, golf

Maui Island

Hana Kai-Maui Resort (18 r.), II, P.O. Box 38, HI 96713; tel. 248–8426; minimum age 25   **Hana**

Maui Eldorado Resort Kaanapali (C–120 r.), I, 2661 Kekaa Drive, HI 96761; tel. 661–0021, SP, golf   **Kaanapali**

Maui Beach Hotel (148 r.), III, 170 Kaahumanu Ave., HI 96732; tel. 591–2235, SP   **Kahului**

Kapalua Bay Hotel and Villas (294 r.), I+, One Day Drive, HI 96761; tel. 669–5656, SP, T, golf   **Kapalua**

Kapalua Golf Villas (C–160 r.), I, 500 Kapalua Drive, HI 96761; tel. 669–4144/800–326–6775, SP, T, golf; minimum booking 5 days

Kamaole Sands (C–250 r.), II–I, 2695 S. Kihei Road, HI 96753; tel. 874–8700, SP, T   **Kihei**

Kihei Beach Resort (C–35 r.), II, 36 S. Kihei Road, HI 96753; tel. 879–2744/ 800–367–6034, SP; minimum booking 3 days

Kihei Surfside Resort (C–30 r.), II, 2936 S. Kihei Road, HI 96753; tel. 879–1488, SP

Maui Lu Resort (120 r.), 575 S. Kihei Road, HI 96753; tel. 879–5881/ 800–321–2558, SP, T

Maui Vista (C–279 r.), 2191 S. Kihei Road, HI 96753; tel. 879–7966/ 800–321–2558, SP, T

Shores of Maui (C–50 r.), III, 2075 S. Kihei Road, HI 96753; tel. 879–9140, SP, T

Embassy Suites Resort (413 r.), I+, 104 Kaanapali Shores Plaza; tel. 861–2000/800–GO–2–MAUI, SP, minigolf   **Lahaina**

Hyatt Regency Maui (815 r.), 200 Nohea Kai Drive, HI 96761; tel. 661–1234/800–233–1234, SP, T, golf

Hotels

Kaanapali Beach Hotel (430 r.), I, 2525 Ka'anapali Parkway, HI 96761;
 tel. 661–0011/800–233–1014, SP, golf
Kaanapali Shores Resort (C–463 r.), II, 3445 L. Honoapiilani Road,
 HI 96761; tel. 800–854–8843, SP, T; minimum booking 3 days
Kahana Village (C–42 r.), I, 4531 L. Honoapiilani Road, HI 96761;
 tel. 669–5111, SP; minimum booking 5 days
Lahaina Shores Beach Resort (C–199 r.), II–I, 475 Front Street, HI 96761;
 tel. 661–4835/800–642–6284, SP
Mahana (C–15 r.), III–II, 110 Kaanapali Shore Plaza, HI 96761;
 tel. 800–854–8843, SP, T; minimum booking 3 days
Maui Kaanapali Villas (C–250 r.), I, 45 Kai Ala Drive, HI 96761;
 tel. 667–7791/800–321–2558, SP, windsurfing
Napili Kai Beach Club (165 r.), I, 5900 Honoapiilani Road, HI 96761;
 tel. 669–6271/800–367–5030, SP, whirlpool
Napili Shores Resort (C–152 r.), III, 5315 L. Honoapiilani Road, HI 96761;
 tel. 854–8843/800–854–8843, SP; minimum booking 3 days
Pioneer Inn (48 r.), II, 658 Wharf St., HI 96761; tel. 661–3636/
 800–4457–5457
Papakea Resort (C–364 r.), III–II, 3543 L. Honoapillani Road, HI 96761;
 tel. 800–484–9884, SP, T; minimum booking 4 days
Polynesian Shores (C–52 r.), 3975 L. Honoapiilani Road, HI 96761;
 tel. 669–6065, SP; minimum booking 3 days

Wailea Maui Inter-Continental Resort (516 r.), I–I+, 3700 Wailea Alanui Drive,
 HI 96753; tel. 879–1922, SP
The Palms at Wailea (70 r.), 3200 Wailea Alanui, HI 96753; tel. 879–5800/
 800–688–7444, SP

Molokai Island

Colony's Kaluakoi Hotel and Golf Club (114 r.), II–I, P.O. Box 1977,
 Maunaloa, HI 96770; tel. 552–2555/800–777–1700, SP, golf
Kaluakoi Villas (C–135 r.), IV, Kuluakoi Road, Maunaloa, HI 96770;
 tel. 800–225–7978, SP, T, golf
Molokai Shores Suites (C–100 r.), I, Kamehameha Highway, Star Route,
 Kaunakakai; tel. 800–219–9700, SP

Oahu Island

Honolulu Best Western Plaza Hotel (274 r.), II, 3253 N. Nimitz Highway;
(near airport)   tel. 836–3636/800–800–4683, SP

Honolulu Aston Waikiki Beach Tower (C–140 r.), I+, 2470 Kalakaua Ave., HI 96815;
(Waikiki)   tel. 926–6400/800–321–2558, SP
Aston Waikiki Beachside Hotel (79 r.), 2452 Kalakaua Ave., HI 96815;
 tel. 931–2100/800–321–2558
Colony's Hawaii Polo Inn (72 r.), from IV, 1696 Ala Moana Blvd.,
 HI 96815; tel. 949–0061, SP
Diamond Head Beach Hotel (57 r.), 2947 Kalakaua Ave., HI 96815;
 tel. 922–1928/800–923–1928
Edmund's Hotel Apartments (8 r.), IV, 2411 Ala Wai Blvd., HI 96815;
 tel. 923–8381/732–5169
Halekulani (456 r.), I+, 2199 Kalia Road, HI 96815–1988; tel. 923–2311/
 800–367–2343, SP, T
Hawaiian Monarch Hotel (C–439 r.), 444 Niu St., HI 96815; tel. 949–3911,
 SP
Hawaiian Regent (1346 r.), 2552 Kalakaua Ave., HI 96815; tel. 922–6611,
 SP, T
Hilton Hawaiian Village (2542 r.), I–I+, 2005 Kalia Road, HI 96815;
 tel. 949–4321/800–HILTONS, SP

Honolulu Prince (125 r.), III, 415 Nahua St., HI 96815; tel. 931–1400/
   800–321–2558
Hyatt Regency Waikiki (1230 r.), I–I+, 2424 Kalakaua Ave.; tel. 923–1234/
   800–233–1234, SP
The Ilikai Hotel Nikko Waikiki (800 r.), I, 1777 Ala Moana Blvd., HI 96815;
   tel. 949–3811/800–NIKKOUS, ST. T
Ilima Hotel (99 r.), II, 445 Nohonani St., HI 86815; tel. 923–1877, SP
Inn on the Park (238 r.), III, 1920 Ala Moana Blvd., HI 96815;
   tel. 946–8355/800–321–2558
Island Colony (C–740 r.), III, 445 Seaside Ave.; tel. 854-8843, SP;
   minimum booking 5 days
The New Otani Kaimana Beach Hotel (124 r.), II–I, 2368 Kalakaua Ave.;
   tel. 923–1555/800–356–8264; minimum booking 5 days

Note: all Outrigger Hotels have the same dial-free number 800–688–7444
   for reservations

Outrigger Coral Sea Hotel (109 r.), III, 250 Lewers St., HI 96815;
   tel. 923–3881, SP
Outrigger East Hotel (445 r.), II, 150 Kaiulani Ave., HI 96815;
   tel. 922–5353, SP
Outrigger Edgewater (184 r.), III, 2168 Kalia Road, HI 96815;
   tel. 922–6424, SP
Outrigger Hobron (612 r.), II, 343 Hobron Lane, HI 96815; tel. 942–7777,
   SP
Outrigger Maile Sky Court (596 r.), 2058 Kuhio Ave., HI 96815;
   tel. 947–2828, SP
The Outrigger Prince Kuhio, A Royal Outrigger (626 r.), I, 2500 Kuhio
   Ave., HI 96815; tel. 922–0811, SP
Outrigger Reef Towers (479 r.), II, 227 Lewers St., HI 96815; tel. 924–8844,
   SP

Sheraton Moana Surfrider, the oldest hotel in Waikiki

The swimming pool and gardens of the Turtle Bay Hilton Hotel

Outrigger Royal Islander (101 r.), III–II, 2164 Kalia Road, HI 96815;
tel. 922–1961, SP

Outrigger Waikiki Surf (303 r.), III, 2200 Kuhio Ave., HI 96815;
tel. 923–7671, SP

Outrigger West Hotel (663 r.), II, 2330 Kuhio Ave., HI 96815; tel. 922–5022,
SP

Park Shore Hotel (227 r.), II–I, 2586 Kalakaua Ave., HI 96815;
tel. 923–0411/800–367–2377, SP

Queen Kapiolani Hotel (315 r.), II, 150 Kapahulu Ave., HI 96815;
tel. 922–1941, SP

Royal Grove Hotel (80 r.), IV–III, 151 Uluniu Ave., HI 96815; tel. 923–7691,
SP

Royal Hawaiian Hotel (526 r.), I+, 2259 Kalakaua Ave., HI 96815;
tel. 923–7311/800–782–9488, SP

Sheraton Waikiki Hotel (1852 r.), I+, 2255 Kalakaua Ave., HI 96815;
tel. 922–4422/800–325–3535, SP

Tradewind Plaza (C–80 r.), IV, 2572 Lemon Road, HI 96815;
tel. 923–4835

Waikiki Beach Condominium Suites (C–100 r.), IV–III, Waikiki, HI 96815;
tel. 800–446–6248, SP, minimum booking 2 days

Waikiki Beachcomber Hotel (495 r.), I, 2300 Kalakaua Ave., HI 96815;
tel. 922–4646, SP

Waikiki Gateway Hotel (190 r.), III, 2070 Kalakaua Ave., HI 96744;
tel. 955–3741, SP

Waikiki Parc Hotel (298 r.), I, 2233 Helumoa Road, HI 96815;
tel. 921–7171/800–422–0450, SP

Waikiki Parkside Hotel (250 r.), II, 1850 Ala Moana Blvd.; tel. 955–1567,
SP

Waikiki Prince Hotel (30 r.), IV, 2431 Prince Edward; tel. 922–1544

White Sands Waikiki Resort (78 r.), III, 431 Nohonani St., HI 96815;
tel. 923–7336/800–634–6431, SP

Ilikai Marina Apartments-Condos (256 r.), IV–III, 1765 Ala Moana Blvd., HI 96815; tel. 946–0716, SP, T

444 Nahua Condominium Suites (192 r.), IV–III, 444 Nahua St., HI 96815; tel. 923–9458; minimum booking 2 days

Pacific Monarch Condo Rentals (216 r.), III, 142 Uluniu Ave., HI 96815; tel. 923–4402/800–655–6055; minimum booking 3 days

Waikiki Banyan (860 r.), III, 201 Ohua Ave., HI 96815; tel. 854–8843, SP, T

Waikiki Lanais (160 r.), I, 2452 Tusitala St.; tel. 923–0994, SP

Honolulu
Waikiki
(Condominiums)

Turtle Bay Hilton Golf and Tennis Resort (485 r.), I. P.O. Box 187, HI 96763; tel. 293–8811, SP, T, golf, horse-riding

Kahuku

Makaha Surfside (450 r.), IV, 85–175 Farrington Highway, #B–-310, HI 96792; tel. 696–8282; minimum booking 2 days

Sheraton Makaha Resort and Country Club (185 r.), 84–626 Makaha Valley, Waianae, HI 96792; tel. 695–9511, SP, T, golf, horse-riding

Makaha

Information

Information outside the Hawaiian Islands

United States Travel Service
22 Sackville Street
London W1X 2EA. Tel. (0171) 439 7433

United Kingdom

HVB,
Empire State Building, Suite 808, 350 Fifth Ave.
New York NY 110118
Tel. (212) 947–0717, fax (212) 947–0725

USA

HVB,
3975 University Dr., Suite 335
Fairfax, VA 22030
Tel. (703) 691–1800, fax (703) 691–4820

HVB,
180 N. Michigan Ave., Chicago IL 60601
Tel. (312) 236–0632, fax (312) 385–2513

HVB,
3440 Wiltshire Boulevard, Suite 610
Los Angeles CA 90010
Tel. (213) 385–5301, fax (213) 385–2513

HVB,
50 California Street, San Francisco CA 94111
Tel. (415) 392–8173

Normal opening times are Mon.–Fri. 9am–5pm, closed on official public holidays.

Information on the Hawaiian Islands

In addition to numerous private travel offices, the official Hawaii Visitors Bureau will provide information: offices will be found at:

Hawaii Visitors Bureau (HVB)

Waikiki/Oahu Visitors Association, 1001 Bishop Street, Suite 477. Pauahi Tower, Honolulu, HI 96813; tel. (808) 524–0722, fax (808) 538–0314

Oahu

Maui Visitors Bureau, 1727 Wili Pa Loop, Wailuku, HI 96793; tel. (808) 244–3530, fax (808) 244–1337

Maui

Hawaii	HVB, 250 Keawe Street, Hilo, HI 96720; tel. (808) 961–5797, fax (808) 961–2126
	HVB, 75–5718 W. Alii Drive, Kailua-Kona, HI 96740; tel. (808) 329–7787, fax (808) 325–7563
Kauai	HVB, Lihua Plaza Building, Lihue, HI 96766; tel. (808) 245–3971, fax (808) 246–9235

Insurance

It is essential to take out short health and accident insurance since the costs of medical treatment are high. It is also advisable to have baggage insurance and, particularly if a package holiday has been booked, cancellation insurance. Arrangements can be made through a travel agent or an insurance company; many companies operating package holidays now include insurance as part of the deal.

Island Tours

Visitors without a car who wish to get to know the islands better can always join an organised tour by coach – some small, some large – or jeep. Most such tours last a half or a whole day.

The coastlines can also be viewed from a helicopter. Such flights are expensive and normally last between one and three hours. However, quite understandably, such flights have been the subject of criticism from nature conservationists because the noise and aircraft exhaust fumes are causing much damage to the natural environment. Some species of plants have already disappeared altogether while others are threatened with extinction, and the fauna is being seriously disturbed. Therefore visitors may well wish to ask themselves whether they can do without this (they are also very expensive) attraction. For this reason no such flights have been recommended here; however, those who wish to view the islands from the air will have no difficulty in finding plenty of brochures in the hotels and public squares.

In addition, there is a wide choice of trips by boat or ship along the coast, to the neighbouring islands, or for deep-sea fishing (see also Sport). Brochures can be found at the airport, in hotels and at the premises of car rental firms.

Hawaii Island

Information about excursions can usually be obtained at hotels, from where clients will normally be picked up.

Coach trips   Coach tours of the islands, usually taking a half or a whole day, usually visit all the main places of interest. Of course, participants can never spend as much time as they would like at each, but this is partly compensated for by commentaries provided during the journey, which are usually fairly comprehensive.

Gray Line Hawaii, 74–5487 Kaiwi St., Kailua-Kona; tel. 329–9337/
800–367–2420
Waipi'o Valley Shuttle and Tours, Kukuihaele; tel. 775–7121

Trips by boat and ship   There is a wide variety of such trips, ranging from pleasant and informal boat-trips along the west coast (Kohala, Kailu-Kona and Puna) to fishing trips and excursions between November and March to observe the whales.

Captain Dan McSweeney's Year-Round Whale-Watching Adventures,
  P.O. Box 139, Holualoa; tel. 322–0028
Red Sail Sports, 69–425 Waikoloa Beach Drive, Kamuela; tel. 885–2876/
  800–255–6425

Those who would like to survey the underwater world without getting wet   Submarine trips
are recommended to take a trip in a special submarine; these go down to
about 160ft/50m and enable the passengers to observe marine life through
viewing windows.

Atlantis Submarines Kona, 74–5590 Alapa St., Kailua-Kona;
  tel. 329–6626/800–548–6262

In the south-east of Hawaii there is a wine-cellar where visitors can taste the   Wine-tasting
wines free of charge.

Volcano Winery, 35 Pilmauna Drive (at the end of Volcano Golf Course
  Road), P.O. Box 843, Volcano; tel. 967–7772

Kauai Island

A number of coach firms offer half and whole day trips; brochures and   Coach trips
information can be obtained and seats booked at hotel reception.

Gray Line Kauai, P.O. Box 1551, Lihue; tel. 245–3344 or 800–367–2420
Kauai Island Tours, Ahukini Road–Lihue Airport, Lihue; tel. 245–4777/
  800–525–6706
Kauai Mountain Tours, Lihue; tel. 245–7224/800–452–1113
Kauai Paradise Tours, 3971 Hunakai St., Lihue; tel. 246–3999

Most boat trips and cruises ply in summer along the Na Pali coast – which is   Boat trips
inaccessible from the land side – and also along Kauai's south coast.
    Some firms also offer trips in catamarans, which are fast but said to be
safe from capsizing. A large number of operators also provide trips in small
and larger boats to remote swimming and snorkelling spots which similarly cannot be reached by land (see Sport). From November to the end of
March it is also possible to observe whales from special boats which leave
from Nawiliwili harbour at Lihue. (However, the chances of seeing whales
are better from the coasts of Maui and Hawaii.)

Captain Zodiac Raft Expeditions/Na Pali Zodiac, P.O. Box 456, Hanalei;
  tel. 825–9371/800–422–7824
Catamaran Kahunu, 1 Kauhale Center, Hanalei; tel. 826–4596
The Exploration Company, 9633 Kaumuali'i Highway, Waimea;
  tel. 335–9909/800–852–4183
Hanalei Sea Tours, P.O. Box 1437, Hanalei; tel. 826–7254/800–733–7997
  (catamarans)
Smith's Motor Boat Service Inc., Wailua Marina, 174 Wailua Road,
  Kapaa; tel. 822–4111/822–3467/822–5213
Sundancer Cruises, Eleele Shopping Center, Eleele; tel. 335–0110/
  800–359–3057 (catamarans)

Maui Island

As there is hardly any public transport in Maui the various travel firms offer
a large nunber of half- and whole-day trips on the island. The most popular
are cruises to the neighbouring islands of Molokai and Lanai and to the
smaller island of Molokoni.

Coach trips across the island concentrate on its two major attractions, Hana   Coach trips
Highway and Haleakala Crater.

Language

Akina Aloha Tours/Akina Bus Service, 140 Alahele Place, Kihei;
tel. 879–2828/800–3989
Gray Line Maui, 273 Dairy Road, Kahului; tel. 877–5507/800–367–2420

Cruises

There are so many cruises to the neighbouring islands of Molokai, Lanai and Molokini that the best course to follow is to see what is on offer at Lahaina harbour, where a choice can be made between motor-yachts, sailing boats, catamarans, glass-bottomed boats, and so on. There are also trips available from Kihei, Maalea and Kanapali.

Pacific Whale Foundation, Kealia Beach Plaza, 101 North Kihei Road,
Kihei; tel. 879–8860/800–WHALE (observing whales)
Maui Classic Charters, 1215 S. Kinei Road, Kihei; tel. 879–8188/
800–736–5740 (including glass-bottomed boats)
Atlantis Submarines, 505 Front St., Lahaina; tel. 667–2224/800–548–6262
(submarines)

Wine-tasting

There is a daily free wine-tasting in Ulupalakua:

Tedeschi Vineyards Ltd., Highway 37, Ulupalakua; tel. 878–6058

Oahu Island

Oahu Island offers a particularly wide choice of excursions. The following is just a selection; details of others can be obtained from the various advertisements and brochures available.

Coach tours

E Noa Corporation, 1141 Waimanu St., Honolulu; tel. 591–2561/
800–824–8804
Gray Line Hawaii, 435 Kalewa St., Honolulu; tel. 836–1883/800–367–2420

Cruises

There are pleasure cruises by ship and boat and also trips on sailing boats mainly for diving, snorkelling and deep-sea fishing. The following is a selection:

Aloha Ocean Charters, 4112-A Puumalu Plaza, Honolulu; tel. 734–4300
(exclusive yachts, weddings performed)
Dream Cruises, 1085 Ala Moana Blvd.–Kewalo Basin, Honolulu;
tel. 592–5200 (observing whales, dancing)
Leahi Catamaran, 2255 Kalakaua Ave., Honolulu; tel. 922–5665/
800–462–7975
Navatek I, Honolulu, Pier 6; tel. 848–6360/800–852–4183 (observing
whales)
Royal Hawaiian Cruises, P.O. Box 29816, Honolulu; tel. 848–6360/
800–852–4183

The Tradewinds Estate, 53–012 Halai St., Hauula; tel. 293–2175 (sailing
boats for charter, weddings performed)
Windjammer Cruises, Aloha Tower Pier 7A, 181 Ala Moana Blvd.,
Honolulu; tel. 537–1122/800–1122/800–367–5000

Submarine trips

Submarine trips are also available on Oahu. Besides marine life, visitors can usually see a sunken wreck.

Atlantis Submarines Hawaii, LP, 1600 Kapiolani Blvd., Honolulu;
tel. 973–9811/800–548–6262

Language

General

Although the official language of Hawaii is English, visitors will also hear Hawaiian and "pidgin English" spoken, the latter being quite widespread in all the South Sea islands, but varying somewhat from island to island. It is a simplified everyday language with little grammar, which enables peoples speaking various native tongues to make themselves understood. Some examples are: lesgo (let's go, let's get on with it), an'den (then what?), bimbye (after a time, by and by), li'dis an' li'dat (like this and like that), waddascoops (what's up?).

The following are some of the main differences between "American English", as spoken in Hawaii, and that spoken in the UK and elsewhere.

American English

British	American
attractive, dainty	cute
autumn	fall
bill	check
billion – 1000 million (now widely accepted in Britain where traditionally a billion was a million million)	billion
biscuit	cracker, cookie
bonnet	hood (of car)
boot	trunk (of car)
boot polish	shoeshine
braces	suspenders
caravan	trailer
carry-out	"to go" (in cafeteria, etc.)
chemists	drugstore
Christian name	first name
cinema	movie (theatre)
cloakroom	checkroom
cupboard	closet
dustbin	garbage can
first floor	second floor
flat	apartment
football	soccer
fortnight	two weeks
gangway	aisle
"gents" (lavatory)	men's room
graduation (university, etc.)	commencement
ground floor	first floor
handbag	purse
holidays vacation label	sticker
"ladies" (lavatory)	ladies' room, powder room
lavatory	rest room
lavatory (roadside)	comfort station
lift	elevator
lorry	truck
luggage	baggage
maize	corn
nappy	diaper
open square	plaza
pavement	sidewalk
personal call (on telephone)	person to person call
petrol	gas, gasoline
policeman	cop
post	mail
post code	zip code
queue	stand in line
railway line, platform	track
refrigerator	icebox
return ticket	round trip ticket
reversed charge	collect (on telephone)

233

British	American
ring (up)	call (on telephone)
scone	biscuit
second floor	third floor
shop	store
single ticket	one-way ticket
spanner	wrench
spectacles	eyeglasses
subway	underpass
summer time	daylight saving time
surname	last name
tap	faucet
tin	can (e.g. of food)
tram	streetcar
trousers	pants
trunk call	long distance call
underground	subway
viewpoint, viewing platform	observatory
Whitsun	Pentecost

The Hawaiian language

General

The visitor is likely to come across the Hawaiian language only in context of the few words which have become absorbed into everyday colloquial speech and in the various place names. For those interested in hearing Hawaiian spoken the best way do so is to attend one of the Sunday services in Kawaiaho Church in Honolulu (see entry), where sermons are delivered in that language.

Pronunciation

Pronunciation of Hawaii is not too difficult. Most consonants are pronounced as expected, except that the letter w is like a v, but more like an f after e and i. In the dipthongs ei, eu, oi, ou, ai, ae, ao and au, the first letter is always emphasised, and the two vowels do not melt into one sound, as in English. The same applies to double vowels aa, ee, ii, oo and uu; these are always pronounced as two separate syllables. A horizontal line above a vowel means that it is stressed. Most words have the stress on the penultimate syllable, but five syllable words without a horizontal line are stressed on the first and fourth syllables.

Hawaiian dictionary

The following brief Hawaiian-English vocabulary should explain the meaning of some of the most commonly used words. For example, anyone finding himself on Ala Moana Boulevard will now know that it means "the road by the sea". In Honolulu many place-names have been taken from history; for example, Kalakaua, Kuhio, Likelike and Kapiolani are names which go back to the time of the Hawaiian monarchy.

a'a	thick, viscuous lava
ae	yes
ahi	tuna fish
ala	road, path
alii	chieftain, ruler, king, of royal blood
aloha	in general use to mean good day, goodbye, all the best, etc.
aumaka	family
aole	no
halau	school of hula dancing
hale	house, building
hana	work
haole	white man, foreigner

haupia	pudding made from coconut milk
heiau	temple, place of worship
hoku	star
holomu	long dress
huhu	annoyed, angry
hula	Hawaiian dance
ilio	dog
imu	underground oven, earth-oven
ipo	man or lady friend, lover
kahuna	priest (also magician)
kalua	roasted in an imu (earth-oven)
kamaaina	a native
kane	man (seen on door of men's toilets)
kapu	taboo, forbidden
keiki	child
kona	on the lee side, west, also a sultry wind
lanai	veranda, balcony
lei	garland of flowers
limu	seaweed
lomilomi	traditional Hawaiian massage
lua	toilet
luau	party, banquet
mahalo	thank you
makai	seawards
malihini	newcomer
mana	power of god
mauka	towards the mountains
mauna	mountain
moana	sea
muumuu	long, loose dress
ohana	family
ono	palatable, pleasant-tasting; also the name of a fish
opu	belly, stomach
pali	cliff, precipice
paniolo	Hawaiian cowboy
pau	ready, finished (pau hana = party evening)
pele	lava, goddess of fire
poi	porridge made from taro
pua	flower
puka	hole
punee	bed, sofa
pupu	hors d'œuvre, starter
tapa	material produced from the bark of a tree
tutu	grandmother
wahine	young lady, girl (seen on door of ladies' toilets)
wai	fresh water, drinking water
wiki	fast, quickly (wikiwiki = very fast)

Medical Assistance

General

As the costs of medical treatment are high it is essential to take out short-term sickness and accident insurance (see Insurance).

If a visitor needs to consult a doctor the "Doctors on call" service, available 24 hours a day should be contacted; (Hotel Outrigger Waikiki, Kalakauha Avenue, Waikiki, HI; tel. 971–6000). A consultation will cost at least $100. On other islands the relevant telephone number can be found in the telephone book provided in every hotel room, or at the reception desk, where any further information can be obtained.

Hospitals

All the islands are well equipped with hospitals. The main ones are as follows:

Oahu
Honolulu

Queen's Medical Center
1301 Punchbowl Street. Tel. 538–9011

Straub Clinic and Hospital
Royal Waikiki Shopping Center, 3rd floor. Tel. 522–4000

Kuhiu Walk-in Medical Clinic
2310 Kuhiu Avenue (Mon.–Sat. 9am–6pm)

Hawaii

Hilo Hospital, 1190 Waianuenue Avenue. Tel. 969–4111

Kona Hospital, Keealekekua, Kona. Tel. 322–9311

Kauai

Wilcox Memorial Hospital
3420 Kuhiu Highway. Tel. 245–1100

Molokai

Molokai General, Kaunakakai. Tel. 553–5331

Lanai

Lanai Community Hospital
7th Street, Lanai City. Tel. 565–6411

Motoring

Motoring assistance

Automobile club

American Automobile Association (AAA) Hawaii
590 Queen Street, Honolulu HI 968 13. Tel. 808–528–2600

Breakdown assistance

If a hire car (see Car Rental) should break down the first thing to do is to telephone the rental firm concerned and await their further instructions. Generally speaking, the American Automobile Association (AAA) will provide assistance in the event of a breakdown.

Addresses and telephone numbers of repair garages can also be found in the "Yellow Pages" of the telephone directory under "Automobile Repairing and Servicing". Note that towing away a car can be a very costly procedure unless the driver is a member of a motoring organisation allied to the AAA.

Precautions to take

Important documents

The following will provide a useful check-list to ensure that visitors have all the necessary papers before leaving home.

A valid passport and visa if required (see Travel Documents)

Driving licence and international driving licence if required (see Car Rental)
Automobile club membership card
Insurance (see entry)
Tickets and booking confirmation, etc.
Inoculation certificates
Photocopies of all important papers (in your suitcase)
Traveller's cheques, credit cards, money
Maps and guides

Make sure that a small first-aid box to deal with minor accidents and injuries is taken, as well as any normal medication. Visitors should consult their doctor about any inoculations or special medicine they may require. | Medication and first-aid equipment

Remember that driving under the influence of drugs and medicines can affect a driver's reactions and ability and can be a punishable offence.

Remember to take a spare pair of spectacles.

Safe driving

A visitor who wishes to rent a car should go to a firm with an international reputation (see Car rental), to ensure that the vehicle conforms in every way with accepted standards. A credit card is very useful when renting a car. | Car Rental

Always wear seat belts and make sure that front and rear seat passengers do the same. Belts should fit tightly across the body; a badly fitted seat belt can result in additional injuries in the event of an accident. | Seat belts

Seat belts can only perform their function if used in conjunction with correctly adjusted head-retraints, the upper edge of which should be at or above eye-level in order to protect the cervical spine.

Wearers of spectacles can drive more safely at night if wearing those fitted with special reflective glass, rather than tinted glass.

What to do in the event of an accident

Always remain calm and polite and carry out the following measures in order:

1. Make the scene of the accident safe from other road-users, by switching on warning lights and setting up a warning triangle at a suitable distance. | Safety

2. Attend to any injured persons; if necesary, send for an ambulance. | Injured persons

3. To be on the safe side, inform the police. | Police

4. Take down the name and address of other parties, as well as the registration number and make of the other vehicle(s) and name and address of their insurance company together with policy number(s). It is also important to note down the exact time and place of the accident and the address of any police station involved. | Personal details

5. Obtain any available evidence, particularly the names and addresses of independent witnesses. Make a sketch of the scene or – better still – take a number of photos from various angles. | Evidence

6. Do not admit any blame for the accident or sign any written admission of responsibility or any other form which is not fully understood. | Signing

Newspapers and Periodicals

Honolulu has two excellent newspapers, the "Honolulu Star Bulletin" and the "Honolulu Advertiser", each with a circulation of about 100,000. Of less importance are the "Hawaii Tribune-Herald" in Hilo (Hawaii), the "Maui News" in Wailuku (Maui) and the "West Hawaii Today" in Kailua-Kona. "Hawaii Hochi" is a newspaper in Japanese and English, printed in Honolulu. There are also daily papers in Chinese and Korean.

American newspapers from the mainland, such as the "Los Angeles Times", "San Francisco Chronicle", "San Francisco Examiner", the West Coast edition of the "Wall Street Journal" and the "New York Times" are also obtainable every day in Honolulu and frequently on the other islands too.

Naturally, all periodicals from the mainland are also on sale in Honolulu; of the Hawaiian periodicals, only "Honolulu Business" and "Hawaii Business" are of general interest. A selection of European newspapers and periodicals can be found in "Nene Travel", in the Hawaiian Shopping Center (2201 Kalakana Ave., Waikiki).

Opening Times

Chemists	See entry
Banks	See Currency
Shops and offices	As elsewhere in the USA, there are no official business hours in Hawaii. Many shops remain open from 7am until well into the night, and even on Sundays and public holidays.
Shopping centres	The opening times of shopping centres vary. Shops on Kalakaua Avenue, Waikikis' main street, are usually open until midnight; those in the Royal Hawaiian Shopping Center close at 10pm. All such shops open seven days a week, although usually for fewer hours at week-ends than on other days.
Museums	The opening times of museums vary greatly, so the museum concerned (see A to Z) should be telephoned in advance.
Post Offices	See Postal Services
Restaurants	The opening times of restaurants vary. Many open only in the evening, others from 6am onwards. Visitors can usually get something to eat at any time of day or night in the larger hotels. Restaurants normally close at 10pm or midnight.

Personal Papers

See Travel Documents and Motoring

Postal Services

General	As in Great Britain, the postal and telephone services are run by separate undertakings (see also Telephone and Telegraph).
Tariffs	Postage for letters within the USA is 25 cents for the first ounce (28g) and 21 cents for each further ounce; postcards cost 15 cents. Airmail rates for letters to Europe are 45 cents per half ounce (14g); for postcards 36 cents. Pre-stamped printed air-letter forms cost 35 cents.
Stamps	Visitors are advised to buy stamps at a post office, either at the counter or from one of the automatic machines there, because in many hotels stamps from machines may cost more (for example, for one dollar you may get only three 25 cent stamps).

Express delivery is possible by way of "Priority Mail" and "Federal Express"; details of rates can be obtained from the "Information" desk in post offices.

Main Post Office in Honolulu: Post offices
3600 Aolele Street; tel. 423–3990
   In Waikiki the post office is on Kalakaua Avenue; tel. 941–1062, with a further one in the Ala Moana Center; tel. 946–2020. For addresses of post offices on the other islands it is best to ask at the hotel.

Letters sent poste restante should be marked "general delivery" and can be   Poste restante
collected from the main post office. Holders of American Express cards can also have letters addressed to them c/o American Express, 2222 Kalakaua Avenue, Honolulu, HI 96815 (in the Hyatt Regency Hotel), and can collect them from there.

The postal code (zip code) is put after the name of the place and the   Post codes
abbreviation HI for Hawaii. The code consists of five digits; for Oahu these are 90968, and for the other islands 90969.

Post boxes are blue with "US Mail" in white lettering. Times of collection   Post boxes
are shown on the box.

Public Holidays

Official American public holidays apply on the Hawaiian islands as well.   General
Banks, government and municipal offices remain closed on those days, but most shops stay open; they close only on New Year's Day, Easter Sunday, Thanksgiving Day and Christmas Day. Even on those days some shops open.

New Year's Day; Martin Luther King Day (third Monday in January);   USA official
Washington's Birthday (third Monday in February); Easter Sunday; Memo-   holidays
rial Day (fourth Monday in May); Independence Day (July 4th); Labor Day (first Monday in September); Election Day (first Tuesday in November, every other year); Veterans' Day (November 11th); Thanksgiving Day (fourth Thursday in November); and Christmas Day.

Hawaii celebrates the following public holidays as well: Hawaiian official
Prince Kuhio Day (March 26th, in memory of Hawaii's first delegate to the   holidays
United States Congress, 1898–1922); Kamehameha Day (June 11th, in memory of King Kamehameha I, founder of the Kingdom of Hawaii) and Admission Day (third Friday in August, in memory of the day on which Hawaii was declared the 50th state of the USA in 1959).

Public Transport

Apart from Oahu Island and its capital Honolulu the public transport sys-   Bus network
tem on the Hawaiian islands leaves much to be desired. On the sparsely inhabited islands of Molokai and Lanai there are hardly any buses at all, so a car is almost a necessity. One way of seeing the islands without personal transport is to join one of the organised tours (see Island Tours).

The island of Hawaii is rather short of public transport. In Hilo itself there **Hawaii**
are municipal buses covering six routes, and overland coaches run from Hilo, leaving from the corner of Kamehameha Avenue and Mamo Street, Mon.–Sat. 6am–6pm. The "hele-on-bus", as it is generally known, runs at irregular times but covers the whole of the island. It is cheap but slow; for details of fares and departure times tel. 961–6722 or 935–8241. There is also

a bus which runs six times a day between 9.30am and 6pm from the post office in Kailua-Kona to the Kona Surf Hotel.

Maui

There are a number of bus services on Maui, but these cover only short distances and are rather expensive. Blue Shoreline plys between Lahaina and Kaanapali, with connections to Napili and Kapalua (Mon.–Fri. 8am–5pm at fifteen minute intervals, and 5pm–10pm at 30 minute intervals. Three times a day there is a bus between Lahaina and Wailea.

Kauai

Kauai has no public transport system. There is only one route: from the Westin Kauai Hotel by way of Lihue and Wailua to Kapaa (Aloha bus, Mon.–Sat. 8.15am–4.20pm).

Oahu
Honolulu

The island of Oahu – and Honolulu in particular – boasts an excellent bus network, by which almost every point on the island can be reached. "The Bus", as the municipal service is known, travels around the whole of the island – each journey costs only 60 cents, which must make it the cheapest bus line in the whole of the USA. Transfer tickets can be obtained free of charge from the driver. When buying tickets on the bus the exact fare should be tendered as the driver will not give any change. All the buses are air-conditioned. Visitors who are staying in Honolulu for any length of time will find it worth their while to purchase a monthly ticket, which costs only US$ 15, or the equivalent of 25 journeys.

Bus companies

The Bus, Oahu, Honolulu, 1585 Kapiolani Street; tel. 942–3702
MTS, Hawaii, Hilo, 25 Aupuni Street; tel. 961–6722 or 935–8241
Aloha Bus, Kauai; tel. 822–9532
The Blue Shoreline Bus, Maui; tel. 661–3827

Radio and Television

Radio

Of the current 38 radio stations on the Hawaiian islands, 24 are in Honolulu (seventeen AM and seven FM stations). The KCCN channel plays Hawaiian music day and night. Radios are not often provided in hotel rooms.

Television

Of the twelve Hawaiian TV channels five are in Honolulu, four on Hawaii Island and three on Maui. Programme details are published in the daily newspapers.

As there are TV sets in most hotel rooms there are ample opportunities to sample Hawaiian programmes.

One word of warning; as on the US mainland, the programmes are constantly interrupted by advertising.

Restaurants

General

There are a vast number of restaurants on the five islands, to suit every taste and every pocket, ranging from fast-food restaurants such as McDonald's and Burger King to exclusive French establishments. The latter are found mainly in the luxury hotels, and it is worth pointing out that it is not usually any more expensive to eat in a hotel than in other restaurants. In many hotels there are inexpensive breakfast, lunch and evening buffets, sometimes several. In almost all restaurants guests will find a "wait to be seated" sign at the entrance; to avoid any unpleasantness, visitors are advised to obey this notice and to wait to be shown to an empty table by a waiter. Oahu, in particular, boasts a large number of "fast-food" establishments, including sixteen Burger Kings, seventeen Jack in the Boxes, 31 McDonald's, eighteen Pizza Huts and ten Wendys, most of them in Honolulu, as might be expected.

Authentic Hawaiian or Polynesian cooking is not easy to find; the best way is to join in a traditional luau (see Food and Drink). A luau meal normally lasts from 6pm to 9pm, and is usually combined with a performance of hula dancing. Reservations are essential for these, as they are for restaurants in Groups I and II.

The selection of restaurants in the following lists are divided into five groups, based on the cost per person of an evening meal excluding drinks and tips:

Group I	more than US$ 45	Price categories
Group II	US$ 30–45	
Group III	US$ 15–30	
Group IV	below US$ 15	

To these prices must be added the Hawaiian sales tax, which is currently 4·17 per cent, as well as a service charge of about 15 per cent, so that overall the above prices are increased by about one-fifth. In all restaurants of groups I to III customers can pay by credit card, and in some of those in Group IV as well.

The type of cuisine is indicated by a letter inserted after the name of the restaurant, as follows:

Type of cuisine

A = American	C = Continental	CH = Chinese
F = Fish	FR = French	H = Hawaiian
I = Italian	J = Japanese	P = Polynesian

Addresses of restaurants inside hotels can be found in the list of hotels (see Hotels).

Hawaii Island · Big Island

Manago Restaurant (A), IV, Manago Hotel; tel. 323–2642 **Captain Cook**

Nihon Restaurant (J), IV, 123 Lihiwai St.; tel. 969–1133 **Hilo**
Restaurant Fuji (J), III, Hilo Hotel, 142 Kinoole St.; tel. 961–3733
Sandalwood Room (C), IV, Hawaii Naniloa Hotel; tel. 969–3333
Uncle Billy's Hilo Bay Restaurant (F), IV, Uncle Billy's Hilo Bay Hotel;
   tel. 935–0861/800–442–5841

Captain's Deck (F), IV, Kona Inn Shopping Village, 57–5744 Alii Drive; **Kailua**
   tel. 326–2555
Fisherman's Landing (F), III, 75–5744 Alii Drive; tel. 326–2555
Jolly Roger Kona (A), III, 75–5776 Alii Drive; tel. 329–1344
Kona Galley (F), IV–III, 75–5663 Palani Road; tel. 329–5550
Pele's Court (A), III, Kona Surf Resort, 78–128 Ehukai St.; tel. 322–3411

Ka Ohelo Dining Room (C), III, Volcano House, P.O. Box 53; tel. 967–7321 **Volcanoes National Park**

Batik Room (C), II, Mauna Kea Beach Hotel, One Mauna Kea Beach Drive; **Kamuela**
   tel. 882–7222
Donatoni's (I), II, Hilton Waikoloa Village, 425 Waikoloa Beach Drive;
   tel. 885–1234
Hakone (J), II, Hapuna Beach Prince Hotel, 62–100 Kaunaoa Drive;
   tel. 880–1111
Merriman's Restaurant (H), IV–III, Opela Plaza/Waimea; tel. 885–6822
Orchid Café (A), IV, Hilton Waikoloa Village, 425 Waikoloa Beach Drive;
   tel. 885–1234
The Royal Lu'au (H), I, Royal Waikoloan Hotel; tel. 885–6789

Kauai Island

Al & Don's Restaurant (A), IV, Kauai Sands Hotel, 420 Papaloa Road; **Kapaa**
   tel. 822–4221

Restaurants

Flying Lobster Restaurant (F), III, Kauai Coconut Beach Resort; tel. 800–22–ALOHA
Smith's Tropical Paradise (H), II, Wailua Marina; tel. 822–4654

Lihue
Cafe Portofino Italian Restaurant (I), IV, Pacific Ocean Plaza, 3501 Rice St.; tel. 245–2121
Jacaranda Terrace (C), III, Outrigger Kauai Beach, 4331 Kauai Beach Drive; tel. 245–1955
Lihue Barbecue Inn (A), IV, 2982 Kress St.; tel. 245–2921
Fisherman's Galley (F), IV, 3–1850 Kaumuali Highway

Koloa
Brenneckes (F), III, 2100 Hoone Road, Poipu Bach; tel. 742–7588
Dondero's (I), II, Hyatt Regency Kauai Resort & Spa, 1571 Poipu Road; tel. 742–1234
Ilima Terrace (C), III, Hyatt Regency Kauai Resort & Spa (see above)
The Dock (A), IV, Hyatt Regency Kauai, 1571 Poipu Road; tel. 800–233–1234

Princeville
Chuck's Steakhouse, III, 54280–F Kuhio Highway; tel. 826–6211
La Cascada (I), III–II, Princeville Hotel, 5520 Ka Haku Road; tel. 826–9644

Lanai Island

Lana'i City
Experience at Koele Clubhouse (A), III, The Lodge at Koele; tel. 565–4605
In the Manele Bay Hotel (tel. 565–2230) there are four restaurants:
Challenge at Manele Clubhouse (C), III; Hulopo'e Court (C), I; Ihilani (F), I; The Pool Grille (C), II

Maui Island

Lahaina
Beach Club (A), IV, Kaanapali Shores, 3455 Honoapiilani Highway; tel. 669–2211
Beachcombers (P), III, Royal Lahaina Resort, 2780 Kekaa Drive; tel. 661–3611
Chez Paul Restaurant Français (F), II, 820B Oluwalu Village; tel. 661–3843
Golden Palace (CH), IV, Lahaina Shopping Center; tel. 661–3126
Hard Rock Café (A), IV, 900 Front St.; tel. 667–7400
Moana Terrace (A), II, Maui Marriott; tel. 667–1200
Hecocks Ocean Front Dining (C, I), III, 505 Front St.; tel. 661–8810
Nikko Steakhouse (J), III, Maui Marriott, 100 Mohea Kai Drive; tel. 667–1200
Old Lahaina Café & Luau (H), III, 505 Front St.; tel. 661–3303
Sea House Restaurant (A), III, Napili Beach Club, 5900 Honoapiilani Road; tel. 669–1500
The Villa Seafood Buffet (F), III, The Westin Maui, 2365 Kaanapali Parkway; tel. 667–2525

Kaanapali
Leilani's On The Beach (F), II, Whaler's Village, 2345 Kaanapali Parkway; tel. 661–4495
Mona Terrace (A), III, Maui Marriott, 100 Nohea Kai Drive; tel. 667–1200
Tiki Grill (A), IV, Kaanapali Beach Hotel, 2525 Kaanapali Parkway

Kapalua
The Beach House (A), IV, The Ritz-Carlton Kapalua, One Ritz Carlton Drive; tel. 669–1665
The Grill & Bar at Kapalua (H), II, 200 Kapalua Drive; tel. 669–5653

Kihei
Hula Moons (F), III, Maui Inter-Continental, 3700 Wailea Alanui; tel. 879–1922
International House of Pancakes (A), IV, Azeka Plaza, South Kihei Road; tel. 879–3445

Lanai Terrace (K), III, Maui Inter-Continental (see above)
Satoru, Diamond Resort Hawaii (J), II, 555 Kaukahi St.; tel. 874–0500

Hakone (J), II, Maui Prince Hotel; tel. 874–5888   **Makena**

Bistro Molokoni (I), III, Grand Wailea Resort, 3850 Wailea Alanui Drive;   **Wailea**
  tel. 875–1234
Hana Gion (J), I, Stouffer Wailea Resort, 3550 Wailea Alanui;
  tel. 879–4900
Humuhumunukunukuapua's (F), II, Grand Wailea Resort (see above)
Maui Onion (A), IV, Stouffer Wailea Resort (see above)
Polo Beach Grille & Bar (A), IV, Kea Lani Hotel, 4100 Wailea Alanui Drive;
  tel. 875–4100

Molokai Island

Ohia Lodge (A), IV, Colony's Kaluakoi Hotel & Golf Club, Kepuhi Beach;   **Maunaloa**
  tel. 552–2555

Oahu Island

Flamingo Chuckwagon (A), IV, 1015 Kapiolani Blvd.   **Honolulu**
John Dominis Restaurant (F), I, 43 Ahui St.; tel. 523–0955   **Downtown**
Kincaid's Fish, Chop & Steakhouse, 1050 Ala Moana Blvd.; tel. 591–2006
Studebaker's All American Diner & Bar (A), IV, 500 Ala Moana;
  tel. 526–9888
The Wisteria (J), IV, 1206 S. King St.; tel. 591–9276
Wo Fat (CH), IV, 115 N. Hotel St.; tel. 533–6393
In the Kahala Hilton, 5000 Kahala Ave. (tel. 737–7938) there are two
  restaurants: the Hala Terrace (A), III, and the Maile Restaurant (C), II
Yum Yum Tree Kahala (A), IV, 4211 Waialae Ave.; tel. 737–7938

Captain's Table (C), III, Hawaiian Waikiki Beach Hotel, 257 Kalakaua Ave.;   **Honolulu**
  tel. 922–2511   **Waikiki**
Ciao Mein (I), III, Hyatt Regency Waikiki, 2424 Kalakaua Ave.;
  tel. 923–CIAO
Daruma (J), III, Royal Hawaiian Shopping Center, 2201 Kalakaua Ave.;
  tel. 926–8878
Golden Dragon (CH), II, Hilton Hawaiian Village; tel. 946–5336
Hard Rock Café (A), IV, 1837 Kapiolani Blvd.; tel. 955–7383
Hee Hing Restaurant (CH), IV, Hee Hing Plaza, 449 Kapahulu Ave.;
  tel. 735–5544
House Without A Key (A), IV, Halekulani , 2199 Kalia Road; tel. 923–2311
La Mer (FR), I, Halekulani, 2199 Kalia Road; tel. 923–2311
Lotus Room (CH), III, Princess Kaiulani Hotel; tel. 922–5811
Momoyama (J), III, Sheraton Princess Kaiulani Hotel, 120 Kaiulani Ave.;
  tel. 922–5811
Top of Waikiki Revolving Restaurant (C), III, Waikiki Business Plaza, 2270
  Kalakaua Ave.; tel. 923–3877
Royal Luau (H), I, Royal Hawaiian Hotel, 2259 Kalakaua Ave.;
  tel. 931–7194
Wailana Malia Restaurant (A), IV, 2211 Kuhio Ave.; tel. 922–4769

Safety

See Insurance, Motoring

Shopping

General

There are ample opportunities for shopping in Hawaii, especially in Honolulu. Along Kalakaua Avenue are all sorts of souvenir shops, and shopping centres – with everything under one roof – are very convenient and popular.

Department stores

Honolulu, Hawaii's only city, also boasts the only large department store on the islands, Liberty House in Bishop Street. This store has numerous outlets in Honolulu and on the other islands, often in the larger hotels or nearby shopping centres.

Shopping centres

The lack of choice of department stores in Honolulu is compensated for by the array of shopping centres:

Ala Moana Shopping Center, Ala Moana Boulevard, is the oldest and largest, with more than 100 shops, a dozen restaurants, three banks and a post-office.
Open: Mon.–Fri. 9.30am–9pm, Sat. 9am–5.30pm, Sun. 10am–5pm.

Ward Warehouse/Ward Center, 1050 Ala Moana Boulevard, is a converted old factory building.
Open: Mon.–Fri. 10am–9pm, Sat. 10am–5pm, Sun. 11am–4pm.

Both are within walking distance of Waikiki, or can also be reached by a No. 8 bus.

The new Royal Hawaiian Shopping Center in Waikiki at 2201 Kalakaua Avenue, has about 100 shops, eleven restaurants and a large number of travel bureaux.
Open: Mon.–Sat. 9am–10pm, Sun. until 9pm.

Souvenirs
Aloha shirts

Of all the souvenirs on sale one in particular should be mentioned: aloha shirts. Hawaiian fashion is, of course, also exemplified by the women in their "muuumuus", loose-fitting dresses reaching to the ground, but aloha shirts are famous world-wide. Decorated with hibiscus flowers, palm trees, whole landscapes, human figures, mountains and seas, these brightly-coloured shirts express better than anything the exotic atmosphere of the Hawaiian islands. They seem to glow with every colour of the rainbow, and the new arrival will soon realise that they represent just what is meant by the word aloha, symbolising as it does all that is fine and good and happy in Hawaiian life. Outside Hawaii, especially in California where they are very popular, they are usually known as Hawaiian shirts.

Aloha shirts as we see them today originated in the time of the missionaries, whose prudish ideals led them to insist that the Hawaiians, who were accustomed to going around topless, should henceforth be "properly" dressed. The shirts they provided were at first of one colour only, and were known as "palakas". The first multi-coloured shirts displayed traditional geometric Polynesian motifs, usually in warm colours. It was not until the 1920s and 1930s that designers ventured into shirts of a louder design, which were snapped up by tourists. The patterns were often small island scenes, such as hula-dancers under palm-trees up which young men were climbing. Those shirts, made mainly of a silk and cotton mixture, are now sought-after collectors' items.

In the 1930s, when mass production came in, rayon was the favourite material used, because the colours and motifs showed up more clearly on it. Rayon continued to be used for the next twenty years or so, but now cotton is preferred, as well as new man-made fibres such as polyester.

Buying aloha shirts

In Honolulu, in particular, there are a number of shops where the old-type shirts can still be bought, with the original designer labels, such as Kame-

Aloha shirts in Hilo Hattie's store

hameha, Duke Kahanamoku, Paradise, Kahala and Shaheens's; for these prices are more than twenty times as much as for the mass-produced variety. In Bailey's Antique Clothing, 2051 Kalakaua Avenue, Waikiki, these shirts sell like hot cakes. Another good shop is Clothes Addict in Paia Maui, on the road to Hana.

The most expensive are those with a black, light-blue, red or yellow background, with designs based on pineapple motifs, palms waving in the wind, fishing boats or surf-riders. To distinguish these rayon shirts from later ones – and firms such as Kahala and Cooke Street are now also selling modern reproductions – look for double-stitching, long pointed collars and complex designs, which tend to be lacking in modern shirts.

New aloha shirts are on sale by the thousand in many shops; prices vary between 20 and 50 US dollars. Good places to buy them are the many branches of the "Liberty House" department store, "Andrade" and "Rayns", to be found in most shopping centres. "Hilo Hattie's" factory shops – named after one of the most famous among Hawaiian hula-dancers and singers – have outlets on all the islands and are generally cheap. Some of the best-known makes are Cooke Street, Malihini of Hawaii, Princess Kaiulani, Tori Richards and Rayns.

Sightseeing

See Island Tours

Souvenirs

See Shopping

Surfers in Honolua Bay, Maui

Sport

Surfing

Surfing was originally invented on the coasts of the Hawaiian islands, and is the oldest and most popular sport enjoyed here today.

When Captain Cook arrived off the coast of Kauai in 1778 the British sailors were amazed to see the natives paddling towards them on long boards and then skilfully negotiating the high breakers as they returned to the shore. At that time the boards were made from the wood of the koa tree. Rock-drawings of these early "surfers" exist, as well as drawings made by artists among Captain Cook's crew.

Surfing became known world-wide thanks mainly to one man, Duke Kahanamoku (see Famous People), one of the most successful Olympic competitors of all time. In 1925 he saved the lives of eight fishermen off the coast of Newport Beach, California by rescuing them from their capsized boat and bringing them ashore on his surf-board through mountainous seas. Surfing spread initially from Hawaii to California.

While the original boards used by the Hawaiians were made from hard koa wood, measured some 6km/20ft in length and weighed up to 70kg/150lb, much lighter materials are used today. Modern surf-boards are only about 2m/7ft long and weigh about 5kg/11lb. They can be hired on all the beaches where there is surfing.

To become a skilled surfer requires years of training. Not only must the practitioner be a good swimmer but must also have a good sense of balance. On some beaches instruction is available, and there are also some quiet beaches well suited to beginners (see Beaches). Waikiki, with its shallow beach, is ideal for the novice. Along the beach can be found the many huts where surf-boards are for hire – usually for about US$ 5 per hour. Beginners can usually get some lessons from the legendary "beach boys".

Two of the best known surfing beaches, Sunset Beach and Ehukai Beach Park, are to be found in the north of Oahu. Every year at the end of November or early in December this is where the international surfing championships, the Triple Crown of Surfing, are held, with the best professional surfers in the world taking part.

Snorkelling is another popular form of water sport, and much easier and cheaper to learn than scuba diving (see below). Diving goggles, a pair of flippers and a snorkel are required, all of which can be rented from the hotel or from the beach stalls. Anyone interested in marine photography can hire a special underwater camera for US$ 10–20.

Snorkelling

Scuba diving – scuba stands for self-contained underwater breathing apparatus – is somewhat more complicated than snorkelling. A diving certificate, which is awarded after completion of four or five days' instruction, is required before diving equipment can be rented for diving in Hawaiian waters. Anyone not fully familiar with the Hawaiian diving grounds should preferably never dive alone. Boat trips (see below) are available to the most attractive spots, such as that from Maui to the uninhabited volcanic island of Molokini.

Scuba diving

There are opportunities to go on boat excursions to some particularly beautiful snorkelling and diving spots – the following is a selection (I = from US$ 45, II = under US$ 45):
Leahi Catamaran, II, 2255 Kalakau Ave.; tel. 800–462–7975
Body Glove Cruises, I, Kailua-Kona/Hawaii; tel. 800–551–8911
Eco-Adventures, I, 75–5744 Alii Drive, Kailua-Kona/Hawaii; tel. 800–949–3483
Red Sail Sports, I, 69–425 Waikoloa Beach Drive, Kamuela/Hawaii; tel. 800–255–6425
Frogman Charters, I, 888 Wainww St., Lahaina/Maui; tel. 800–700–FROG
Trilogy Ocean Sports, I, 1036 Lanai Ave., Lanai City/Lanai; tel. 565–2387

Boat trips for snorkelling and scuba diving

Keen deep-sea anglers can hire a boat for half a day or a whole day, complete with captain and crew – but it will not be cheap. The cost for a whole day for up to six people can be as much as US$ 450 (about £250); for firms which organise such trips see Island Tours.
In Honolulu most of the boats are moored in the Kewalo Marine Basin.

Deep-sea fishing

As well as surfing, wind-surfing – invented in the United States – is becoming very popular in Hawaii also. The strong trade winds and high waves in the winter months – especially on the coast of Maui – present a constant challenge to competitors from Europe and the American mainland. A favourite surfing beach is Hookipa Beach on Maui.

Wind-surfing

A number of surfing schools provide tuition in wind-surfing and rent out surf-boards; the following is a selection:
Captain Nemo's Ocean Sports, Royal Waikoloan Hotel, Kohala Coast (Hawaii); tel. 885–5555
Hanalei Surf Company, Hanalei Center, Hanalei (Kauai); tel. 826–9000
Maui Windsurf Company, 520 Keolani Place, Kahului (Maui); tel. 877–4815
Robbie Naish, 155A Hamakua Drive, Kailau (Oahui); tel. 800–767–6068
Surf-N-Sea, Halawei (Oahu); tel. 637–9887
The Kailua Sailboard Company, 130 Kailau (Oahu); tel. 262–2555

Another old Hawaiian sport is paddling in outriggers. Various competitions are held by canoe clubs; the best-known are the two long-distance races through the Kaiwi Channel from Molokai island to Oahu.

Paddling

The strong trade winds make the Hawaiian islands a sailor's paradise, whether he indulges in it as a competitive sport or simply for pleasure. Sailing schools offer courses and yachts and catamarans can also be hired.

Sailing

Taxis

Walking/ hiking	The best way to discover the hidden beauties of the Hawaiian islands is to go on a walking tour. Although there is a network of well-marked trails hiking is not without its dangers, and certain rules should be followed. The main points to bear in mind are to set out fairly early in the day, take maps and sufficient food and drink and not to stray from the marked trails. Climbing shoes are essential, and do not undertake a mountain walk alone. A number of organisations offer guided walks, and there is also a good selection of suggested routes in the National Parks on Maui and Hawaii. Those interested in walks with a guide on the islands of Oahu, Maui, Kauai or Molokai can obtain information from the Sierra Club Hawaii, 212 Merchant St., Honolulu; tel. 538–6616. The following is a selection of firms offering guided walks. Discover Molokai, P.O. Box 123, Maunaloa (Molokai); tel. 552–2975 Hawaiian Nature Center, Makiki (Oahu); tel. 955–0100 Hawaiian Walkways, 73–1307 Kaiminani Drive, Kailua-Kona (Hawaii); tel. 325–6677 Hike Maui, P.O. Box 330969, Kahului (Maui); tel. 879–5270 Tortoise and Hare Adventure Tours, P.O. Box 637, Kilauea (Kauai); tel. 800–538–4453
Maps	Suitable maps for walking can be obtained from all good bookshops in Honolulu or from the University Press, 2840 Kolowalu Street, Honolulu, HI 96822. State Department of Land and Natural Resources, 1151 Punchbowl St., Honolulu; tel. 587–0393.
Riding	There are a number of riding-stables which offer opportunities to discover the islands on horseback; the following is a selection: Charley's Trailride and Pack Trips, Kaupo Store, Hana (Maui); tel. 248–8209 CJM Country Stables, 1731 Kelaukia St., Koloa (Kaui); tel. 742–6096 Paniolo Riding, Ponoholo Ranch, Kohala Mountain Road, Kamuela (Hawaii); tel. 889–5554 Kualoa Ranch, 49–560 Kamihameha Highway, Kuaolo (Oahu); tel. 237–8515 Molokai Horse & Wagon Ride, Hoolehua (Molokai); tel. 567–6773 Pony Express Tours, Kula (Maui); tel. 667–2200 Sheraton Makaha Lio Stables, Makaha; tel. 695–9511
Tennis	Thanks to the pleasant climate tennis has grown in popularity and is now played on all the islands. On Oahu, the island with the most tennis courts, there are some run by the local council which are available to the public free of charge. Examples of these are the Diamond Head Tennis Center and Kapiolani Tennis Courts in Ala Moana Park in Waikiki. Further details can be obtained from the Department of Parks and Recreation; tel. 923–7927. In addition many courts owned by tennis clubs can often be rented by non-members for a fee. Most of the larger hotels have their own courts. Some are reserved for hotel residents only, but most are open to the public; charges vary. A list of tennis courts with more detailed information is obtainable from the Hawaiian Tourist Bureau (see Information).
Other kinds of sport	The Hawaiian Islands are a veritable paradise for numerous sports, on land, on sea and in the air. These include gliding, hang-gliding, para-gliding, body-surfing, body-boarding, water-skiing. fresh-water fishing, hunting, jogging, cycling and skiing, to name only a few.

Taxis

General	Taxis can be found on all the islands except Lanai. Generally speaking they are very expensive, the result mainly of the long distances involved and lack of competition from public transport (with the exception of Oahu).

Apart from those at the airport there are no taxi-stands in Honolulu, although most taxis line up in front of the larger hotels. Although they are not supposed to stop in the street to pick up passengers they all seem to do so nevertheless.

The best way to order a taxi on Oahu is by telephone; it will usually arrive within a few minutes. On the other islands a longer wait should be expected.

The basic fare for a taxi on Hawaii Island is up to US$ 2, plus US$ 1.75 or so for each additional mile. **Fares**

The following are some of the taxi firms which can be recommended as reliable:

Sida Taxis & Tours; tel. 836–0011 **Oahu**
Aloha State Taxi; tel. 847–3566
The CAB; tel. 533–4999 or 422–2222
Charley's Taxi; tel. 995–2211
Americabs Taxi; tel. 988–5733 and 848–8133
Century Cab; tel. 528–4655

Kona Airport Taxi; tel. 329–7779 **Hawaii**
Bob's Taxi in Hilo; tel. 959–4800 Big Island

Kuai Cab; tel. 246–4622 **Kauai**
Garden Isle Taxi; tel. 245–6161

Mita Taxi; tel. 871–4622 **Maui**
Kahului Taxi; tel. 242–6404
Red and White Cab; tel. 661–3684
Alii Taxi; tel. 661–3688 and 661–0133

Molokai Off Road Tours & Taxi, Kaunakakai; tel. 553–3369 **Molokai**
Molokai Limousine Taxi Service, Kaunakakai; tel. 553–3979

Lanai City Service; tel. 565–7227 **Lanai**
Oshiro Service; tel. 565–6952

Temperatures

See Facts and Figures; Climate

Telephone and Telegraph

As a result of the increase in the number of telephones and the use of fax machines, sending a telegraph is now somewhat old-fashioned, but they can still be sent over the telephone. Dial 1411 to enquire about the number. **Telegrams**

The dialling code for all the Hawaiian islands is 808. In addition to their normal telephone number, many hotels, restaurants and firms which offer leisure activities have a number beginning with 800. Using this number, the establishment concerned can be phoned free of charge. Hawaii dialling code

Local calls from coin boxes, which can be found almost anywhere, cost 25 cents, but hotels generally charge 50 or 60 cents. Calls from one island to another rank as long-distance calls and cost correspondingly more; for example, a three-minute call from Honolulu to Kauai costs over two dollars. Local calls

From Great Britain to Hawaii dial 001, followed by 808 and the customer's number. Long distance calls

From Hawaii to Great Britain dial 011–44, followed by the local code (omitting the initial zero) and the customer's number.

When using a call-box remember to have available a handful of 25 cent coins if you are not using a credit card telephone, which is considerably more expensive. A three-minute call to the UK should cost about US$ 8.

Since the charge for a long-distance call made from an hotel can be quite high, it is best to use a credit card – preferably one from the American Telephone & Telegraph (AT & T).

In Honolulu only there is a company (Phone Line Hawaii; tel. 923–1214, open daily 8.30am–11pm), from the two branches of which calls can be made to the UK for US$ 6·95 plus 4 per cent sales tax for the first three minutes. Each additional minute is then charged for, depending on the time of day. These two branches are at:

International Market Place, Kalakaua Avenue, 1st floor
Discovery Bay Center, 1778 Ala Moana Boulevard, opposite the Hotel Ilikai.

Time difference | When making an overseas call do not forget to bear in mind the time difference (see below).

Time

Time difference | Local time in Hawaii is two hours behind the west coast of America, five hours behind the east coast and ten hours behind Greenwich Mean Time. In contrast to the UK, Europe and all other US states, Hawaii does not advance its clocks in summer (daylight saving time), so during the six summer months the above differences are increased by a further hour, to three, six and eleven respectively. As Hawaii lies east of the International Date Line, clocks on the islands are almost a full day behind those of Asiatic and Pacific countries (Singapore 18 hours, Japan 19 hours, Sydney 20 hours, New Zealand and Fiji 22 hours).

Tipping

In Hawaii, in contrast to European countries, tips are only rarely included in the total bill and have to be offered separately. In restaurants and night-clubs the normal tip is 15 to 20 per cent, and for taxi drivers is 15 per cent.

For items of luggage taken into your hotel room or removed from it the rate is normally one dollar. If the stay lasts more than three days it is customary to give the room maid 50 cents to one dollar for each day. If a porter calls a taxi he should be given 50 cents to a dollar.

Tourist Information

See Information

Travel Bureaux

General | Some agents in Honolulu specialise in selling "package tours" to the islands of Hawaii, Kauai, Maui and Molokai, which provide several days' stay on the islands inclusive of flight, hotel and car rental. Organising an itinerary in this way is both convenient and sometimes cheaper. Almost all the agencies can be telephoned between 8am and 8pm.

Addresses (a selection) | Ali's Tickets and Tours, 234 Beachwalk, Honolulu; tel. 922–0772
American Express Travel, Hilton Hawaiian Village Hotel, Honolulu-Waikiki; tel. 947–2607

American Express Travel, Kailua-Kona/Hawauu, King Kamehameha
   Hotel; tel. 326–4631
American Express Travel, Lihue/Kauai, Hotel Westin Kauau; tel. 246–0627
American Express Travel, Lahaina/Maui, 658 Front St.; tel. 667–4381, or
   in the Hyatt Regency Hotel; tel. 667–7451
Friendly Isle Travel Inc.; Kaunakakei/Molokai; tel. 553–5357

Travel Documents

For a visit to Hawaii (as to any of the United States of America) a passport is   Passport
required; this must be valid for at least six months after the planned date of
return from the islands.

From July 1989 the compulsory visa was abolished, but before arrival the   Visa
tourist or businessman must complete Form 1–791 which will be provided
in the aircraft. Those whose passport includes an unrestricted B-1 or B-2
visa need not complete the form.
   A visa is still required in the following cases: people who intend to stay
more than 90 days in the USA, students, journalists, exchange visitors, civil
servants on official visits, those engaged to American citizens, and
aircrews.

When to go

As the Hawaiian islands do not really have a rainy season, and the four
seasons vary comparatively little climate-wise, they can in fact be visited at
any time of the year (see Facts and Figures; Climate). The high season
really lies between December and April, the Christmas holidays being the
highlight, even though it does rain more during those months than at other
times. July and August are other seasonal months. In the high season most
hotel prices are somewhat higher than during the remainder of the year.

Youth Hostels

Youth hostels are something of a rarity on the Hawaiian islands, but they do   General
offer economic accommodation for younger visitors. To use youth hostels
it is normally necessary to be in possession of a valid membership card of
the American Youth Hostels Federation or of an International Youth Hostel
Federation. Usually, however, anyone not in possession of such a card will
be accepted on payment of a small surcharge.
   The five hostels shown below are mainly AYHs (American Youth Hostels)
or YMCAs (Young Men's Christian Association) hostels. Bookings can be
made by letter. Depending on the time of year and how full they are, stays
may be restricted to between 7 and 14 days.

Hilo Bay AYH-Hostel,   **Hawaii**
311 Kalaniangole Ave.,   Hilo
Hilo, HI 96720.
Tel. 935–1383
(outside Hilo, near the airport)

Honolulu International AYH-Hostel,   **Oahu**
2323A Sea View Ave.,   Honolulu
Honolulu, HI 96822.
Tel. 946–0591 (above Waikiki)

Youth Hostels

Hale Aloha AYH-Hostel,
2417 Prince Edward Street
Honolulu, HI 96815.
Tel. 926–8313
(in Waikiki, 5 minutes from the beach)

Kauai

YMCA Kauai. Camp Naue,
P.O. Box 1786, Lihue HI 96799
Tel. 246–9090
(at Haena, near the beach)

Maui

Banana Bungalow & International Travellers Hostels
310 North Market St., Wailuku, HI 96793.
Tel. 244–5090

Index

Index

Imprint

108 illustrations, 9 general maps, 7 town plans, 4 drawings, 3 information maps, 2 location maps, 2 ground plans. 1 information plan, 1 special plan, 1 large map

Original German text: Henry Marx, Claudia Smettan

Editorial work: Baedeker Redaktion (Anja Schliebitz, Barbara Branscheid)
English language edition: Alec Court

General direction: Dr Peter Baumgarten, Baedeker Stuttgart

English translation: Julie Bullock, David Cocking, Julie Waller

Cartography: Ingenieurbüro für Kartographie Harms, Erlenbach bei Kandel/Pfalz

Source of Illustrations: Archiv (1), Drechsler-Marx (73), Hawaii Visitors' Bureau, Waterfall (1), Historia-Photo (4), IFA-Bilderteam (5), Lade (9), Schuster (6), Simon (1), Steenmans (1), Strüber (4), Ullstein-Bilderdienst (Haeckel) (1)

2nd English edition 1995

© Baedeker Stuttgart
Original German edition 1995

© 1995 Jarrold and Sons Ltd
English language edition worldwide

© 1995 The Automobile Association: United Kingdom and Ireland

Published in the United States by:
Macmillan Travel
A Simon & Schuster Macmillan Company
1633 Broadway
New York, NY 10019–6785

Macmillan is a registered trademark of Macmillan, Inc.

Distributed in the United Kingdom by the Publishing Division of the Automobile Association, Fanum House, Basingstoke, Hampshire RG21 2EA

Licensed user: Mairs Geographischer Verlag GmbH & Co., Ostfildern-Kemnat bei Stuttgart

The name *Baedeker* is a registered trademark

A CIP catalogue record of this book is available from the British Library

Reproductions: Eder Repro GmbH, Ostfildern (Scharnhausen)

Printed in Italy by G. Canale & C.S.p.A – Borgaro T.se –Turin

ISBN UK 0 7495 1263 6
US and Canada 0–02–860483–0